CRUMB

CRUMB

THE BAKING BOOK

Ruby Tandoh

Photographs by Nato Welton

Berkeley

Published in the United States by Ten Speed Press, an imprint of the
Crown Publishing Group, a division of Random House LLC,
a Penguin Random House Company, New York.
www.crownpublishing.com
www.tenspeed.com

Ten Speed Press and the Ten Speed Press colophon are registered
trademarks of Random House LLC.

Originally published in hardcover in slightly different form in
Great Britain by Chatto & Windus, an imprint of The Random House
Group Ltd., London, in 2014.

Grateful acknowledgment is made to the following to reprint
previously published material:

Anchor Books: Excerpt from *The Unabridged Journals of Sylvia Plath
1950-1962: Transcribed from the Original Manuscripts at Smith College*
by Sylvia Plath, edited by Karen V. Kukil, copyright © 2000 by The
Estate of Sylvia Plath. Reprinted courtesy of Anchor Books, an imprint
of the Knopf Doubleday Group, a division of Random House LLC.

Puffin Books and David Higham Associates: Excerpt from Matilda by
Roald Dahl, copyright © 1988 by Roald Dahl (Jonathan Cape Ltd.,
London, and Puffin Books, New York). Rights for eBook administered
by David Higham Associates, London. Reprinted by permission of
Puffin Books, a division of Penguin Group (USA) LLC and David
Higham Associates.

Library of Congress Cataloging-in-Publication Data
Tandoh, Ruby.
  Crumb : the baking book / Ruby Tandoh ; photographs by Nato
Welton. — First American edition.
     pages cm
  Includes bibliographical references and index.

1. Baking. I. Welton, Nato. II. Title.

TX763.T36 2015

641.81'5--dc23

                              2014043873

Hardcover ISBN: 978-1-60774-836-6
eBook ISBN: 978-1-60774-837-3

Printed in China

Design & Art Direction: Hyperkit
Photography: Nato Welton
Index: Ben Murphy

10 9 8 7 6 5 4 3 2 1

First American Edition

" Instead of studying Locke, for instance,
or writing - I go make an apple pie."
Sylvia Plath

There's a lot more to baking than meets the eye. Millions of air bubbles suspended in a bowl of beaten egg whites can make a meringue melt on the tongue. There's science behind the deep brown crust of a brioche loaf and the tenderness of a pastry shell. Just a few degrees can nudge a pot of boiling sugar from sweet syrup to caramel (or to bitter cinder, if you're unlucky). I've taken great care here to explain the whys and hows of baking, in the hope that this will give you the confidence to get started and adapt recipes to suit your tastes and preferences.

But science alone won't bake a cake. It can't replicate the feeling of cool pastry under your fingertips or completely describe the consistency of the perfect custard. Something happens between the numbered steps of a recipe and the end result that can't be predicted or prepared for. This is where baking soars clear of plain chemistry. It's not the kind of thing that can be dissected under bullet-pointed headings or jargon — it has to be witnessed firsthand. For that reason I urge you to dive in, make a mess, and not be squeamish about getting your hands dirty. Enjoy the sensory pleasures that baking has to offer, from the exertion of a long knead to the crackle of a rustic loaf cooling on the countertop. You'll soon find that the processes of baking are every bit as exciting as tucking in to the finished product.

This sensuous side of baking is about more than just hedonism. A finger gently pressed into a rising loaf can tell you whether it's ready for baking; a piece of dough is well kneaded if you can stretch it so thinly that, when it's held up to the sun, you can almost see straight through it. Baking isn't just about the tasting: prod, sniff, listen to, and squeeze your food. This is not baking by rote.

The recipes in this book aren't grand or highly decorated; their roots lie in the thrill of a new ingredient or the comfort of a familiar food. They aim to please, rather than to impress. I hope that they'll make it to your table over and over again. I may digress at points, singing the praises of black currants or writing an ode to doughnuts. I make no apologies for this. I bake for the love of it, and I hope that you will, too.

INTRODUCTION

Crumb started long, long before it was bound into the book you hold now. Perhaps the story begins with childhood birthday cakes, or at three years old — felt-tip pen clutched between my stubby fingers as I circled each and every dessert in my parents' illustrated cookbook. Maybe it was *The Very Hungry Caterpillar* — so well thumbed that its pages wore thin at the edges — or Bruce Bogtrotter's chocolate cake in *Matilda*. Later there were food supplements torn out of newspapers and messily archived, lunchtime feasts in the school cafeteria, homemade bundles of fudge, and a whole summer spent rereading the Great Hall feast scenes in *Harry Potter*. Teenage romances played out against a backdrop of cake: to charm, to celebrate, to appease, and to soothe the hurt of the breakup.

It could be that this book started while I was in college, at the Christmas market baking stall that I spent three months preparing for and made about $50 from. Or maybe it was in a Lisbon backpackers' hostel, where a cheesecake landed me a kitchen job and where, from that point onward, I spent every second of each day jotting down recipes, writing shopping lists, and planning menus in what felt like a dream come true. Then again, it could've been in the park at Belém, eating the fabled *pastéis de nata,* that the penny finally dropped.

I was living in a dank London flat when I saw a TV baking show and wondered whether it was something I could do. Perhaps the book really began to take shape there: in the pages of scrawled notes on baking theory and chemistry that I made in a bid to learn all that I needed to know to survive in the competition. Before long, I was spending my weekends on the set of *The Great British Bake Off* as a season 4 contestant, and during that time some of the recipes in these pages began to crystalize. Notes still stored on my phone ("try coffee & black currant. do washing. make croissants") are the reminders of this baking storm.

By the time season 4 of *The Great British Bake Off* began to air, I had dozens of books of notes: paeans to profiteroles, half-finished recipes, flavor combinations, diary entries fondly recounting good meals, sketches of cakes, breads, and cookies, and scores of shopping lists. This book is built from those musings, experiments, and memories. It's the distillation of my obsession with food. It's been a pleasure.

GETTING STARTED

There's a misconception that baking is different from cooking. I hear friends sincerely proclaim that they can cook but not bake, or bake but not cook, as though it makes any sense to abstract one from the other. Baking *is* cooking. If you enjoy food — if you can operate an oven and follow a recipe — you're most of the way there already. Don't overthink it, and don't assume the worst before you've even gotten started.

That said, I'll admit that the equipment, methods, and vocabulary of baking can be daunting if you're new to it. To take out the guesswork, I've explained some of the baking-specific equipment, ingredients, and techniques in this introduction. If you're a seasoned baker, just head straight to the recipes — you'll find that there's a mix of easier and more involved recipes in each chapter, and a progression through the book from familiar cakes to meringues, tarts, and pastries.

EQUIPMENT

As someone who has always baked in tiny kitchens and student apartments, I have little tolerance for unnecessary culinary clutter. You'll find no heart-shaped cupcake molds or cake turntables in this book, and where a recipe calls for an unusual shape or size of pan (such as the madeleines on page 29), I've given advice on alternatives, including adjustments to baking times, for those who don't have that piece of specialized equipment. There are some pieces of (cheap, easy to source) equipment that I would recommend, though.

Electronic kitchen scale

I can't overstate just how important an electronic scale is. I've used various mechanical scales for baking in the past and suffered a string of disappointments. They're not sensitive enough for small measurements, they distort when too heavily loaded, and there's the worry of manually resetting to zero. Most irritatingly of all, there's the agonizing over the needle on the dial as it flickers between one number and another, depending on which eye you squint through. Unless you have saintlike patience and the Rolls-Royce of mechanical scales, you really should go electronic. There's no need to break the bank, though: a $15 electronic scale will do just fine.

Teaspoon and tablespoon measures

Don't use your normal cutlery to approximate teaspoons and tablespoons, as the quantity measured by the sort of teaspoon you use to stir your tea can range widely. It may not seem like much, but a cake can stand or fall on as little as ¼ teaspoon too much or too little baking powder. Measuring spoons are inexpensive, and if you plan to do much baking, they'll prove invaluable.

Oven thermometer

Do your cakes often emerge from the oven either burnt or raw, despite having followed the recipe to the letter? Your oven might not be operating at the correct temperatures. Oven thermostats are notoriously unreliable — they may cook 35°F warmer or cooler than the temperature shown on the dial, and for foods as temperamental as cakes and meringues, this can spell disaster. Luckily, there's no need to invest in a new oven. An oven thermometer costs less than $10 and will sit happily on your oven shelf, giving you peace of mind. (Whether you have a convection, gas, or electric oven, an oven thermometer should read the temperature that you've set your oven to. If a recipe specifies 350°F, your thermometer should display 350°F.

Coffee grinder

A coffee grinder isn't essential, but I find it useful for grinding nuts, seeds, and spices. A food processor is an alternative. If you have neither, use a mortar and pestle instead for spices and small seeds and buy already ground nuts, or nut meal.

And the rest
Flat baking sheets
9 by 13-inch baking pan
8-inch round loose-bottomed or springform cake pan
Standard loaf pan, about 5 by 9 inches at its base
Approximately 1-quart pudding basin, steam bowl, or pudding mold
Large pie pan
12-cup muffin tin
Pie weights, dried beans, or rice (for blind baking)
Handheld blender
Grater
Wire whisk
Wooden spoons
Rolling pin
Spatula
Heavy saucepan
Large mixing bowls
Parchment paper
Plastic wrap
Ruler
Pastry brush
Fine-mesh sieve
Disposable pastry bags

Useful but inessential extras
Electric handheld mixer
Fluted flan or tart pan
Candy thermometer
Individual pudding molds
Round pastry cutters, in different sizes
Madeleine pan
Bundt pan
Dough scraper
Frosting spatula
Piping nozzles

INGREDIENTS

Most ingredients used in these recipes can be found in any large supermarket. The occasional ingredient that is hard to find outside the UK (such as black currants, clotted cream, stem ginger, or digestives) can be ordered online.

Eggs
Wherever I use eggs in this book, they're large ones, but there are some instances where you can swap in medium eggs instead if that's all you've got. As a rule of thumb, I'd recommend that you don't fiddle with egg quantities in anything whisked (that includes sponge cakes and meringues), but in most other cakes, cookies, pastries, and bread doughs, you can use medium eggs, adding a dash more milk or water if the mixture looks a little dry as a result.

Whatever size you use, make sure the eggs are free-range at the very least, and organic if possible.

Milk
Always use whole or 2% milk for baking. Sometimes the higher fat content of whole milk is important for helping something to mix, set, or bake as it should. Where this is the case, I have specified whole milk in the recipe.

Butter
Butter should always be unsalted. It doesn't keep as well as salted butter, but it gives you far greater control over the amount of salt you add to the food. This is particularly important in breads and buns, where too much salt will adversely affect both taste and texture, preventing the dough from rising properly. You really don't need to spend a fortune on the best-quality butter for most cakes, cookies, or even butter-rich short-crust pastries. I invest in good butter only for puff and Danish pastries — the lower water content of European-style butter gives crisper layers.

Sugar
I always specify the type of sugar to use, but do feel free to play around with it to achieve subtly different flavors and textures. Superfine sugar, which has crystals much smaller than those of the slightly cheaper granulated sugar, is most commonly used in this book. It's quick to dissolve and versatile and won't distract from other flavors. Light and dark brown sugars are less intensively refined than white sugar, leaving them with a soft, crumbly texture and toffee flavor (the darker the sugar, the more intense a molasses flavor it has). They are the taste of gingerbreads, moist chocolate cakes, and sticky toffee puddings. Demerara is slow to dissolve — good for sprinkling on top of cakes or sweet pies for a crunch. Confectioners' sugar is very finely ground and perfect for making smooth, glossy icing.

Flour
Most of the recipes here use all-purpose flour, by which I mean the most common type of white flour. Note that it is different from white bread flour, which has a higher protein content and is better suited to breads, because it helps the dough to stretch as it rises. Whole wheat flour has the bran from the wheat grain left in, giving it a lightly nutty taste and coarser texture. There are also flours made from different grains, including rye and spelt. These have very different properties than wheat flour, and are discussed further in the Bread chapter. You can buy self-rising flour, which

is white flour with added leavening agents. This usually does away with the need for separately added baking powder or baking soda, but I prefer not to use self-rising flour, and you won't find any recipes that use it here — adding your own leavening agents affords you far greater control.

Baking powder and baking soda

Chemical leavening agents help to produce the air bubbles that make a cake rise. Baking powder activates upon contact with water and again when it enters the oven, meaning that even if you leave a cake batter standing for a while before you bake it, it'll have a second lease on life when it hits the heat. You don't have this luxury with baking soda, which reacts the instant that it's mixed in (there's more on baking soda on page 178), so make sure that you bake items leavened with baking soda soon after the batter has been prepared.

Yeast

Yeast is a natural leavening agent and the force behind bread. It ferments bread dough, feeding on starches and producing tiny air bubbles as it works. It's these air bubbles that expand in the oven to give bread its rise. Yeast adds complex flavors, too. You can read more about it on page 73.

Cornstarch

Cornstarch is a pure starch and a potent thickener. Added to liquids and then heated, it absorbs water and releases a network of starch molecules, which thicken sauces and creams. You can see it in action in the pastry cream on page 312. Don't confuse cornstarch with cornmeal, which is often yellow and has grittier particles.

Salt

Wherever salt is called for, I mean standard table salt. Although there's a romance to fleur de sel or crystalline flakes of sea salt, quick-dissolving table salt is far better suited to baking, and cheaper, too. You'll find that many of my recipes have a little salt added to them (even sweet dishes benefit from a pinch of salt to bring out their flavor).

MEASURING

There are as many ways of measuring ingredients as there are recipes. However, in baking, weight measures are so much more accurate than volume for dry ingredients such as flour and sugar, and easier to accomplish for certain ingredients, such as butter. Therefore, this book uses grams as the primary measure for most ingredients. This explains why some of the volume measures may seem quite awkward. There's really no way around this. The plain and simple truth is that a nicely round metric measure often becomes quite convoluted in US measures. For example, 200 milliliters becomes ¾ cup + 1½ tablespoons; or 200 grams of all-purpose flour becomes 1½ cups + 1½ tablespoons. If you find these measures frustrating, perhaps I will have set you on the road to more accurate baking by spurring you to begin weighing your dry ingredients in grams with a digital scale — and that's a good thing.

MIXING

The way that you mix a pastry, batter, or dough can be every bit as important as the way you actually bake it. There are a few different mixing techniques involved in baking, and you'll see these key words pop up again and again. Take a moment to run through the list and check that you know your beating from your whisking.

Beat

Use a wooden spoon to vigorously stir the mixture in a roughly circular motion. This combines two ingredients and incorporates air at the same time.

Cream

Creaming is much the same as beating, but specific to the stage at the beginning of preparing a batter when you mix softened butter with sugar until thick and creamy (see page 27).

Crumb

Rub cubes of butter into flour using your fingertips, continuing until no visible pieces of butter remain.

Fold in

Folding in is a delicate operation. When you fold two mixtures together, you're aiming to combine them without knocking the air out of them. Use a spatula or large metal spoon to cut across the middle of the bowl then sweep around the side. Twist the bowl slightly, then repeat. It's something like a figure-eight motion. Work quickly but lightly, and remember to dig right to the bottom of the bowl.

Stir

There's nothing difficult about stirring — just use a wooden spoon to mix the ingredients until combined.

Whisk

Use a wire whisk to rapidly beat the mixture. The point of whisking (sometimes referred to as whipping) is either to aerate the mixture or to break up clumps. If you're trying to incorporate air into the ingredients, it can help to hold the bowl at a slight angle and lift the whisk partially out of the liquid with every stroke.

A NOTE ON HEALTHY BAKING

The thought of baking a cake, a stack of chunky cookies, or a bittersweet crème caramel with anything less than complete joy in the excess it embodies is, for me, a very sad one. There are plenty of areas in your culinary life where compromises can be made, but if you have a choice in the matter, baking shouldn't be one of them.

It's difficult to slim down baked foods. Where there isn't butter, you might find oil; where there's no cream, there could be half a dozen eggs; where flour is whole grain, there'll still be salt. There is no such thing as a healthy cake and you should be suspicious of anything that claims to be one. If what you're eating really is low in fat, sugar, carbs, and salt, it's probably a vegetable.

But that's not to suggest that you can't make health-conscious changes to your baking. Where one ingredient can be swapped for a healthier one, I do just that. Heavy cream, for example, can be left out in favor of half-and-half, or even whole milk, depending on the recipe (although, I beg you, hands off the skim milk). I've slimmed down certain recipes with this in mind, avoid slathering icing on everything, and experimented with nonwheat flours. What I'm not willing to do is whittle down the calories (and taste) where the sensible option is just to cut oneself a slightly smaller slice.

CONVERSIONS

VOLUME

1 tablespoon	½ fl oz	15ml
2 tablespoons	1 fl oz	30ml
¼ cup	2 fl oz	60ml
⅓ cup	3 fl oz	80ml
½ cup	4 fl oz	120ml
¾ cup	5 fl oz (¼ pint)	180ml
1 cup	6 fl oz	240ml
1¼ cup	8 fl oz (⅓ pint)	300ml
2 cups, 1 pint	10 fl oz (½ pint)	480ml
1 fl oz	16 fl oz (⅔ pint)	28ml
2½ cups	20 fl oz (1 pint)	600ml
1 quart	32 fl oz (1⅔ pints)	1L

WEIGHT

½ oz	15g
1 oz	30g
2 oz	60g
¼ lb	115g
⅓ lb	150g
½ lb	225g
¾ lb	350g
1 lb (=16 oz)	450g

OVEN TEMPERATURES

Fahrenheit	Celcius / Gas mark
250°F	120°C / gas mark ½
275°F	135°C / gas mark 1
300°F	150°C / gas mark 2
325°F	160°C / gas mark 3
350°F	175 or 180°C / gas mark 4
375°F	190°C / gas mark 5
400°F	200°C / gas mark 6
425°F	220°C / gas mark 7
450°F	230°C / gas mark 8
475°F	245°C / gas mark 9
500°F	260°C

LENGTH

¼ inch	6 mm
½ inch	1.25 cm
¾ inch	2 cm
1 inch	2.5 cm
6 inches (½ foot)	15 cm
12 inches (1 foot)	30 cm

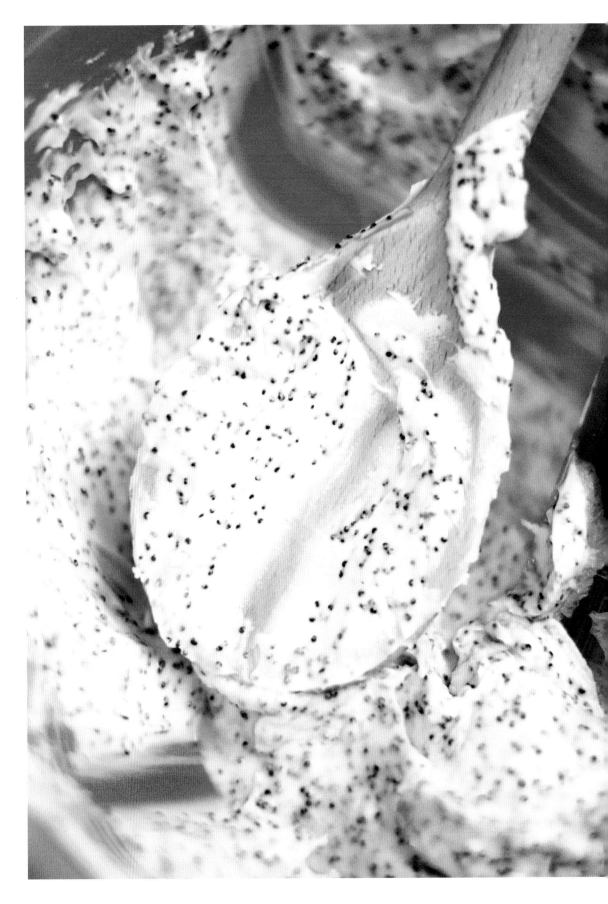

CAKE

LITTLE CAKES

LEMON & MARZIPAN CUPCAKES • HONEY MADELEINES

MORNING MUFFINS • CHAMOMILE VANILLA CUPCAKES

LOAF CAKES

ORANGE & WHITE CHOCOLATE LOAF CAKE • DATE MALT LOAF

BANANA BREAD • FIG, ORANGE & STAR ANISE TEA LOAF

SOUR CREAM MADEIRA CAKE

EVERYDAY CAKES

LEMON SEMOLINA CAKE • RYE APPLE UPSIDE-DOWN CAKE

CARAWAY CARROT CAKE WITH POPPY SEEDS

STOUT GINGERBREAD • GOOSEBERRY ELDERFLOWER CAKE

CHOCOLATE FUDGE CAKE

SPONGE CAKES

CHOCOLATE LIME MUD CAKE • TIRAMISU CAKE

PASSION FRUIT CURD JELLY ROLL

COFFEE & BLACK CURRANT OPERA CAKE

A slice of birthday cake cradled in a greasy napkin — a thick layer of fondant over buttercream over yellow cake, with bright red jam sandwiched in the middle. This is my first definitive memory of cake, and I'm sure that it's the reason why, to this day, I feel a little cheated by anything less than the most cheerful, blandly saccharine of confections. Nonetheless, I've grown to appreciate a few more grown-up flavors, too: rye flour with crisp apples, marzipan (its sweetness tempered with a kick of lemon), black coffee, passion fruit, and grassy caraway seeds. As you look through this chapter, you'll notice that the cakes become slightly bigger and more complex as you progress, from small cakes to loaf cakes, everyday cakes, and then sponge cakes, with the climactic opera cake at the end. This isn't a rigid syllabus but a friendly guide. Tackle the recipes in whatever order you please and don't feel intimidated by the trickier recipes — it's only cake, after all.

WHEN'S MY CAKE DONE?

After sliding a pan of cake batter into a hot oven and tenderly shutting the door, it's tempting to turn the kettle on, kick back, and congratulate yourself on a job well done. But, without wishing to be a scaremonger or fuss: don't speak too soon. Far from being the closing credits in your cake's story, its time in the oven will prove pivotal: baked well, it'll rise to great heights; baked poorly, even the most fastidiously prepared cake batter will proceed to disappoint, emerging perhaps gummy, perhaps dry.

Cooking time and temperature are the important variables to consider at this point. Rapid, high-temperature cooking will set an airy sponge batter, whereas a deeper, heavier cake — a fruitcake, for instance — is better suited to a longer, gentler stint in the oven. As I mentioned in the introduction, oven temperatures can be checked by using a cheap oven thermometer. The baking time, however, is slightly more difficult to pin down. Variations in pan sizes and thicknesses, different ambient and ingredient temperatures, and oven peculiarities can all have an impact on how long it takes a cake to cook.

With this in mind, it's important to be able to look beyond the suggested baking times and learn how to read a cake, judging for yourself whether your creation is baked or not. If you can do this — by ogling, prodding, and stabbing your cake — you'll be able to scale up or down or swap pans with confidence, making these recipes your own. Here are a few tests, which will, I hope, make the process more intuitive and less fraught.

KNIFE TEST

The knife test is the most used test, and the most effective. I always use a small knife for this, but you can use a proper cake tester if you have one, or even a skewer or toothpick. If the cake is ready, a knife inserted into the middle will come out with no more than a couple of moist crumbs sticking to it. If the knife emerges coated with batter, the cake isn't yet done. This is the best way of being sure that the cake is cooked through. Just don't be overzealous: the knife needs to come out cleanish, but if you wait until it comes out bone-dry, then you will have baked the cake too long. Remember, the center of the cake will continue to cook in its own heat for a short while after it's taken out of the oven, so it's better to bake slightly too little than too much.

CHECK THE EDGES

Large cakes, particularly whisked ones such as genoise sponges, will pull away from the edges of the pan when fully baked. Watch for the rim of the cake just starting to separate from the pan. This won't hold true for all cakes, particularly very moist ones such as banana bread or dense chocolate cakes, but it's not bad as a rule of thumb.

SPRING

Surface spring won't tell you definitively whether the cake is ready, but it will give you an indication. If, under the gentle press of a fingertip, the cake is left dented or feels fragile and spongy, it almost certainly needs a while longer in the oven. If it's springy to the touch, it may well be ready, or very nearly there.

COLOR

Recipes will often specify that a cake ought to be golden brown when done. This is fair enough as an observation, but a very inaccurate way of actually judging the cooking time in practice. Some very thin cakes might cook through before they have a chance to brown on top; some cakes, such as gingerbread or chocolate cake, will remain much the same color when baked; some have higher sugar content and therefore color more easily. But the fundamental problem here is that most cakes will begin to take on a deeper hue long before their center is cooked. The only time you need to heed the color of your cake as it's baking is if it's beginning to burn.

RISE

The amount of rise isn't very conclusive either. If the cake is well risen, fantastic. But that doesn't mean that it's cooked through just yet.

WHY IS MY CAKE . . .

Not all things in baking, as in life, can be foreseen. There will be times when even tried-and-tested, hand-me-down recipes fail. These disasters can, however, be explained. I can certainly relate to anyone who, as they despairingly attempt to salvage a burnt birthday cake in the early hours of the morning, doesn't much want to dwell on precisely when and how it all went wrong. But if you can face it, it's well worth taking a moment to look back and pinpoint the problem. Not only will this make it less likely that the mistake will repeat itself, but you'll also be able to gain some peace of mind. More often than not, it will come down to something as seemingly inconsequential as a teaspoon of baking powder or an egg too many. Here are some of the most common cake problems, their causes, and solutions.

... TOO DENSE?

— Too much liquid. Reduce the amount of liquid and be careful if adding any fresh fruit to the batter before baking.

— Underbaked, causing the cake to fall back on itself as it cools.

— Too little leavening agent. In most standard butter-based cakes you'll need about 1 teaspoon of baking powder per 100 grams (¾ c) of all-purpose flour, but you might need more if the batter is laden with ingredients such as fruit, nuts, or chocolate.

— In sponge cakes, you may have underbeaten or deflated the eggs. Be sure to whisk the eggs to the specified stage, whether ribbon, soft peak, or stiff peak, and fold the other ingredients in very carefully to avoid bashing the air out and deflating the mixture.

... TOO DRY?

— This will almost certainly be because your cake is overbaked. You can salvage a dry cake with a generous dose of syrup, though, or even by slicing it into thinner layers and sandwiching with buttercream.

... SUNKEN IN THE CENTER?

— Too much leavening agent. Believe it or not, too much baking soda or baking powder can result in a cake that rises and then falls again in the oven. The cake starts off with too much energy, tires itself out before it has a chance to set, and slumps back down again, exhausted.

— Underbaked. The cake's structure hasn't had a chance to firm properly and therefore has fallen back on itself under its own weight. But you might just be able to hurry the cake back to the oven to finish baking before it collapses completely.

— Bear in mind that some cakes do sink in the center as they cool — flourless cakes, for example, or very rich cakes such as the Chocolate Lime Mud Cake (page 60) are particularly prone to this. Most standard flour-based cakes shouldn't suffer from this problem.

...STEEPLY DOMED OR CRACKED?

— Usually this happens when the oven temperature is too high, causing the crust to set before the inside of the cake has cooked through. The raw batter then erupts through the surface as it continues to heat and expand, resulting in a domed, ruptured top. Bake at a slightly lower temperature next time (325°F will be sufficient for most cakes, with a longer cooking time factored in accordingly). One novel solution to this problem is to wrap the outside of the cake pan in well-soaked kitchen towels or rags prior to baking. These shield the sides of the cake from the direct heat of the oven, slowing the setting and therefore ensuring a more uniform rise.

— Counterintuitively, domed or cracked tops can also be caused by using too little leavening agent. Leavening agents slightly weaken the structure of the flour, resulting in a cake batter that can stretch and rise more before it begins to set. When there's too little of this weakening, the cake will grow more and the crust will set too soon, as above.

...BROWNED OR BURNT OUTSIDE BUT RAW INSIDE?

— It's very likely that your oven temperature is too high. Turn the oven down low, to 285°F and continue to bake until the cake is just set inside. Next time, bake at a slightly lower heat or invest in an oven thermometer (they're inexpensive and worth their weight in burnt cakes) to check that your oven is operating at the right temperature.

— Too much sugar can also be at the root of this problem, causing the outside to caramelize too quickly. Some sweeteners brown more quickly than others, too — agave nectar, for instance.

LITTLE CAKES

CREAMING BUTTER & SUGAR

I'm guilty of laziness when it comes to beating together butter and sugar. The cold butter has barely combined with the sugar before I throw up my hands in defeat and add the rest of the ingredients. This way lie curdled batter and heavy cakes. It's a boring job but you mustn't cut corners; as the butter and sugar are mixed, air is beaten into the mixture and the sugar begins to dissolve. You'll really notice the difference if you do it properly: a transformation from a heavy, greasy lump to a fluffy mixture, far lighter in both color and texture than before. This will take around 5 minutes if you work by hand, or as little as 2 minutes using an electric handheld or stand mixer. Dip a finger in and you'll notice that the mixture is almost mousse-like in texture, and far less gritty. The millions of air bubbles held in suspension by the fat and sugar are responsible for this metamorphosis, and this is what makes a cake particularly light and tender once baked.

LEMON & MARZIPAN CUPCAKES

In Portugal, there is a a light-colored, bitter almond liqueur called *amarguinha* that is typically mixed with a very generous measure of lemon juice. Bitter almond and lemon partner together wonderfully, and this very simple recipe is proof of that.

Makes 12
120 grams (8½ tbsp) unsalted
   butter, softened
75 grams (⅓ c) superfine sugar
½ teaspoon almond extract
Zest of 2 lemons
120 grams (scant 1 c)
   all-purpose flour

60 grams (½ c + 2 tbsp) ground almonds
1½ teaspoons baking powder
½ teaspoon salt
2 large eggs
3 tablespoons milk
200 grams (7 oz) marzipan, homemade
   (page 319) or store-bought

12-cup muffin tin

1   Preheat the oven to 350°F. Line the muffin tin with paper liners.

2   Cream the butter and sugar together until light and fluffy. Stir in the almond extract and lemon zest. Combine the flour, ground almonds, baking powder, and salt in a separate bowl. Break one egg into the butter mixture and then add a couple of tablespoons of the flour mixture. Stir to combine and then repeat. Stir in the rest of the flour along with the milk.

3   Grate in half of the marzipan, then break the remaining marzipan into small pieces and stir into the batter. Spoon the mixture into the lined muffin cups and bake for 17 to 20 minutes. A knife test is tricky with these cupcakes as the melted marzipan inside looks suspiciously like the uncooked cake batter. But use your instincts — if the cupcakes are well risen and golden and spring back when gently pressed with a finger, they are ready.

BROWN BUTTER

Peel back the wrapper of a heavy, pallid block of butter. Put the butter in a small pan over low heat and watch it slip and slide, leaving crisscrossing trails of yellow fat across the pan. Before long, the last island of butter will disappear into the golden liquid. Milky specks will settle at the bottom, while the fat — which is now clarified butter — begins to sizzle. It'll grow fragrant and nutty, deepening to an amber color. Snatch it off the heat now: this is brown butter. A few seconds later, the smell will turn bitter, the milk residue will char, and it'll be too late. If you thought that butter was butter, plain and simple — think again.

Brown butter is commonly found in recipes for *financiers*: little French cakes typically baked into tiny portions, each — fantastically, immodestly — the shape of a gold ingot. Used in place of normal butter it will impart a welcome warmth and roundness of flavor, especially when showcased against the neutrality of milk, cream, or simple sponge cakes. It has a natural affinity with nuts, too, hazelnuts being a particularly good match. The madeleine recipe that follows uses brown butter to complement the flavor of the honey.

It's important to substitute with care, however, if using brown butter in place of the usual stuff. During the cooking process, brown butter loses almost all of its water content (up to 20 percent of its original weight). This moisture must therefore be reintroduced into the recipe, with a splash of milk, for instance.

HONEY MADELEINES

Quite enough florid food prose has been written on the subject of these delicate little French cakes already, so I'll resist the temptation to wax lyrical about them here. All I will say is that they really are every bit as good as Proust and co. would have you believe.

If you have a madeleine pan only large enough to make 12 at a time, don't worry: the batter won't suffer if left standing while you cook the cakes in batches. And if you don't have a madeleine pan at all, you can use a standard muffin tin instead. The end result won't be any less delicious.

Chilling the filled pan seems to help the cakes develop their characteristic nipple. I think it brings an element of interest to the teatime table . . .

Makes 20 to 24 traditional madeleines, or 12 in a muffin tin
130 grams (½ c + 1 tbsp) unsalted butter
75 grams (⅓ c) superfine sugar
2 tablespoons honey
2 large eggs
100 grams (¾ c) all-purpose flour

½ teaspoon baking powder

12-cup madeleine pan or 12-cup muffin tin

📷 page 28

1 Melt the butter over low heat. As soon as it's melted, transfer 2 tablespoons of it to a small bowl. Return the remaining butter to the heat, stirring continuously while it sizzles. Before long it'll turn a light brown color and smell slightly toasted — as soon as it reaches this stage, remove it from the heat or else it'll burn. Set aside to cool for a few minutes.

2   Use the reserved tablespoons of melted butter to brush the cavities of the madeleine or muffin tin. You may not need all of it. Put the tin in the fridge (or freezer, if you have the space) while you make the batter.

3   Combine the sugar, honey, and eggs in a bowl, whisking for a minute or so until foamy. In a separate bowl, combine the flour and baking powder, then add to the sugar mixture. Fold in the slightly cooled brown butter.

4   Remove the buttered pan from the fridge. If making traditional shell-shaped madeleines, fill each hole no more than three-quarters full. Set the remaining batter aside until the next batch, remembering to grease and chill the pan again before using. If using a muffin tin, just divide all of the mixture between the 12 holes (they won't be anywhere near full — these are going to be dainty morsels, not full-sized cupcakes). Place the filled pan in the fridge for 20 minutes while you preheat the oven to 400°F.

5   Bake the shell-shaped madeleines for 8 to 9 minutes, or the cupcakes for 9 to 12 minutes. Remove from the pan and let cool.

MORNING MUFFINS

These muffins are what I like to eat with a mug of black coffee on a lazy weekend, as the morning pushes into the afternoon. They're substantial without being stupefyingly rich — a welcome alternative to buttery pastries or a full breakfast, yet without the dour frugality of a bowl of porridge. The whole wheat flour lends them a reassuringly virtuous edge (although you can swap this for all-purpose flour if you really must). Grapefruit, zested into the batter and decorating the tops of these muffins, gives a citrus kick. Don't be fooled into thinking that they're a healthy breakfast superfood, though: no matter how you dress it up, it's still cake for breakfast.

You can make the batter in the evening, so it will be ready to cook the next morning. Just cover it with plastic wrap and refrigerate overnight. But it is a quick batter to make, and not unfeasible for breakfast-time — you can prepare the batter in 15 minutes and have freshly baked muffins, ready to eat, within an hour.

These muffins are best eaten right away (they're at their lightest and fluffiest while still slightly warm), which is why I have given the quantities for a batch of only 6 here — enough for three people. If you're feeding more, or serving people with very healthy appetites, the recipe can very easily be doubled or even tripled, according to your needs.

Makes 6
1 grapefruit (I use pink grapefruit)
3½ tablespoons unsalted butter
100 grams superfine sugar (7 tbsp)
   or light brown sugar (½ c)
1 large egg
¾ cup plain yogurt
40 grams (½ c) quick oats
60 grams (½ c) all-purpose flour

¼ cup whole wheat flour
½ teaspoon baking powder
½ teaspoon baking soda
¼ teaspoon salt
4 teaspoons sugar (preferably demerara),
   for sprinkling

6- or 12-cup muffin tin

📷 page 31

1   Preheat the oven to 350°F. Line the muffin tin with paper liners.

2   Grate the zest of the grapefruit into a large bowl. Cut one half of the grapefruit into six segments, trim away the peel and pith from each, and set aside. (You can wince your way through the remaining half grapefruit while you wait for the muffins to bake.)

3   Melt the butter in a small pan over low heat. Add the butter and sugar to the zest and beat to combine. Stir in the egg, yogurt, and oats. In a separate bowl, combine the flours, baking powder, baking soda, and salt. Add the flour mixture to the zest mixture and stir briefly until just combined, being careful not to stir any more than is absolutely necessary, as any excess mixing can strengthen the structure of the batter, resulting in chewy, heavy muffins.

4   Spoon the batter into the paper liners. It shouldn't reach any higher than two-thirds up each liner; otherwise the muffins will overflow while baking and you will get far more muffin top than you bargained for.

5   Perch a grapefruit segment on top of each muffin and sprinkle with the 4 teaspoons of sugar. Bake for about 25 minutes, until well risen and springy.

Variations
If the thought of grapefruit sets your teeth on edge, swap it for a small handful of raisins stirred into the batter, and possibly a little cinnamon, too. Blueberries could also be used for a more traditional morning muffin.

BAKING WITH TEA

I once worked in a small London tearoom. It was a steep learning curve for someone who, until then, thought that tea came in just four ways: with milk, sugar, both, or neither. And so I learned about cups, saucers, strainers, and brewing tea in dainty teapots rather than steeping it in a stained mug. The tea was loose-leaf, stored in heavy glass jars clustered on the shelves: fine Earl Gray, feathery chamomile, gray-green Darjeeling . . . The lid of the jar would open with a pop, and up came the smell of rose, fragrant jasmine, or smoky Lapsang souchong. It was an education.

And, excitingly, the very things that make tea so good to brew — the aromatics, the concentrated flavor — also make it perfect to cook with. Earl Gray can complement a citrus tea loaf, and green tea lends a bright green color and delicate flavor to a shortbread cookie. Even gentle chamomile tea can be effective, as in the soothing chamomile cupcakes opposite. It's a change from the usual flavoring formula of essence, spice, or zest. Tea does, however, benefit from being infused in a liquid first if it's to release its flavor most effectively. This is best done in butter or milk, bringing the tea and liquid to a boil, then letting it cool and infuse.

CHAMOMILE VANILLA CUPCAKES

Chamomile might not be an obvious flavor for a cake, but it's one that works remarkably well. It is subtly grassy, fragrant, and — bolstered by the vanilla — mellow and warm. On days when comfort food is called for, you could do worse than one of these sunny cupcakes. There's not an excessive amount of buttercream on these — just enough to cap each one. But if you have a very sweet tooth, you can of course make extra.

I've called for chamomile tea bags here rather than the better-quality loose tea only because the bagged stuff is so much easier to source. But if you can get ahold of the more aromatic loose leaves, then by all means use those instead.

Makes 12
225 grams (1 c) unsalted butter
⅔ cup milk
6 chamomile tea bags
160 grams (scant ¾ c) superfine sugar
3 large eggs
1½ teaspoons vanilla extract
210 grams (1⅔ c) all-purpose flour

1½ teaspoons baking powder
Pinch of salt
200 to 300 grams (1⅔ to 2⅓ c) confectioners' sugar

12-cup muffin tin

📷 page 35

1   Preheat the oven to 350°F. Line the muffin tin with paper liners.

2   Put the butter, milk, and tea bags in a small pan over low heat. Once the butter has completely melted, let the mixture simmer for a couple of minutes. Set aside to cool for 5 minutes, then strain out the tea bags, collecting the chamomile-infused liquid in a bowl. Some of it will have evaporated and some will get lost in the tea bags, but you should still have 1 to 1¼ cups of liquid. Divide the liquid into two bowls — the first bowl containing two-thirds (⅔ to 1 c), the other containing the remaining third. Set both bowls in the fridge for 20 minutes to slightly firm the butter.

3   Beat the larger portion of the chilled milk mixture with the sugar for a couple of minutes until slightly lighter in color. Add the eggs and vanilla extract. In a separate bowl, stir the flour, baking powder, and salt together, then fold this mixture into the egg mixture until all is combined. You'll end up with a thick batter, which drops softly off an upturned spoon. If it stays clinging to the spoon, add a splash of milk to thin it and reach that dropping consistency.

4   Divide the batter among the lined muffin cups and bake for 15 to 20 minutes, testing at the lower end of this interval and keeping a close eye on the cupcakes until they're done. Small cakes such as these go from under to overbaked very quickly, so it's important to be present during the latter part of the cooking time.

5   To make the buttercream, beat the reserved chamomile-infused milk mixture until smooth, gradually adding the confectioners' sugar until the buttercream is thick. Buttercream shouldn't be hidebound by rules and ratios — just use enough sugar to produce a good texture and flavor, balancing the butter's richness with

sweetness and testing as you go. Chill the buttercream in the fridge while you wait for the cupcakes to cool.

6 Once the cupcakes have cooled, top each one with a slick of buttercream. I like to go for maximum coordination, serving them (to myself) with a pot of matching chamomile tea.

Variations
This recipe can be adapted to play host to almost any tea spin-off (Lady Gray tea with orange zest is a favorite).

LOAF CAKES

ORANGE & WHITE CHOCOLATE LOAF CAKE

Sometimes a cake is a cake is a cake, not to be fussed over or tampered with. This is one such cake: moist, sweet, and citrus scented. It is worth it for the joy of zesting alone.

Makes 1 medium loaf, serving 6 to 8
150 grams (⅔ c) unsalted butter, softened
150 grams (⅔ c) superfine sugar
Zest of 2 oranges
Zest of ½ lemon
2 large eggs, lightly beaten
225 grams (1¾ c) all-purpose flour
1½ teaspoons baking powder
¼ teaspoon salt
5 tablespoons milk
150 grams white chocolate chips (⅔ c) or a block chopped into very small ¼-inch chunks (5.25 oz)

Syrup
Juice of 1 orange
Juice of ½ lemon
3½ tablespoons superfine sugar

Drizzle
50 to 100 grams (1.75 to 3.5 oz) white chocolate

5 by 9-inch loaf pan

📷 page 36

1   Preheat the oven to 350°F. Grease the loaf pan and line it with parchment paper.

2   Cream the butter and sugar together until light and fluffy (this takes some elbow grease or an electric mixer). Beat in the zests, then gradually beat in the eggs. In a separate bowl, combine the flour, baking powder, and salt, then gently fold into the butter mixture. Stir in the milk.

3   Toss the chocolate in a couple of tablespoons of extra flour to help ensure that it doesn't sink straight to the bottom of the pan, then stir them into the batter.

4   Spoon the mixture into the prepared pan, smooth the top and bake for 50 to 60 minutes, until a knife inserted into the middle comes out with only a few crumbs sticking to it.

5   While the cake is baking, prepare the syrup by gently heating the orange and lemon juices in a pan and then stirring in the sugar until dissolved. As soon as the cake is out of the oven, pierce it all over with a small, sharp knife, toothpick, or skewer, then spoon the syrup over the top. You may not need to use all of it, but do be generous. Let the cake cool in the pan before turning it out.

6   To make the drizzle, heat the white chocolate in 10-second bursts in the microwave, or in a bowl suspended over — but not touching — a pan of simmering water, stirring often until melted. Drizzle over the top of the cake, using either a spoon or a piping bag.

DATE MALT LOAF

This is more a bread than a cake in spirit, I suppose; there's little lightness or refinement to it. It's possibly the only cake that ever survived my childhood raiding of the kitchen cupboards, regarded with the same suspicion reserved for things like brown rice and fresh fruit. But when it comes to not judging a book by its cover, this squat, heavy little loaf is a case in point. It is densely chewy, deeply malted, and heavy with fruit and has an almost toffee flavor . . . . Forget the tiered, turreted, palatial centerpieces of the cake kingdom: it's this cake — all substance and no style — that really steals the show.

Malt extract is everywhere. It creeps into breads, beers, cereals, and chocolates, bringing with it a unique flavor that I can really only describe, apologetically, as maltiness. It's a taste somewhere between roasted, toasted, caramel, and coffee, and it's delicious. Yet for something so quietly ubiquitous in our foods, malt extract can prove tricky to find in its most basic state: a thick, brown syrup, as viscous as molasses, sold by the jar. But thanks to a folkloric belief in the nutritional power of the stuff (a power which I'm not convinced would stand the scrutiny of nutritionists nowadays) you should be able to find it in well-stocked natural food stores.

Makes 1 medium loaf, serving 6 to 8
60 grams (¼ c) unsalted butter
½ cup strong black tea
150 grams (7 tbsp) liquid malt extract
120 grams (½ c + 1½ tbsp) dark
 brown sugar
2 large eggs, lightly beaten

260 grams (2 c + 1 tbsp) all-purpose flour
2 teaspoons baking powder
¼ teaspoon salt
150 grams (1 c) coarsely chopped dates

5 by 9-inch loaf pan

📷 page 39

1   Preheat the oven to 325°F. Grease the loaf pan and line it with parchment paper.

2   Put the butter, tea, and malt extract in a small pan over low heat. Once the butter has melted, remove from the heat, stir in the sugar, and add the beaten eggs. Stir to combine.

3   Mix the flour, baking powder, and salt together in a bowl, then pour in the tea mixture and stir lightly to combine. Stir in the dates. The satiny batter might be slightly runnier than you're used to, but this is no cause for concern.

4   Pour the mixture into the prepared loaf pan and bake for 60 to 75 minutes, until a knife inserted into the center comes out with nothing but a crumb or two on it. Let cool completely before eating, if you can resist. And for those with powers of moderation and restraint that I can barely dream of, wrap the loaf tightly in foil and store at room temperature for a couple of days before eating, during which time its flavor will deepen and mature.

Variations
You can swap the dates for golden raisins, raisins, or currants if you want, although I quite like the caramel flavor of the dates here. You might also try using brown ale, porter, or even stout instead of the tea — it's an unusual but completely logical

combination, the mellow maltiness of the ale bolstering the malt flavor of the cake. Some things, however, are not up for negotiation, and when it comes to the eating there is only one sensible way to proceed: cut the loaf into generous slices, spread each thickly with salted — always salted — butter, and eat with your fingers.

BANANA BREAD

Banana bread has a magnetic pull. Don't be surprised if its sweet, deep banana scent draws you nose first into the kitchen as it bakes. This is one of the best-smelling cakes I've made. The misty sugar glaze is an inessential but delicious afterthought. You can, of course, omit it if sugar levels are a concern.

This banana bread is made with agave nectar. It's an alternative to traditional sugars and syrups but does call for some fine-tuning of the other ingredients to get the ratios right. Although light, agave nectar has its own distinctive taste, which in a plainer cake might be an unwelcome distraction, but here subtly complements the banana.

If you'd rather make this with "normal" sugar, just swap the agave for 140 grams of superfine sugar (½ c + 2 tbsp) or light brown sugar (½ c + 3 tbsp) and then add 3½ tablespoons of milk with the rum or brandy. Similarly, you can omit the cardamom if it's not to your taste, although I really like the citrusy spice alongside the banana's creamy sweetness.

Makes 1 medium loaf, serving 6 to 8
125 grams (½ c + 1 tbsp) unsalted butter, softened
⅓ cup agave nectar
2 medium bananas, well mashed
2 tablespoons rum or brandy
2 large eggs
190 grams (1½ c) all-purpose flour
1½ teaspoons baking powder
½ teaspoon ground cinnamon
¼ teaspoon salt
4 cardamom pods, seeds only, crushed

Glaze (optional)
1 tablespoon + 2 teaspoons water
100 grams (¾ c + 1 tbsp) confectioners' sugar

5 by 9-inch loaf pan

📷 page 40

1   Preheat the oven to 350°F. Grease the loaf pan and line it with parchment paper.

2   Cream the butter, then stir in the agave nectar. Beat in the bananas and rum, then the eggs and a couple of tablespoons of the flour. Beat until smooth, but don't worry if the mixture looks a little curdled at this stage. Combine the remaining flour with the baking powder, cinnamon, salt, and cardamom in a separate bowl then add to the banana mixture. Fold the ingredients together, then stir lightly until fully combined.

3   Spoon the batter into the prepared pan and bake for 45 to 55 minutes, until a knife inserted into the center of the cake comes out clean. While the cake is baking make the glaze: stir the water into the sugar, a teaspoonful at a time, until combined. Set aside.

4   Let the cake cool in the pan for 5 minutes, then turn it out onto a wire rack set over a tray (to catch any drips). Spoon the glaze over the top of the cake while it's still hot. It will cover the top and run down the sides in thick rivulets, but it will set to a cracked sugar crust as the cake cools.

FIG, ORANGE & STAR ANISE TEA LOAF

This is my favorite recipe in this book. If you buy dried figs just once in your life, let it be for this. It's a headily perfumed loaf that is, quite impossibly, at once floral, citrus, licorice, spice, and caramel and yet not definitively any one of those things. It sits happily outside the tea loaf status quo. I love it.

Makes 1 medium loaf, serving 6 to 8
1¼ cups milk
250 grams (1⅔ c) dried figs,
    coarsely chopped
75 grams (6 tbsp) light brown sugar
Zest of 1 orange
1 teaspoon finely ground star anise*
1½ teaspoons vanilla extract
2 large eggs
275 grams (2 c + 3 tbsp) all-purpose flour

2½ teaspoons baking powder
1 teaspoon ground ginger
¼ teaspoon salt

5 by 9-inch loaf pan

* grind 3 to 4 whole star anise, sift out
    the grit, and measure what you need

page 43

1   Preheat the oven to 350°F. Grease the loaf pan and line it with parchment paper.

2   In a large bowl, combine the milk, figs, sugar, orange zest, star anise, vanilla extract, and eggs.

3   In a separate bowl, combine the flour, baking powder, ginger, and salt. Add to the milk mixture and stir lightly until combined. Spoon into the prepared pan and bake for 50 to 60 minutes. Let rest in the pan for 15 minutes or so before turning out onto a wire rack to cool completely.

SOUR CREAM MADEIRA CAKE

This unadorned cake doesn't need any drizzle, dusting, or decoration — any such messing around will only distract from the meltingly soft, yellow sponge. The sour cream works wonders here, offsetting the buttery richness and creating a tender texture. It's a firmer cake than some, but this is precisely what makes Madeira cake, allowing it to be cut cleanly into proud, even slices.

Makes 1 medium loaf, serving 6 to 8
150 grams (⅔ c) unsalted butter,
    softened
150 grams (⅔ c) superfine sugar
2 large eggs
Zest of 1 lemon

½ cup + 2 tablespoons sour cream
175 grams (1⅓ c + 1 tbsp)
    all-purpose flour
1½ teaspoons baking powder
¼ teaspoon salt

5 by 9-inch loaf pan

1   Preheat the oven to 350°F. Grease the loaf pan and line it with parchment paper.

2   Beat the butter and sugar together for about 5 minutes. Although stubbornly heavy to start with, the butter will soon become soft, light, and fluffy as the sugar dissolves into it and air is incorporated. Stir in the eggs, lemon zest, and sour cream, beating well until the mixture is completely combined.

3   Combine the flour, baking powder, and salt in a separate bowl, then stir into the butter mixture. Don't mix for any longer than is necessary or you risk a heavy, chewy cake.

4   Spoon the mixture into the prepared pan and bake for about 45 minutes, until a knife inserted into the middle of the cake comes out with no more than a crumb or two on it. Let cool completely in the pan before turning out and serving.

EVERYDAY CAKES

LEMON SEMOLINA CAKE

Lemon drizzle cake should teasingly tread the sweet-sharp line; if it doesn't make your mouth pucker just a little, then, to my mind, it's all wrong. For this, a generous hand with the syrup is essential, and using both the juice and zest of the lemons helps, too. The semolina makes for a far more interesting texture and leaves the cake exuberantly, sunnily yellow.

Makes one 8-inch round cake, serving 8
125 grams (½ c + 1 tbsp) unsalted
    butter, softened
125 grams (½ c + 1 tbsp) superfine sugar
2 large eggs, lightly beaten
Zest and juice of 2 large or 3 smaller
    lemons
100 grams (½ c + 1½ tbsp) semolina
60 grams (½ c) all-purpose flour
1 teaspoon baking powder
Pinch of salt

Syrup
60 grams (¼ c) superfine
    or granulated sugar
Lemon juice
2½ tablespoons confectioners' sugar,
    for dusting (optional)

**8-inch round cake pan, preferably
loose-bottomed or springform**

1   Preheat the oven to 340°F and grease the pan. If the pan isn't loose-bottomed, be sure to line the bottom with parchment paper.

2   Cream the butter and sugar until pale and fluffy, then add the eggs, lemon zest, semolina, and 1 tablespoon of the lemon juice. Reserve the remaining lemon juice for the syrup, to be made later. In a separate bowl, combine the flour, baking powder, and salt. Add the flour mixture to the butter mixture and stir to combine. Spoon into the prepared pan, smooth the top, and bake for 25 minutes, until a knife inserted into the middle comes out clean.

3   While the cake is in the oven, make the syrup. Combine the reserved lemon juice and the sugar in a pan over low heat. Let bubble for just a couple of minutes, until it looks a bit more . . . well, syrupy. Remove from the heat.

4   As soon as the cake is out of the oven, pierce deeply through the top with a fork or skewer a few times then slowly spoon the syrup over the top, giving it time to seep into the cake. Let cool slightly, then remove the cake from the pan and put it on a wire rack to cool completely. A liberal dusting of confectioners' sugar is a glorious (but admittedly unnecessary) finishing touch.

RYE APPLE UPSIDE-DOWN CAKE

This nutty, caramel-crusted apple cake is only a single-tier cake by design: why go to such pains to achieve a layer of toffee-apple splendor if it's going to be dwarfed by the mass of cake underneath? The rye flour enhances the flavor and gives a more interesting texture, too. If your 8-inch round pan is quite shallow, with sides less than 2 inches high, I recommend making two-thirds of the quantity to avoid overflow.

Makes one 8-inch round cake, serving 8

Caramel Layer
100 grams superfine sugar (7 tbsp)
   or granulated sugar (½ c)
2 tablespoons water
2 teaspoons unsalted butter
1 to 2 medium eating apples
   such as Golden Delicious, peeled,
   cored, and thinly sliced

Cake
160 grams (scant ¾ c) unsalted butter,
   softened
150 grams superfine sugar (⅔ c)
   or light brown sugar (¾ c)

3 large eggs, lightly beaten
2 medium eating apples, peeled and
   coarsely grated
90 grams (⅔ c + 1 tbsp) all-purpose flour
90 grams (¾ c + 2 tbsp) rye flour
1½ teaspoons baking powder
1 teaspoon ground cinnamon
¼ teaspoon salt
100 grams (about ¾ c + 2 tbsp)
   chopped nuts
100 grams (⅔ c) raisins or golden raisins

Deep 8-inch round cake pan

📷 page 46

1   Preheat the oven to 350°F. Grease the pan and line it with parchment paper.

2   To make the caramel layer, combine the sugar and water in a small pan (preferably not nonstick) over low heat. Cook, stirring occasionally, until the sugar is dissolved and then — and this really is important — do not stir or otherwise touch it. Turn up the heat to medium-high and let it simmer until the sugar has turned golden. Add the butter (careful — it may spatter!) and stir until melted. (See page 316 for advice on making caramel.) Pour the caramel into the prepared pan, covering the entire bottom.

3   Arrange the apple slices in concentric circles on the caramel while it's still warm and sticky then set aside.

4   To make the cake batter, cream the butter and sugar until light and fluffy, then gradually stir in the eggs. Stir in the grated apple. Don't worry if the mixture seems slightly curdled.

5   Combine the flours, baking powder, cinnamon, and salt in a separate bowl, then add to the wet ingredients. Finally, stir in the nuts and raisins. Spoon the batter into the pan and very carefully level it with the back of the spoon.

6   Bake for 35 to 45 minutes, until a knife inserted in the middle comes out with no more than a crumb or two sticking to it. Let cool in the pan for a few minutes before turning out onto a wire rack, turning it upside down (or the right way up now, I suppose). Peel back the parchment paper to reveal the caramelized apple top.

CARAWAY CARROT CAKE WITH POPPY SEEDS

Despite being an unusual addition to a carrot cake (typically flavored with cinnamon), caraway seeds work very well in this recipe. They're not much to look at — tiny, banana-shaped brown seeds — but their taste is unique. If you haven't ever done so, chew on a seed before you get to work on this cake; you'll find it sharp yet earthy, bitter but surprisingly bright. It's often used in rye breads. You can increase the amount of caraway here to taste, or even leave a few of the seeds whole, for a bolder flavor. Be sure to use good-quality cream cheese — cheaper ones will have a higher water content, leaving the icing runny and thin.

Makes one 8-inch round cake,
   serving 8 to 10
150 grams (⅔ c) unsalted butter,
   softened
150 grams (¾ c) light brown sugar
125 grams (1⅓ c) grated carrots
   (from about 2 carrots)
2 large eggs
2 tablespoons milk
150 grams (1 c + 3 tbsp) all-purpose flour
Pinch of salt
1½ teaspoons baking powder
1 teaspoon ground coriander

1½ teaspoons caraway seeds, coarsely
   ground or crushed
3 tablespoons poppy seeds

Icing
300 grams (10.5 oz) full-fat cream cheese
75 grams (½ c + 2 tbsp) confectioners'
   sugar
Zest of 1 lemon
3 tablespoons poppy seeds

**Deep 8-inch round cake pan, preferably
   springform or loose-bottomed**

📷 page 49

1   Preheat the oven to 350°F and grease the pan.

2   In a large bowl, beat the butter and brown sugar until fluffy. Add the carrots, eggs, and milk, along with a tablespoon or two of the flour. Mix the remaining flour with the salt, baking powder, coriander, caraway seeds, and poppy seeds in a separate bowl then add to the butter mixture. Stir until just combined.

3   Pour the batter into the prepared pan and bake for 25 to 35 minutes, until a knife inserted into the center of the cake comes out with no more than a crumb or two stuck to it. Let cool for a few minutes in the pan before unmolding and transferring to a wire rack to cool completely.

4   To make the icing, strain any excess liquid from the cheese to avoid a runny icing. Stir the cream cheese until smooth, then add the sugar, lemon zest, and poppy seeds and stir until just combined.

5   Halve the cooled cake horizontally using a large serrated knife. Perfectly even layers aren't always easy to achieve — I tend to just remedy the inevitably wonky cake by using icing to level out the layers.

6   Dollop half of the icing on the bottom circle of cake and spread gently to cover the top. Sandwich with the upper layer and spread the remaining icing over the top and sides.

LIQUID FLAVORINGS

Using liquids to add flavor to a cake is a difficult maneuver. They can't simply be added to a standard cake mix — that skews the ratios of ingredients and potentially results in a dense, gummy texture in the finished cake. It's often safer and easier to use dry flavorings or highly concentrated liquid ones, hence lemon zest rather than juice, a dash of ground spices, or a scant teaspoon of potent vanilla extract.

But some cakes have a more liquid batter, such as gingerbreads, malt loaves, banana breads, some chocolate cakes, and heavy fruitcakes. With these cakes, you're freer to experiment. If a fruited loaf cake calls for a cup of milk, perhaps try strong black tea instead. It's not unusual to find recipes for chocolate cake that use Guinness to deepen the flavor. The gingerbread below works on exactly this principle. Have a go with your own substitutions — tea, ale, spirits, liqueurs, coffee. Just steer clear of acidic liquids such as fruit juice, which can curdle the batter.

STOUT GINGERBREAD

This isn't brittle, cookie-like gingerbread — this one is moist, cakey, and deliciously dark. It's a very wet batter, easier to pour than to spoon into the pan, so don't be alarmed. The smooth, almost chocolaty stout rounds the flavor of the cake and keeps it beautifully tender. You can use milk instead, if you prefer, but the result won't have quite the same molassesy depth.

This cake tastes even better in the days after baking, so a little self-restraint will really pay off if you can bear to leave it untouched for a day or two. That said, it rarely lasts longer than a few hours at my house.

Makes one 8-inch round cake,
  serving 8 to 10
60 grams (¼ c) unsalted butter
¼ cup molasses
60 grams (5 tbsp) dark or light
  brown sugar
2 to 2½ inches fresh ginger, grated
7 tablespoons stout, porter, or
  brown ale

1 large egg, lightly beaten
120 grams (scant 1 c) all-purpose flour
2 teaspoons ground ginger
½ teaspoon baking soda
¼ teaspoon salt

8-inch round cake pan

📷 page 50

1   Preheat the oven to 350°F. Grease the pan and line it with parchment paper.

2   Combine the butter, molasses, and sugar in a pan over low heat and cook just until the butter is melted. Stir in the fresh ginger and stout. Using a whisk or fork, beat in the egg.

3   Mix the flour, ground ginger, baking soda, and salt together in a large bowl. Add the molasses mixture gradually, whisking all the time, and continue to mix until well combined and clump-free.

4   Pour the batter into the prepared pan and bake for 25 to 30 minutes until the top is springy and a knife inserted into the middle comes out clean.

WHIPPING CREAM

Whipping cream is at once very simple and unexpectedly tricky: it's dangerously easy to move from smooth, proud crests of cream one moment to a grainy mess the next. If you really bully the cream, it'll separate, clump, and turn into butter. To avoid a cream calamity, go slowly when whisking and stop just before you think it's thick enough, particularly if you plan to pipe the cream; when forced through the nozzle of a piping bag, even loosely whipped cream can, bewilderingly, churn itself. Although it's hard work, I like to whip cream the old-fashioned way, with a wire whisk. It gives you a far keener sense of the texture of the cream as it thickens than an electric mixer does, and minimizes the risk of overwhipping. And let's face it: if you're going to be eating any of this gloriously thick, whipped cream, a little preliminary workout can't do any harm.

GOOSEBERRY ELDERFLOWER CAKE

This is the archetypical summer fête cake: two thick layers of buttery cake sandwiching cream and fruit. It's an old-fashioned slice of collective nostalgia.

If you can't get your hands on fresh gooseberries (they're best from June to August and even then aren't always easy to find), you could try canned gooseberries, reducing the amount of sugar they're simmered with, but they're rarely very good. You could also opt for a different filling altogether (see the variations on page 54).

It is best not to make this too far in advance — the cream will spoil if left at room temperature for too long, but the cake will go stale if stored in the fridge. The only option is to gobble it quite soon after baking. That shouldn't be too hard.

Makes one 8-inch round cake,
 serving 8 to 10
175 grams (¾ c) unsalted butter,
 softened
175 grams (¾ c) superfine sugar
175 grams (1⅓ c + 1 tbsp)
 all-purpose flour
Pinch of salt
1½ teaspoons baking powder
3 large eggs
1 teaspoon vanilla extract
3½ tablespoons milk
7 tablespoons elderflower liqueur

Filling
250 grams (1⅔ c) gooseberries,
 trimmed if fresh
40 to100 grams (3 to 7 tbsp)
 superfine sugar
½ cup + 2 tablespoons heavy cream
3 tablespoons elderflower liqueur

Superfine sugar, for dusting

**Two 8-inch round cake tins, preferably
 loose-bottomed or springform**

📷 page 53

1 Preheat the oven to 350°F. Grease the pans and line them with parchment paper.

2 Cream the butter and sugar until light and fluffy. In another bowl, combine the flour, salt, and baking powder. Add one-third of the flour mixture and one of the eggs to the butter mixture and stir to combine. Repeat until all of the flour and eggs are incorporated, then stir in the vanilla extract and milk.

3   Divide the batter between the two pans and bake for 15 to 20 minutes, until golden brown and just starting to shrink away from the sides of the pan. The cakes should feel springy to the touch.

4   Let the cakes cool in their pans for 5 minutes, then carefully turn them out onto a wire rack. Drizzle the 7 tablespoons of elderflower liqueur over both cakes and let cool completely.

5   Meanwhile, make the filling. Simmer the gooseberries over low heat with the sugar, using only about 3 tablespoons of sugar for canned gooseberries, and up to 7 tablespoons for fresh gooseberries, to balance their sharpness. Just add the sugar to taste and cook until the berries split their skins, release their juices, and soften — about 10 minutes for fresh gooseberries and only a couple of minutes for canned ones. Set aside to cool.

6   Whisk together the cream and the 3 tablespoons of elderflower liqueur until just thick enough to spread. This will take anywhere between 2 and 5 minutes, depending on whether you use a manual wire whisk or an electric mixer.

7   Once the cake and the gooseberry mixture are at room temperature, spread the gooseberries over one cake, dollop the cream on top, then sandwich with the other cake. Dust with superfine sugar.

Variations
Strawberries also complement the delicately floral elderflower liqueur. Fill the cake with a few tablespoons of good-quality strawberry jam — or better still, make your own (see page 323) — instead of the gooseberries. If elderflower isn't your thing, omit the elderflower drizzle and spread with raspberry jam for a timeless Victoria sponge cake.

CHOCOLATE FUDGE CAKE

"Suddenly the Trunchbull exploded. 'Eat!' she shouted, banging her thigh with the riding-crop. 'If I tell you to eat, you will eat! You wanted cake! You stole cake! And now you've got cake! What's more, you're going to eat it! You do not leave this platform and nobody leaves this hall until you have eaten the entire cake that is sitting there in front of you!'" Roald Dahl, *Matilda*

Bruce Bogtrotter's triumph over the chocolate cake was perhaps my most read passage in any book throughout my childhood. It's the cake that stands for cake itself, with two thick layers of moist, dark chocolate sponge smothered in fudgy frosting. And if you can turn eating it into an act of defiance against the Trunchbull, or diet culture, or whatever, all the better.

Chocolate is the very essence of this cake, so using a reasonable-quality bar will make a big difference. I do not, however, subscribe to the rather priggish school of cooking that blusteringly dismisses anything but the finest single-origin, artisanally crafted Peruvian chocolate. I've made many a chocolate cake with nothing more fancy than a couple of bars of Bournville and had no complaints thus far.

Makes one 8-inch round cake,
serving 8 to 10
200 grams (7 oz) dark chocolate
200 grams (¾ c + 2 tbsp) unsalted
butter, cubed
4 large eggs
¾ cup + 1½ tablespoons milk
100 grams (½ c) dark brown sugar
160 grams (scant ¾ c) superfine sugar
50 grams (½ c + 1 tbsp) cocoa powder
200 grams (1½ c + 1½ tbsp)
all-purpose flour

2 teaspoons baking powder
½ teaspoon baking soda
¼ teaspoon salt
Chocolate fudge ganache or butterscotch
frosting (recipes follow)

**Two 8-inch round cake pans, preferably
loose-bottomed or springform**

📷 page 56

1   Preheat the oven to 350°F. Grease the pans and line them with parchment paper.

2   Melt the chocolate either in short bursts in the microwave or in a bowl suspended
over (but not touching) simmering water in a pan. Remove from the heat, then stir
in the butter until melted. Whisk in the eggs, milk, and both sugars.

3   In another bowl, combine the cocoa powder, flour, baking powder, baking soda,
and salt. Add to the wet ingredients, gently whisking in for only as long as it takes
to combine. The batter will be thick and satiny, inviting you to take first a little
finger to it, then a teaspoon, then a ladle.

4   Divide the mixture between the prepared pans and bake for 25 to 30 minutes.
Chocolate cakes suffer for being even slightly overbaked, so be vigilant: test
at 25 minutes and keep a close eye on the cakes thereafter. If a knife inserted into
the center of a cake comes out with no more than a couple of crumbs sticking
to it, it's ready.

5   Let the cakes cool in their pans for a few minutes, then turn out onto wire racks
and let cool to room temperature. Layer and frost with one of the following types
of icing.

CHOCOLATE FUDGE GANACHE

This dark, fudgy ganache is an event in itself. The same goes here for the chocolate
as in the cake recipe above: one with a high percentage of cocoa solids (65% or more)
will produce a richer, more chocolaty ganache, while a lower-quality chocolate will
create a frosting with a very different (but no less interesting) flavor — more mellow,
caramelized, and sweet.

Makes enough to fill and cover one
8-inch layer cake
200 grams (7 oz) dark chocolate
¾ cup + 1½ tablespoons heavy cream

100 grams (½ c) dark brown sugar
Pinch of salt
¼ cup light corn syrup

1 Finely chop the chocolate and set aside in a large bowl.

2 Heat the cream, sugar, and salt in a pan over low heat, stirring occasionally, until scalding — it needs to be steaming hot, but you mustn't let it boil. Pour it slowly over the chopped chocolate, let the mixture sit for a minute, then stir to combine. The chocolate should melt into the cream, leaving a smooth, shiny mixture. If any chunks of chocolate remain, heat very gently over a pan of simmering water or in the microwave. Stir in the corn syrup.

3 Let the ganache cool to room temperature before using some to sandwich the cake layers together. Then spread the rest on the top and sides. The ganache itself will set too firm to spread if you refrigerate it, but you can put the whole cake in the fridge once iced if you want a firmer set.

BUTTERSCOTCH FROSTING

It seems laughable that a buttercream could be a "light" alternative to anything, but that's exactly what this is: a lighter, brighter, sweeter alternative to the rich chocolate ganache above. If you're nervous about working with caramel, there's more information on page 316.

Makes enough to fill and cover one
  8-inch layer cake
150 grams (⅔ c) superfine sugar
3 tablespoons water

5 tablespoons heavy cream
125 grams (½ c + 1 tbsp) unsalted butter,
  softened
250 to 300 grams (2 to 2⅓ c)
  confectioners' sugar

1 Combine the superfine sugar and water in a small pan over low heat and cook, stirring only occasionally, until the sugar has just dissolved. Increase to medium-high heat and let bubble, without stirring, until the mixture has a rich amber color. Immediately remove from the heat and stir in the cream and 1½ tablespoons of the butter. Set aside to cool.

2 Cream the remaining butter. Slowly beat in the cooled cream mixture then gradually add the confectioners' sugar until thick, smooth, and a workable consistency. Spread over the layers and sides of the cooled cake.

SPONGE CAKES

This next group of cakes is a little different. Rather than using chemical raising agents such as baking powder or baking soda, these sponge cakes rely solely on whisked eggs for their rise. The ratios of flour, egg, fat, and sugar are very different, too: in order to keep the cake light, only a small amount of butter is used, while the higher volume of egg means that only a little flour is required to set the batter. These cakes are a little trickier than the earlier recipes, but they're well worth the effort. They are generally lighter, less crumbly, and more versatile and therefore well suited for use in desserts such as trifles and fruit puddings, where the cake's role is not to provide richness, but to absorb and marry the other flavors in the dessert, whether inky fruit juices, punchy liqueurs, or rich egg custards.

WHISKING EGG WHITES

Whereas egg yolks are rich, gloriously yellow, neatly spherical, and delicious, the whites are nearly tasteless, slimy, and translucent. But the ugly duckling egg white is nothing short of a baking miracle. When introduced to a whisk and a little sugar, the white will loosen, hold bubbles, grow thick with foam, and slowly expand to a great billowing cloud of meringue. It really is a sight to see.

But egg whites are tricky things. They won't perform this culinary magic without a little wooing. They'll refuse to whip up to stiff peaks unless the bowl and whisk used are scrupulously clean. There can be no moisture, no dirt or grease, and not a single drop of yolk. For this reason, it's often best to use a metal or glass bowl, as grease can cling to plastic after even the most thorough washing. I used to be skeptical about whether this egg white paranoia was strictly necessary, but after my fair share of failed meringues, I can assure you it really does make a difference. Taking 5 minutes to clean and dry your equipment will save you 15 minutes of futile whisking later on.

It may seem like a lot of fuss, but the difference that a few well-beaten egg whites will make to a cake is huge. The air incorporated as you whisk is caught in the egg's protein structure in millions of tiny pockets. During baking, the fierce heat of the oven causes the air in these bubbles to expand, making the cake rise. In the Chocolate Lime Mud Cake (page 60), this happens very quickly in the first half of the cooking time: the cake rises impressively and the uppermost layer sets to form a sugar crust. But the mixture underneath, though aerated, won't set as firm as the crust, so as it cools, the bubbles won't be able to support the weight of the cake and it'll sink in the center. This creates a sublime contrast of textures: a crisp, fractured crust and a gooey interior.

CHOCOLATE LIME MUD CAKE

This is more or less a glorified brownie, I suppose, but I prefer the name mud cake. Unlike a brownie, this isn't something to be cut into fat squares, picked up in paper napkins, and doled out at a children's party — this is a cake to be eaten with reverence, with a fork. It is moist, almost mousse-like, and elegantly dark.

Makes one 8-inch round cake,
  serving 8 to 10
120 grams (4.25 oz) dark chocolate
100 grams (7 tbsp) unsalted butter,
  cubed
Zest of 3 limes
Generous pinch of salt

3 large eggs, separated
150 grams (⅔ c) superfine sugar
50 grams (6½ tbsp) all-purpose flour

8-inch round cake tin

📷 page 58

1   Preheat the oven to 350°F. Grease the pan and line with parchment paper.

2   Gently melt the chocolate, either in short bursts in the microwave or in a bowl perched over a pan of simmering water, taking care not to let the bowl touch the water. Turn off the heat and stir in the butter until melted. Add the lime zest and salt. Set aside to cool a little.

3   Whisk together the egg yolks with 50 grams (3½ tbsp) of the sugar for a couple of minutes, until thick and creamy. It's the right consistency when the mixture falling from the whisk leaves a ribbon on the surface of the mixture. (See opposite for more information on this elusive "ribbon stage.") Make sure you whisk the yolks and sugar together promptly — if the sugar just sits on top of the yolks, it will react with the egg, resulting in rubbery bits of yolk that you'll have to sift out later.

4   In a clean, dry bowl, with an equally clean, dry whisk, beat the egg whites until completely foamy. Continue to whisk, adding the remaining 100 grams (7 tbsp) of sugar 1 tablespoon at a time. Whisk well after each addition of sugar. The mixture will become thicker and glossier until, after several minutes of elbow grease, slowly lifting the whisk out of the mixture will leave a soft peak — a tapering curl of meringue, slightly droopy at its tip.

5   Fold the egg yolk mixture into the chocolate with a large spoon, then fold one-third of this chocolate mixture into the egg whites. As soon as basically combined but still marbled, fold in the next third of the chocolate mixture, and then the final third. Sift in half of the flour. Gently fold in until nearly combined, then sift in the remaining flour and fold in until just combined. The most important thing here is to keep as much air as possible in the batter — gently cut through with the spoon, don't beat it, and mix only for as long as necessary.

6   Spoon the batter, which should feel light, aerated, and wobbly, into the prepared pan and bake for 30 minutes. It should be well risen and crisp on top, and a knife inserted into the center should come out barely clean. Let cool in the pan before carefully turning out. It's very good while still warm, served with a scoop of good-quality ice cream.

RIBBON STAGE

When whisking sugar into whole eggs or yolks — whether for a custard, cake, or cream — you'll often be told to keep going until the "ribbon stage" is reached. Ribbon stage is the point at which, when you lift the whisk from the egg and sugar, the mixture is sufficiently thick and creamy that a ribbon of it will sit for some seconds on the surface before sinking back in. If the mixture sinks immediately into the bowl, it's not yet ready. You'll notice other changes en route, too: the eggs will grow paler and their texture will move from slimy, to foamy, to velvety thick.

It can take a good 8 to 10 minutes (depending on the ratio of egg to sugar) to reach ribbon stage if using an electric mixer, and a bit longer if whisking by hand. The process can be catalyzed somewhat by suspending the bowl over a pan of simmering water to gently heat it as you whisk, but it's not a method I've recommended here. It's easy to accidentally cook the mixture if the water is at too vigorous a simmer, and I find it's not much of a shortcut at all once you've gone to the effort of finding the right size pan and bringing the water to a boil. Whisking at room temperature works fine — it just takes a little patience.

Halfway through the whisking process, when the mixture is still resolutely liquid and your arm is beginning to cramp, you might start wondering whether it's really that important to reach ribbon stage. You might convince yourself that I'm either a pedant or a sadist for insisting upon it. But I promise that all the whisking isn't for nothing: it dissolves the sugar and, crucially, aerates the mixture. The result will be springy cake with impressive rise and open structure. The alternative is a pancake-flat disappointment.

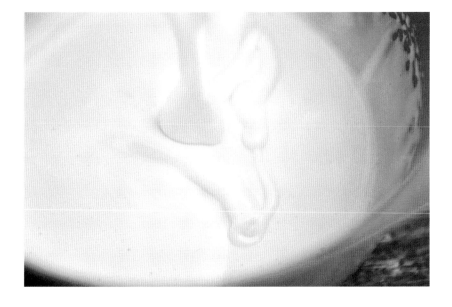

TIRAMISU CAKE

All of the elements of tiramisu — thick mascarpone cream, coffee-sodden sponge, a scattering of chocolate — are rearranged, neatened, and stacked into this impressive dessert cake. A sponge cake (this one is called a genoise) is the perfect base for this: it's easily cut into thin layers; it absorbs the coffee, and it's light enough that, miraculously, this cream-slathered, boozy cake still manages to resist feeling heavy. This certainly feels like a special sort of cake — one to be cut into slender slices, eaten with the good cutlery, and washed down with strong coffee. Somehow, it's a cake that commands respect.

Makes one 8-inch round cake,
  serving 8 to 10
Cake
2 tablespoons + 2 teaspoons
  unsalted butter
4 large eggs
125 grams (½ c + 1 tbsp) superfine sugar
125 grams (1 c) all-purpose flour

Filling
400 grams (14 oz) mascarpone
75 grams (⅓ c) superfine sugar

½ cup + 2 tablespoons heavy cream
½ cup + 2 tablespoons sweet dessert
  wine, such as muscat or marsala

¾ cup + 1½ tablespoons strong
  black coffee
50 grams (1.75 oz) dark chocolate

**Deep 8-inch round cake pan, preferably
  springform or loose-bottomed**

📷 page 62

1   Preheat the oven to 350°F. Grease the pan and line it with parchment paper.

2   To make the cake, melt the butter and set aside to cool slightly.

3   Whisk the eggs and sugar together in a large bowl until very thick and creamy. The mixture needs to reach the stage where, as the whisk is lifted out, it will leave a thick ribbon that sits on the surface for a short while before sinking back in (see page 61). This will take a good 8 to 10 minutes with an electric mixer and much longer by hand.

4   Sift one-third of the flour into the egg mixture and very gently fold it in, taking care to sweep right to the bottom of the bowl, as the flour can easily sink through. Sift and fold in the next third of the flour, and then the final third. Drizzle the butter over the mixture and carefully fold it in.

5   Lightly spoon the batter into the prepared pan and bake for 25 to 30 minutes, until well risen, golden brown, springy, and — most importantly — shrinking away from the sides of the pan. Let cool completely in the pan, then unmold.

6   To make the filling, beat the mascarpone with the sugar until smooth. Add a little of the cream to loosen the mixture and stir to combine. Pour in the remaining cream and whisk for a minute or two, until smooth and luxuriantly thick. Gradually stir in the wine.

7   Using a large, serrated knife or cake-cutting wire, cut the cake horizontally into three thin layers. It can be tricky to cut them evenly, but just go slowly and breathe deep. It's not an issue if the layers are slightly irregular or even if they break: they'll be smothered in cream soon enough, masking all manner of sins. If you have a completely flat, rimless baking sheet, a sturdy sheet of plastic, or a thin cutting board, you can use this to help move each fragile cake layer: just shimmy it underneath the cake, and slide the cake off afterward. This is far more secure than using your hands, which risks puncturing or tearing the cake in the process. If the thought of cutting the cake into three layers makes you nervous, just settle for dividing it into two thicker layers — it won't taste any worse for it. Just use slightly less of the mascarpone cream filling if you do.

8   Drizzle one-third of the coffee over one of the layers, then spread with one-quarter of the cream. Grate one-third of the chocolate over the cream, then stack the next cake layer on top. Repeat the layers, then spread the final one-quarter of the cream around the sides of the cake. Use a vegetable peeler to scrape thin curls of chocolate on top.

Variations
Layer the simple genoise sponge above with thick cream, amaretto, and very ripe raspberries. A handful of toasted, sliced almonds wouldn't go amiss either.

PASSION FRUIT CURD JELLY ROLL

This is another variant of the genoise sponge used in the Tiramisu Cake (page 63), this time rolled around a startlingly sharp tropical passion fruit curd. You can make the components of this cake in whatever order best suits you, but I prefer to get the curd made first so that it has ample time to thicken and set in the fridge before using.

Makes one 9-inch roll, serving 6 to 8
Curd
5 or 6 passion fruits
70 grams (5 tbsp) superfine sugar
1 large egg
1 tablespoon + 2 teaspoons unsalted
   butter

Cake
4 teaspoons unsalted butter

3 large eggs
85 grams (6 tbsp) superfine sugar
80 grams (⅔ c) all-purpose flour

A little confectioners' or superfine sugar,
   for dusting

**Jelly roll pan or rimmed baking sheet,
   approximately 9 by 13 inches**

1   To make the curd, halve the passion fruits, scoop out the pulp, and strain through a fine-mesh sieve, collecting the juice in a large heatproof bowl. Squeeze as much juice out of the seeds as you can — you'll need 4 to 5 tablespoons of juice.

2   Add the sugar, egg, and butter to the passion fruit juice. Set the bowl over a pan of barely simmering water, making sure that the bottom of the bowl doesn't touch the water. Patience is critical here: the curd will take a good 10 to 15 minutes to thicken, and it's best to keep stirring it continuously. The curd is ready when

it thickly coats the back of the spoon (see page 325 for more on this). The curd will thicken more as it cools, so don't worry that it's still quite liquid at this point. Once it coats the back of the spoon, remove from the heat and let cool to room temperature, then refrigerate until thick.

3   Preheat the oven to 400°F. Line the pan with parchment paper.

4   To make the cake, melt the butter, then set aside to cool. Whisk the eggs and sugar until very, very thick and creamy. The mixture needs to be thick enough that when the whisk is lifted out, it leaves a ribbon that sits on the surface of the batter for several seconds before sinking back in (see page 61).

5   Sift half of the flour over the surface of the egg mixture, then very gently fold it in. Repeat with the remaining flour. Be sure to dig right to the bottom of the bowl when folding in the flour, as it tends to clump and sink through the mixture unless carefully incorporated.

6   Spoon the batter into the lined pan and bake for 9 to 11 minutes, until well risen, just golden, and springy. Take care not to overbake, which could result in a dry, shrunken cake.

7   Let the cake cool for a minute or two, then turn out onto a sheet of parchment paper dusted generously with confectioners' or superfine sugar. Peel the original piece of parchment paper off the cake. Roll up the cake, along with the sugar-dusted parchment paper — the parchment will prevent the cake from sticking to itself. Roll from short end to short end, creating a roll about 9 inches long. Set it seam side down to prevent it from unfurling, then let cool. Cooling it this way helps the cake "remember" this shape and stay tightly rolled later, once filled.

8   After about 30 minutes the sponge should be cool. Unroll it, spread with the passion fruit curd, and carefully roll it up again, this time without the parchment paper. If you've got a particularly sweet tooth, you could spread with a layer of buttercream, too, to curb the sharpness of the curd.

COFFEE BLACK CURRANT OPERA CAKE

After a crescendo of cakes, a symphony of crumbs, layers, and frostings, and bar upon bar of butter, we reach this, the most complex of the cake recipes in this book and the most refined. It's a take on a French patisserie classic, comprising four layers of light almond sponge cake alternating with coffee, inky black currant jam, and whipped chocolate buttercream with a mirror-shine ganache top. Coffee and black currant are natural partners: both are deeply fruity, robust, dark. It's an unlikely but seductive flavor combination — the stronger, sultrier cousin of chirpy strawberries and cream.

The cake used here is a *joconde* sponge. Unlike a genoise sponge, this one has ground almonds as its base and uses whisked egg whites as well as whole eggs. It's doubly whisked, featherlight, and — unlike the genoise — quite delicious to eat by itself. You could even add a drop or two of almond extract to bolster the almond flavor if you want, but it's a flavor that can overwhelm, so take care.

Because the cake calls for more egg whites than yolks, I've used the remaining yolks for the buttercream to keep them from going to waste. This is a traditional French buttercream — egg yolks are cooked with hot sugar syrup and whisked to an unctuously thick cream before adding butter, and butter, and more butter. Melted chocolate is folded into this mousse-like mixture, and the chocolate buttercream is born. Because of the whisked egg base, this buttercream doesn't require vast quantities of confectioners' sugar to thicken it, so it's not nearly as sickly sweet as British buttercreams.

Scan through the recipe before beginning to familiarize yourself with the components and get a clear idea of the order in which you'll be making them. Neither the individual elements nor their eventual assembly is particularly difficult; organization is the key.

Makes one 6 by 8-inch opera cake, serving 10 to 12 in suitably elegant slices

Cake
1 tablespoon + 2 teaspoons unsalted butter
100 grams (1 c + 1 tbsp) ground almonds
100 grams (¾ c + 1 tbsp) confectioners' sugar
3 large eggs
3 large egg whites (reserve the yolks for the buttercream)
1 tablespoon + 2 teaspoons superfine sugar
50 grams (6½ tbsp) all-purpose flour

Buttercream
100 grams (3.5 oz) dark chocolate
3 large egg yolks
100 grams (7 tbsp) superfine sugar

2 tablespoons water
100 grams (7 tbsp) unsalted butter, very soft
1 teaspoon vanilla extract

Filling
½ cup + 2 tablespoons very strong black coffee
200 grams (3.5 oz) black currant jam (about ⅔ c)

Ganache
½ cup + 2 tablespoons heavy cream
100 grams (3.5 oz) dark chocolate, finely chopped
1 tablespoon light corn syrup

Two 9 by 13-inch rimmed baking sheets or jelly roll pans

📷 pages 66 and 68

For the cake

1 Preheat the oven to 400°F. Line the baking sheets with parchment paper.

2 Melt the butter and set aside to cool. Meanwhile, whisk the ground almonds, confectioners' sugar, and whole eggs together in a large bowl until doubled in volume and very, very thick and creamy. After about 10 minutes of hand whisking, the mixture should just be getting really thick and voluminous.

3 In a separate, scrupulously clean and dry bowl (preferably not plastic, which tends to retain grease even after the most fastidious washing) and with an equally spotless whisk, whisk the egg whites until completely foamy. Add half of the superfine sugar, whisk well, then add the remaining superfine sugar and whisk well again. Continue to whisk until the egg whites just about hold stiff peaks.

66

Take care not to overwhisk, which can easily happen with such a low proportion of sugar in the mix.

4 Sift the flour into the almond mixture and gently fold it in. Watch out for any pockets of flour that may have sunk to the bottom of the bowl. Fold in the melted, cooled butter, then, one-third at a time, fold in the egg whites.

5 Divide this delicate, airy batter between the baking sheets, pushing it gently toward the edges to cover the bottom of each baking sheet. Bake for 5 to 7 minutes, until risen, spongy, and just beginning to color in spots. Let the cakes cool on the baking sheets.

For the buttercream

6 Gently melt the chocolate — either in short bursts in the microwave or in a heatproof bowl perched over a pan of simmering water. Set aside to cool a bit while you prepare the other ingredients.

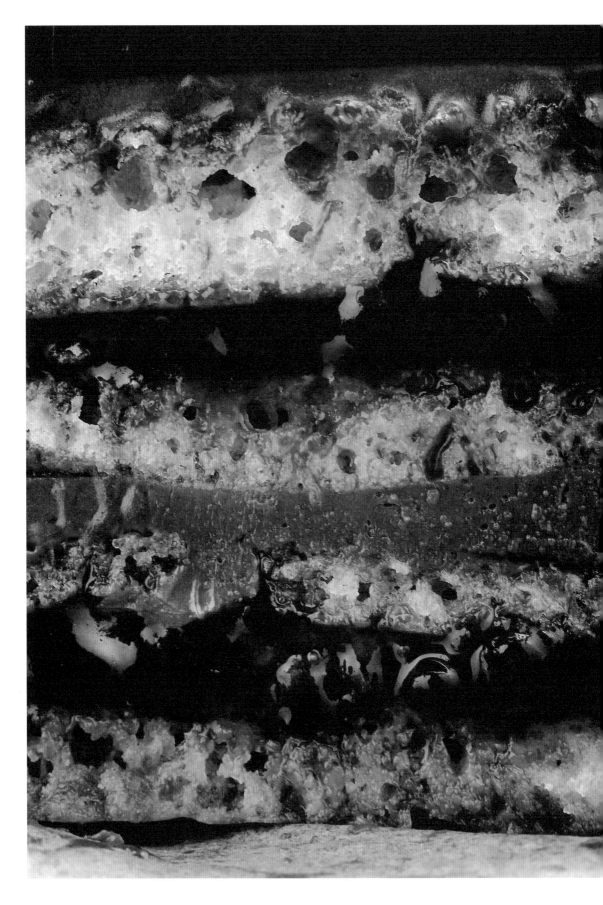

7   Put the egg yolks in a large heatproof bowl. Combine the sugar and water in a small pan and heat, stirring occasionally, very gently. The moment that the sugar has dissolved, stop stirring and let the syrup come to a boil. Let it simmer over medium-low heat for 30 seconds; you don't want it to color at all — you're not making caramel!

8   While whisking constantly, pour the hot sugar syrup in a very thin stream into the egg yolks. Don't add the syrup too quickly, and make sure to keep the mixture constantly moving; otherwise the yolks will cook in parts and the sugar will cool in clumps. Continue to whisk until the mixture is completely cool to the touch. This will take 10 minutes or so. By the time it's cool, the mixture should be thick, creamy, and pale.

9   Cream the butter until completely smooth and soft, then whisk it, bit by bit, into the egg yolk mixture. Keep beating well after each addition until all of the butter has been incorporated. Add the vanilla extract and stir in the slightly cooled melted chocolate.

To fill and assemble the cake

10 Halve each cake crosswise to create four rectangles measuring about 6½ by 9 inches. Put one on a sheet of parchment paper (this will make it easier to move later) and drizzle one-quarter of the coffee over it. Spread with half of the jam.

11 Stack the next rectangle of cake on top. Drizzle with another one-quarter of the coffee, then spread with three-quarters of the buttercream. Stack the next piece of cake on top. Drizzle with another one-quarter of the coffee and spread with the remaining jam.

12 Top with the final layer of cake, soak with the rest of the coffee, and spread the remaining buttercream on top. This layer of buttercream is the undercoat for the ganache glaze to come, so it's good to get it as smooth as possible. Transfer the whole thing to the fridge for around 1 hour to set the layers.

For the ganache

13 Once the cake is thoroughly chilled and set, prepare the ganache. Heat the cream either in a pan over low heat or (vigilantly!) in the microwave until scalding but not boiling. Pour the cream over the chopped chocolate, let the mixture sit for a moment to melt the chocolate, then stir gently until smooth. Stir in the corn syrup. The ganache needs to be at a pouring consistency, so let it cool for a few minutes if it's too runny, or heat it gently in a water bath if it's too thick.

14 Pour the ganache evenly over the top of the chilled cake. Some of it will run down the sides — this is no problem. Put the cake in the fridge for 30 minutes.

15 With a large knife, trim the edges of the cake by about ½ inch. This will remove any ganache overflow and expose the spectacular layers. Cut into slender pieces. And it's done!

BREAD

EVERYDAY LOAVES

DAILY BREAD · FLOURY ROLLS · BATONS · TIGER BREAD

MILK LOAF · SEEDED PAN LOAF · SODA BREAD

WHOLE WHEAT WALNUT BREAD

OLIVE & ORANGE CROWN · CHERRY SPELT LOAVES

SWEDISH CARAWAY RYE BREAD · LEEK & CHEESE TART

SMALL BITES & FLATBREADS

GARLIC DOUGH BALLS · RYE CARAWAY BAGELS

CHICKPEA & CUMIN SEED BUNS · SOCCA

CHORIZO & KALE FLATBREAD · PARATHAS

SLOW & STEADY

THREE-CHEESE BRIOCHE

FRENCH COUNTRY BREAD · CIABATTA

There's something deeply cathartic about baking bread. Some like kneading away their frustration (bread is perhaps the only food that turns out better for being cooked in a foul mood); while for others there's a calm that comes with falling into step with the languorous rhythms of the dough. You might simply find relief in the comforting aroma of the bread as it bakes. But, for me, it's the unpredictability of bread that's so seductive. Yeast is a living organism — it must be fed, watered, treated with care, waited for, and worked around, and even after all this it might create a loaf that's denser, squatter, fatter, or sweeter than you'd hoped for. There's something liberating about having control wrested from your hands like this: perfectionism takes a backseat, and you're left with no choice but to shelve your neuroses, roll up your sleeves, and bake.

THE FOUR ELEMENTS

FLOUR

Flour is the very essence of bread. Bread calls for something more robust than the very fine, soft flours that we use in our cakes and cookies. The sort of chewiness that would mark a truly awful cake is the key to a sublime loaf of bread. For this we use bread flour, known quite literally as strong flour in Britain. It's higher in protein and gluten than all-purpose flour, and resilient in the face of the kneading, pummeling, and stretching that bread dough must endure. You can even find very high-protein flours on supermarket shelves now, but in my experience these are rarely necessary. For most breads, a canny balancing of flours and careful handling should suffice.

As for the quality of the flour, I have to take issue with those who insist that you source organic, stone-ground flour from your local mill, farming cooperative, or somewhere similar. Such standards are unrealistic at best. I rarely use anything more exciting than the $1 per pound white bread flour you can get from the supermarket for the majority of breads, and that works perfectly well. Of course, the fewer chemicals in your flour, the better. Unbleached, organic flours are fantastic if you can afford them, but bread is no snob and it'll bloom all the same even with the cheapest flour fuel.

Yet there's far more to flour than wheat and white. Take a moment to scan the shelves next time you shop: you'll notice whole wheat, pastry, cake, durum, and other flours making the most of wheat, to varying degrees, plus barley and rye flours and flours made from ancient varieties of wheat such as spelt, einkorn, and Kamut. Chickpea, rice, soy, and potato flours are health conscious and gluten-free, and in very well-stocked stores you might find yet more unusual varieties: teff and amaranth, for example. Each one of these flours is very different and can't be straightforwardly substituted in bread making. For this reason it's well worth learning about each flour's properties (Is it high or low in gluten? How absorbent is it? How does it behave?) before heading for the fancy stuff. There are few kitchen disappointments more keenly felt than the sticky, heavy failure of a loaf several hours in the making. You'll find more about spelt and rye flours, and their bread-making qualities, preceding the bread recipes that make use of them, on page 100 and page 102, respectively.

YEAST

Yeast is bread's beating heart. It is the secret to its flavor, texture, and rise. The science of it is difficult and its mastery an exceptional challenge, but, in a nutshell, yeast feeds on the flour, producing carbon dioxide and other by-products. The gases released by the feeding yeast collect in tiny air pockets in the dough. When the dough is baked, the rapid increase in temperature causes these air pockets to expand, pushing the dough upward and outward and accounting for the impressive oven spring in the early stages of baking. Yeast develops gluten and therefore strengthens a bread's structure. But yeast's role in bread making isn't a purely mechanical one — it's also crucial for good flavor. Enzymes in yeast break down complex starches in the flour (starches that have little flavor in themselves) into more basic molecules: sugars. These sugars deepen the flavor of the bread and the color of the crust. In fact, you can often tell if a baked loaf was left to rise for too long by an unusually dark color, the crust having browned too rapidly.

Yeast is sensitive to its environment, acting more quickly, slowly, or not at all depending on the temperature, acidity, and hydration of the dough, among other factors. I'll go into greater depth about these variables a little later, but for now suffice it to say that yeast works well at room temperature, functions very slowly at cool temperatures, is dormant in the fridge, and is dead above about 120°F.

Fresh yeast

Fresh yeast, sold in little blocks, is a sandy beige color, distinctively yeasty in aroma, and rubbery to the touch. There are many who argue that it produces a better-tasting loaf, or at least a more authentic one. I disagree. I've never been able to discern any difference in flavor between loaves made with fresh yeast versus dried. Fresh is also harder to source, shorter lived, and less straightforward to use than dried. You're welcome to use it if you prefer, however; there's certainly a charm to it.

To substitute fresh yeast in any of the recipes in this book, swap in 20 grams for every 2¼ teaspoons of instant yeast. The fresh yeast should first be crumbled into a couple of tablespoons of lukewarm water with a little sugar or honey and left for about 5 minutes, or until bubbles begin to form on the liquid's surface. You can then add this mixture to the flour along with the rest of the water. Any leftover fresh yeast will keep in the fridge for a few days. Once it starts to look blotchy or dry, it is past its prime. If in doubt about the liveliness of your yeast, just activate it by dissolving it as above; if after 5 to 10 minutes there's no sign of bubbles or any action, it's probably dead.

Active dry yeast

Most often sold in little jars, active dry yeast comes in small granules ready to be activated by rehydration in a little warm water with sugar. Prepare it as in the above instructions for fresh yeast. You might want to use slightly more than you would instant yeast: approximately 1 tablespoon for every 2¼ teaspoons of instant yeast. If you don't increase the amount, be prepared to wait a little longer for the dough to rise.

Instant or fast-acting yeast

Instant yeast is the type of yeast called for in every one of the yeasted recipes in this book. You can find it in small jars, similar to those containing active dry yeast, but it's most commonly sold in boxes of 2¼-teaspoon packets — 2¼ teaspoons being conveniently just the right amount to leaven one large loaf of bread. It takes the form of very small, beige-colored granules. The reason that this is my yeast of choice is quite simply because it is easy to use. Unlike both fresh and active dry yeast, instant — or fast-acting — yeast requires no presoaking, no extra stages, no special treatment. Just mix the yeast directly into the flour. One piece of advice: When adding the yeast and salt to the flour in the early stages of the recipe, take care not to pour the salt directly on top of the yeast, or vice versa, as the salt may kill the yeast.

Natural leaven

Natural leaven, spontaneous fermentation, sourdough starter — whatever you'd like to call it — isn't something you'll find in the supermarket baking aisle. Natural leaven makes use of yeasts found naturally in flour and in the air to create a culture that, given plenty of time and a lot of starches, will naturally ferment — no added yeast required. Breads made with natural leaven are called sourdoughs and have a devout following among bread enthusiasts.

WATER

There's no mystery here: plain tap water is all bread needs. If you really want to pamper your loaf, you can feed it mineral water, filtered water, and so on, but it'll ultimately taste no better for the fuss.

Water is crucial for yeast to grow, for the dough's gluten to develop, for the rise and spring of the bread, and for a soft crumb. And the precise amount of water used can make the difference between a chewy, close-textured bagel, a soft sandwich loaf, an open focaccia, and a featherweight ciabatta. In general — and of course without taking into account the effects of different flours and so on — the wetter the dough, the more open the crumb. Naturally there are limits to this: too dry and a dough will barely rise at all and be crumbly and fragile; too wet and it'll be nearly impossible to shape and bake.

Bakers typically calculate bread ingredient quantities based on the ingredients' weights as percentages of the weight of the flour in the recipe. For example, a bread that uses 300 grams (1¼ c) of water, 500 grams flour, and 10 grams each of salt and yeast would have a water percentage of 60 percent, based on the water being three-fifths of the flour weight. For most breads you can expect the amount of liquid to be around 60 to 70 percent of the flour weight.

SALT

Salt can be a contentious topic in bread making. It's sensible to be concerned about salt intake and reasonable to cut excess salt from your diet — prepared foods, cheese, and cured meats all contain a great deal of the stuff. But there are some foods where salt really can't be omitted, and bread is one of them. Salt strengthens the gluten in bread, stabilizing its structure. It also regulates the yeast's activity, preventing the dough from fermenting too quickly. It's an essential component of any loaf (there are one or two exceptions to this rule, but they're unimportant here).

The amount of salt called for in the recipes that follow might seem excessive but it's in line with, and often less than, the amount specified in the majority of bread recipes. A teaspoon of salt weighs approximately 6 grams — an amount that would render a pasta sauce inedible or be disgusting in a cake. But spread through an entire loaf, where the base ingredients are so bland, it is hardly detectable. And to put it into perspective, one medium slice of that bread would contain just 0.3 gram of salt — less than you'd find in most supermarket brands. Moderate consumption is the key to enjoying bread healthfully — a salt witch hunt is not.

As for the type of salt, I always use table salt in my breads and have developed these recipes accordingly. It is practical, potent, and easily dissolved. I can't see the use of pretty, crystalline flakes of sea salt in bread unless they're scattered on top of focaccia or flatbread for flavor.

A LOAF'S LIFE

1 MIX

Fat bags of flour poured into the mixing bowl, yeast packets torn open, a sprinkling of salt, and — to rouse the dormant yeast and nudge the dough into action — a couple of mugfuls of lukewarm water. There's no trick to this part of the process; just take care not to add the yeast directly on top of the salt, or vice versa, and don't be afraid to get your hands dirty.

Bear in mind that the temperature of the ingredients will affect the activity of the yeast: freezing-cold water will dramatically slow the rise, and too much heat risks stressing the yeast. Unless otherwise specified, all ingredients should be at room temperature, with the exception of the liquid, which should lie somewhere in between tepid and lukewarm. Don't feel too hidebound by rules, though. Respond to the needs of the dough (will it be proofed warm and quickly, or cool and slowly?) and the demands of your environment (on a hot day, tap-cold water may suffice), balancing the temperatures of your ingredients accordingly.

2 REST

Resting the just-mixed dough isn't always necessary, but it can be helpul with whole wheat breads or for a particularly wet dough. It gives the flour a chance to absorb more water before you start kneading. During this time the gluten in the flour will also begin to develop, making kneading easier still. Simply let the dough rest for 20 to 30 minutes after mixing.

3 KNEAD

There's plenty of contradictory advice out there on the importance of kneading. For some people, it's crucial; others suggest that you can replace a traditional knead with a less intensive one; and there are those who insist that we can do away with kneading altogether. I'd love to be able to pick a side in this dough debate, but unfortunately there isn't a straightforward answer.

The aim of kneading is to develop and strengthen the dough, building a complex network of gluten strands that will underpin the structure of the bread. Vigorous kneading does just this. But so can a less intensive method of stretching and folding the dough at regular intervals. And so too can doing nothing at all; for some breads, an extended rest (as above) is all it takes. As the yeast swings into action, it begins to develop the gluten itself, relieving you of a job. No-knead bread won't tend to rise quite as high as a well-kneaded one, but you may well be happy to make that sacrifice. There are some breads, however, where kneading is nonnegotiable — Ciabatta (page 120), for instance.

With that in mind, I'll leave it to you to decide when and how to knead. I've given kneading guidelines for all of these recipes and suggested a couple of techniques on page 80, but if it's a step that you choose to omit, there's probably no harm done.

4 RISE OR FIRST PROOF

The least fraught, lowest-maintenance stage of your loaf's life is when you incubate it in a covered bowl and let it ferment. Enzymes will begin to break down some of the flour's starches, and the yeast will feast on the sugars and release — among other things — carbon dioxide into microscopically small pockets in the surrounding dough. The dough will relax and rise, doubling or even tripling in size. How long this takes depends on the temperature of the dough and its surroundings, the amount and type of yeast, and whether the dough contains any enrichments. Butter- or egg-heavy doughs will rise more slowly, as will dough left to rise at cool temperatures.

At normal room temperature (65°F to 70°F) the average dough will take 1 to 1½ hours to complete its first rise. You can speed this up by putting the dough in a slightly warmer place, but this will come at the expense of good flavor; dough that has risen too rapidly has little flavor and risks tasting yeasty. Conversely, rising can happily be slowed by moving the dough to a cooler environment or by using colder water. This won't adversely affect the loaf's flavor — in fact, in the majority of cases a slower rise will yield a better bread. You can take this one step further by moving the dough to the fridge overnight for this first proof, factoring in a little extra time for the dough to regain momentum and complete its second rise at room temperature after shaping.

5 SHAPE

Shaping is a midway point. There's still a ways to go until the loaf is finished, but this is the stage at which the dough — now happily fermenting and active — will finally begin to look something like bread. It's important to shape the dough smoothly and tightly for a good rise, even if baking a simple pan loaf. When it's done well, shaping creates tension across the surface of the bread to act as a sort of skin, controlling the rise and producing an even shape. That said, a lopsided loaf will still taste every bit as good as the most exquisitely braided wreath or hemispheric boule, so I wouldn't worry too much. See pages 80 through 83 for more on how to shape.

6 SECOND PROOF

Consider the second proof the tumultuous teenage stage: it's during this proofing period that the dough will go a great distance toward developing the texture, flavor, and shape that it'll have as a fully baked loaf. It's not always an easy stage to manage. An under-proofed loaf will still feel firm as it enters the oven and will bake into a heavy, close-textured, pale bread. Proof too long and the dough will feel fragile, on the verge of collapse, and the bread will emerge from the oven sunken, crumbly, and dry. A perfectly proofed, oven-ready loaf should be 1½ to 2 times its original size, springy, and soft to the touch yet not fragile. A finger pressed about ½-inch into the dough's surface should leave an indentation that slowly fills out again.

7 SCORE

There's far more to scoring a loaf than just gratuitous decorative flourishes. Scoring the dough is a tactical maneuver, affording the baker some control over how the loaf rises in the oven. The sudden increase in temperature as a loaf hits the preheated oven causes a tremendous surge in yeast activity and a rapid oven spring. If the crust begins to set before this rise is complete, the swelling dough will break through the crust at a point of weakness, resulting in bulging, asymmetrical loaves. But a carefully scored loaf can channel this energy constructively. A deep incision along the length of a pan loaf, for instance, will provide a natural site for the dough to rise from, producing a tall, domed shape. See page 84 for more advice on scoring.

8 BAKE

The finish line is now in sight. During the first 10 minutes of baking, the yeast will have a final surge of energy, working ever faster as the dough's temperature increases until, at around 120°F, the yeast begins to die. This is no sprint finish, though. Even after the bread ceases to rise, it must continue to bake until its interior is cooked, setting the crumb. And still, after that, it must bake a while longer if you want a good, thick crust and deep color. Confronted with the heady aroma of baking bread, and with several hours of mixing, kneading, and proofing already behind you, patience can be difficult, but it's well worth the wait if you can bear it.

In terms of temperature, a good blast of heat as the bread first enters the oven can maximize oven spring, which is why many of the recipes here call for 10 to 15 minutes of baking at a high temperature before decreasing the heat.

And how to tell when the loaf is ready? The most common test is to tap on the underside of the baked loaf; if it sounds hollow, its time is up. This test is far from perfect, but it's not bad, either. Look at the color and thickness of the crust, too; it'll usually be golden brown by the time the crumb inside has set, although small breads and rolls will be cooked through long before a real crust has had the chance to form.

9 COOL
The bread will continue to cook and set as it cools. Resisting the temptation to slice or eat the steaming loaf straight from the oven will pay off in the long run.

HOW TO KNEAD

— Always use as little flour on the work surface as possible. I prefer to use none at all: excess flour incorporated into the dough at this stage risks leaving the bread heavy and uneven.

— Most dough will be sticky, heavy, and frustrating at first. This is to be expected. Only after a vigorous knead will it feel smoother and be easier to handle.

— Be prepared to spend a good 10 to 15 minutes kneading. The dough is ready when it feels robust and elastic and has a satiny sheen to it. The windowpane test (see the photo on page 79) is a good indicator of how well kneaded it is. Tear off a small piece of dough and gently stretch it as far as possible between your fingers. If it can be stretched thinly enough that it lets light through, it's ready. If it tears in the process, knead a little longer.

FOR DRIER DOUGH

Using the heel of your hand, push the dough down and out, stretching out a 4- to 6-inch flap of dough. Fold this piece of dough back over on itself, then rotate the dough 90 degrees and stretch, fold, and turn again. The key is to keep rotating the dough in order to fully develop the gluten.

FOR WETTER DOUGH

Very wet doughs need a different approach. Kneaded the traditional way, as above, they'll cling to the work surface, weld to your hands, and remain flabbily lifeless in the face of even the most enthusiastic knead. Quick, light handling is needed. The photos opposite and the following instructions offer a step-by-step guide.

With splayed fingers, slide both hands underneath the dough from either side. Lift it slightly above the work surface. Stretch the dough outward, pulling sideways until it feels tighter. Fold the elongated dough in half, rotate it 90 degrees (leaving the fold running horizontally), and set it back down on the work surface. Again with fingers splayed, scoop your hands back under the dough from either side, then stretch, fold, and rotate again. You should feel it become gradually more resistant and less sticky.

HOW TO SHAPE

— Surface tension is the most important thing in shaping. Gather any excess dough underneath, leaving the top taut and firm.

— Use only as much flour on the work surface as is absolutely necessary.

— Swift, decisive movements when shaping will minimize sticking.

BOULE 📷 page 83

1   Shape the dough into a very rough ball.

2   Fold the dough in on itself a few times, almost as if lightly kneading it. By doing this, you'll be gathering the loose dough at the top, leaving the underside smooth and taut. You don't want to overdo this, or the dough will become too tight and rupture as it rises. A few folds should suffice.

3   Turn the ball upside down, hiding the seams underneath and exposing the neater surface on top.

4   The next stage is to tighten the skin, smooth out any wrinkles, and ensure even rising. Lay your hands, palms facing upward, on either side of the dough. Bring your hands quickly together to meet underneath the dough, then move them outward in opposite directions — one sliding forward, one sliding back — out from underneath the dough. It's a difficult action to describe, but it's best thought of as a slicing motion, gathering the dough tightly underneath, then deftly sliding your hands back out again before the dough has a chance to stick to them.

ROLLS AND BUNS

1   Shape each portion of dough into a rough ball.

2   For perfectly risen buns, fold the dough over on itself as described above for a boule before proceeding. Otherwise, just roll the dough around on a clean surface in a circle, under a roundly cupped palm. The aim is to keep the ball roughly upright, as you gently smoothe its shape using this motion.

PAN LOAF OR BÂTARD

1   Form the dough into a rough oval shape, about as long as the loaf pan, if using.

2   Gather any loose dough underneath, either by folding the dough in on itself or by slicing it with your hands, as described in steps 2 through 4 above, for a boule.

3   Tuck the tapered ends of the oval neatly underneath to give the dough a smooth upper surface.

BATONS OR BAGUETTES

1   Using both hands, roll the dough backward and forward on a clean (or very lightly floured) surface until it forms a long sausage shape. Remember that it will grow far fatter as it rises, so it's best to start with a piece of dough significantly thinner than the size you envision for the finished bread.

2   Tuck the tapered ends of the dough underneath to create a clean, blunt shape.

HOW TO SCORE

— A very, very sharp knife is crucial: alternatively you could use a razor blade or a lame (a double-edged blade made precisely for scoring dough).

— Use firm, decisive strokes and move quickly. Hesitation and a shaky hand will cause the blade to stick and the dough to snag and tear.

— Hold the blade at a slight angle to the dough's surface — not perpendicular to it. The aim is to cut a sort of flap of dough that will open slowly as the bread rises and bakes.

— Cater the type and depth of incision to the loaf being scored. A loaf that won't rise much in the oven, such as a dark rye, can be scored in a decorative, shallow pattern. Other loaves require greater pragmatism, and should be scored a little deeper and with just a few strokes.

— Always dust with flour before scoring, never after. This is only for the sake of aesthetics, mind you, not practicality.

WHY IS MY BREAD . . .

Here are a few of the most common pitfalls encountered when baking bread. You'll notice that for every complaint, there are a number of potential explanations. A dense loaf, for example, could have started with problems in the ingredients, or could have developed during kneading, proofing, or baking. With so many stages and techniques involved, it can be difficult to pinpoint exactly where and when a loaf went wrong. Yeast's unpredictability and sensitivity — so exciting when they work in your favor — can quickly become infuriating. And yet bread isn't an unsolvable riddle or a sorcerer's trick; both good and bad loaves can be explained. I hope that the explanations and solutions below will help.

. . . DRY AND DENSE?

— A dry, heavy loaf has likely sunk in the oven, having been overproofed. The yeast has exhausted itself before the loaf reached the oven. Try proofing in a cooler place or for a shorter time.

— Too little water in the dough. Most dough should be slightly sticky when you begin to knead it; if it's already perfectly dry and smooth before kneading, you should add a little more water.

— Too much flour was incorporated during the kneading or shaping stage. Dust the work surface and dough as little as possible — or not at all.

. . . WET AND DENSE?

— Underproofed breads tend to be very densely textured, particularly at the base of the loaf, with a sticky, gummy feel. You could bake a little longer to help dry the baked bread, but to prevent this in the future, give the bread a longer second proof.

— Underbaked. Return the loaf to the oven on a medium heat (about 350°F) until it sounds hollow when tapped underneath.

— A wet and dense texture might just be a side effect of the types of flour used. A high proportion of rye (30 percent or more) can do this, and it's common in 100 percent whole wheat loaves, too. A dose of white bread flour in these loaves will go a long way toward lightening the texture.

— If you don't develop the gluten enough, particularly wet doughs might struggle to rise. A vigorous kneading period ought to prevent this.

...CRUST TOO DARK?

— A good, deep golden-brown crust is a fantastic thing, but if it tips over from bronzed to burnt, it may be that the oven temperature was too high or the baking time too long.

— Overproofed loaves have a greater proportion of their starches broken down into sugars, which then brown very quickly in the oven.

— Some glazes darken very quickly; egg washes are applied with just this in mind (see page 129).

...CRUST SO PALE?

— Too few sugars in an underproofed loaf leave the crust looking pasty and sad. Proof longer during the second rise before baking next time.

...POORLY RISEN?

— This is nearly always due to expired or spoiled yeast. Always check the expiration date on the package, be careful if using fresh yeast (which spoils quickly), and if in any doubt, activate the yeast in a little warm water to test it (see page 74).

— It could also be that the yeast has been affected by one of the ingredients added to the dough: if the water was too hot, for instance, or if the salt was added directly on top of the yeast.

...UNEVENLY SHAPED OR TORN?

— Bread that isn't scored, or that's scored too shallowly, is likely to rupture in the oven as it rapidly expands.

— Underproofed loaves rise very quickly, tearing as they bake. Next time, let the shaped dough rise slightly longer, or in a warmer spot, before baking.

...TOO YEASTY?

— A little yeast goes a long way — it's powerful stuff. Too much yeast will leave a loaf tasting distinctively yeasty and put it at risk of overproofing.

— The dough was proofed too quickly or in too warm an environment. Yeast will work just fine at room temperature; don't be tempted to stash the sensitive dough in a warm spot or proofing box.

... DOUGH RISING SO SLOWLY?

— Bread takes time, and slowly proofed bread tastes better, so it's important to be patient. But if the dough is rising very slowly, it may be that the temperature — of either the room or the ingredients used — is too low. Using cold tap water in the depths of winter will naturally slow the action of the yeast.

— Enrichments in the dough, including butter, eggs, or oil, will slow the action of the yeast and result in a lengthier rise. In this case, you will just have to allow extra time for the dough to rise.

— Too much salt will also inhibit the yeast and slow down the rise. A certain amount of salt is necessary to regulate the yeast's growth, but too much — anything over 10 grams (1½ tsp) salt per 500 grams (about 4 c) flour — can result in a longer rising period.

— Too little yeast. It makes sense that the more yeast there is working on the dough, the faster the job of rising will get done. Pre-ferments (see page 118), for instance, which are allowed to ferment in advance to give the dough extra flavor and a better structure, use only a fraction of a teaspoon of yeast and therefore take up to 18 hours to double in size.

EVERYDAY LOAVES

DAILY BREAD

This is a basic loaf, perfect for the novice bread baker. It's a recipe stripped back to the bare bones, with just five ingredients, a simple method, and speedy execution. The only flourish is the addition of a little oil, giving a more tender finished bread and a more malleable, less sticky dough in the meantime. But for all its simplicity, this daily bread still delights: watch it transform from putty, to supple dough, to soft-skinned round, to crusty loaf. There's nothing quotidian about it.

Makes 1 large loaf
500 grams (4 c) white bread flour
2¼ (1 packet) instant yeast
1½ teaspoons salt

1¼ cup + 1 tablespoon lukewarm water
2 tablespoons olive oil

📷 page 88

1   Combine the flour and yeast in a large bowl. Stir in the salt, followed by the water and oil. Bring the dough together into a sticky mass, then let it sit for 20 minutes or so at room temperature. You can skip this resting time if you want, but the dough will be less sticky to knead if you wait.

2   Knead the rested dough for a good 10 to 15 minutes. It ought to feel elastic, smooth, and robust by the time you're done. (See the kneading techniques on page 80 for more guidance.) Put the dough in a large, lightly oiled bowl, cover with plastic wrap or a dampened kitchen towel and let rest until doubled in size — either 1 to 1½ hours at room temperature or overnight in the fridge.

3   Shape the dough into a boule or bâtard shape (see page 82 for instructions on how best to shape the dough) and let proof at room temperature in a draft-free spot until doubled in size. I usually leave mine in the kitchen. How long this takes will depend on the temperature of the room and of the dough, but it'll usually be just under 1 hour. If the dough had its first rise in the fridge overnight, the yeast will still be lethargic from the residual cold. In this case, the proofing period could be as long as 2 hours. Meanwhile, preheat the oven to 425°F.

4   Lightly dust the top of the dough with flour and, using a sharp knife, score either a deep cross or a row of slits into the loaf (see page 84). Bake for 15 minutes then decrease the temperature to 375°F and bake for 30 minutes longer. It'll be baked through after about 35 minutes total, but the extra 10 minutes helps to form a good, deeply colored crust. Give the loaf plenty of time to cool completely before eating, as the inside will still be gummy and moist when first baked.

FLOURY ROLLS

Makes 8 rolls
1 recipe of Daily Bread dough (page 89)

1   Prepare the dough and let it rise as instructed in steps 1 and 2 on page 89.
    Divide the risen dough into 8 portions. Shape each piece into a ball by rolling
    it under your cupped palm on a clean surface (see page 82 for further shaping
    instructions). Place the balls about 1½ inches apart on a large baking sheet and
    lightly pat each one down to a fat circle of dough just under 1 inch thick.

2   Let the rolls proof at room temperature in a draft-free place until visibly puffy and
    almost double their original size. This should take 45 to 60 minutes, and possibly
    a little longer if the dough had its first rise in the fridge overnight. Meanwhile,
    preheat the oven to 350°F.

3   Liberally sprinkle the rolls with flour and bake for 20 minutes. For golden, soft-
    crusted buns, don't dust with flour; instead, brush the tops with whole milk or
    even half-and-half before baking.

BATONS

With batons (short baguettes), crust is key: it should be golden and firm, cracking into
thick shards under the bread knife, in contrast to the soft, white crumb within. A hot
and steamy oven, together with a generous baking time, will help to achieve this. If
crust isn't your thing, baking at 350°F for 20 minutes will suffice, and you needn't
worry about the extra baking sheet with water, either.

Makes 3 batons
1 recipe of Daily Bread dough (page 89)

1   Prepare the dough and let it rise as instructed in steps 1 and 2 on page 89. Divide
    the risen dough into three pieces. On a very lightly floured work surface, roll each
    piece of dough into a sausage shape, about 8 inches long. Set the batons on a large
    baking sheet.

2   Let the batons proof at room temperature until just over 1½ times their original
    size. This should take about 45 minutes, and possibly a little longer if the dough
    had its first proof in the fridge overnight, or shorter in a particularly warm
    environment. Meanwhile, preheat the oven to 475°F, or as high as your oven will
    go. Put a rimmed baking sheet on a low shelf in the oven.

3   Score each baton with three or four diagonal slits (see page 84) and put the batons
    in the oven. Pour a few tablespoons of water onto the rimmed baking sheet on
    the lower shelf of the oven. Bake for 10 minutes, then decrease the temperature
    to 400°F and bake for 15 minutes longer. Surprisingly, the steamy conditions
    created in the early stages of the bake help to create a crustier crust. Just watch
    out for the blast of steam when you open the oven door.

CRUST

Crust is a deeply subjective thing. Some like a very thin, almost papery crust. Others prefer the thick, chewy sort that must be quite forcefully sawed through with a bread knife. Having spent a childhood pushing even the flimsiest crusts to the side of plates, hiding them deep in coat pockets, and throwing them to the ducks, I've now embraced the crust. For me, it must be thin but beautifully crisp, prone to shattering into golden, jagged shards.

The ingredients in a loaf will have some bearing on the caliber of the crust — fat in the dough, for instance, will inhibit crust formation — but most of the magic is in the baking. Most breads will feel crusty immediately after leaving the oven, but all too often they deteriorate as they cool, because steam escaping from the loaf's center softens the crust. Quite simply, crust that lasts requires a long cooking time to dry the crumb and thicken the crust, while a softer crust can be achieved by baking for a shorter time at a slightly higher temperature.

And a loaf baked just right will, quite literally, sing — whispering, snapping, and crackling as it cools and the red-brown crust splits tectonically into an intricate jigsaw. It might just be the most beautiful sound in the world . . . or in the kitchen, at least.

TIGER BREAD

There's something instantly inviting about the fractured, volcanic surface of a loaf of tiger bread. It's an easy finish to achieve and an impressive upgrade from a simple dusting of flour. A paste of rice flour is brushed over the surface of the dough during its final proof prior to baking. This paste cooks more quickly than the bread, splintering into its characteristic crags and rifts as the dough continues to expand beneath it. It also browns quickly, though, so you may have to decrease the oven temperature or reduce the cooking time slightly, especially for larger loaves, if the crust begins to look ominously dark.

Makes 1 large loaf
1 recipe of Daily Bread dough
  (page 89)

Rice Flour Paste
½ teaspoon instant yeast

1 teaspoon sugar
¼ teaspoon salt
60 grams (6 tbsp) white rice flour
7 tablespoons lukewarm water
1 teaspoon oil, preferably sesame

📷 page 92

1   Prepare the dough, let it rise, and shape into a boule or bâtard as instructed in steps 1 through 3 on page 89. During the second proof, prepare the paste. Combine the yeast, sugar, salt, and flour, then stir in the water and oil to create a thick batter. Brush the rising dough generously with this paste and let rest until fully risen (the dough ought to approximately double in size). In the meantime, preheat the oven to 425°F. Bake for 15 minutes, then decrease the temperature to 375°F and bake for about 30 minutes longer; however, you may need to take the loaf out of the oven before the total 45-minute baking time is up, because this crust will brown quickly. As long as a loaf of this size has had 30 minutes in the oven, it will be sufficiently cooked.

THE PAN LOAF

For all the versatility and artisanal aesthetics of free-form loaves, I can't help drifting back to the standard pan loaf. There was always a parade of proud, muffin-topped pan loaves queued neatly along the back wall of the bakery near our family home in Essex, each destined for a whirlwind romance with shades of jam, cheese and pickle, Marmite, or even, on weekends and birthdays, sausages and brown sauce. I like their ungainly top-heaviness, I like the simplicity, and I like that my pan at home — free with some promotion or other — suggestively emblazons Lurpak across the side of each loaf. *Couronne*, croissant, and *kugelhopf* all you like — I know what my desert island loaf would be.

MILK LOAF

I worry we're in danger of forgetting the simple pleasures of the plain sandwich loaf. This isn't a loaf that will confront you on fragile, bleary-eyed mornings with an impenetrable crust and a sterling sourdough lineage. It's a gentler sort of bread: thin crusted and pillowy soft inside. Toast it, mop up gravy with it, or cut it into neat sandwich triangles. Best of all, and incidentally the best hangover cure I have ever had, make French toast with it, dipping it in beaten egg, milk, and cinnamon, then frying it in a little butter and sprinkling it with confectioners' sugar.

I've called for whole milk here, as the higher fat content helps create a more tender crust and crumb. You can use 2% milk if you really want, but the resulting bread won't be quite as delicately soft. Soy milk also works very well.

Makes 1 medium loaf
450 grams (3½ c) white bread flour
2¼ teaspoons (1 packet) instant yeast
1 teaspoon salt

1¼ cups + 2 tablespoons whole milk

5 by 9-inch loaf pan

1   Combine the flour and yeast in a large bowl, then stir in the salt. Over very low heat, warm the milk in a small pan until just lukewarm. Add the milk to the flour mixture and use your hands to mix the ingredients. Once combined, turn the dough out onto a work surface and knead for a good 10 to 15 minutes, until smooth and elastic. It should pass the windowpane test (see page 80).

2   Put the dough in a large bowl, cover with plastic wrap or a plate, and let rise for 60 to 90 minutes, until doubled in size. Exactly how long this takes will depend on the temperature of the room and of the ingredients.

3   Very lightly grease the loaf pan. Shape the loaf into a football shape, or bâtard (see page 82 for shaping tips), making sure to fold it over into itself with the seam underneath, creating a tight skin on the exterior. This will help it keep a good shape as it rises and bakes.

4   Let the dough proof in the pan for 45 to 60 minutes, until it has almost doubled in size again. Meanwhile, preheat the oven to 350°F.

5   Once the loaf has risen, brush it with milk and score, slightly off center, along its length using a razor blade or a very sharp kitchen knife (see page 84). Bake for 50 minutes, brushing with milk again halfway through the baking time. Let cool completely before slicing.

SEEDED PAN LOAF

If you're suffering from the endemic carb concern that's blighting our mealtimes, I beg you to shelve it just for a moment. This loaf is wholesome without being joyless, filling but not heavy. It's packed with goodness. There are, of course, carbohydrates in here, but there's also a hefty dose of fiber plus flaxseeds, pumpkin seeds, and nutty sunflower seeds. Eating a slice ought to be all pleasure, no guilt. Relish it with cheese and a thick spread of mango chutney. It's a meal to make princes of paupers.

Makes 1 medium loaf
300 grams (2⅓ c) white bread flour
100 grams (¾ c + 1 tbsp) whole wheat flour
2¼ teaspoons (1 packet) instant yeast
¾ teaspoon salt
1 cup + 2 tablespoons lukewarm water

150 grams (about 1 c) seeds (sunflower, pumpkin, flax, or sesame are all good)

5 by 9-inch loaf pan

📷 page 95

1   Combine the flours and yeast in a large bowl, then stir in the salt. Add the lukewarm water and mix with your hands until the liquid is well integrated. Let the dough rest for 20 minutes, during which time the flour will absorb more of the water. Knead for 10 minutes, then add the seeds and knead lightly to combine. Set the dough aside in a large, covered bowl and let rise at room temperature for about 1½ hours, until doubled in size.

2   Lightly oil the loaf pan. Turn the dough out, shape it into a fat log, and set it in the pan. Let proof at room temperature in a draft-free spot for about 1 hour, until the loaf is between 1½ and 2 times its original size. Meanwhile, preheat the oven to 400°F.

3   Score the risen loaf with a very sharp knife, cutting an incision about ½ inch deep straight along its length (see page 84). Bake for 10 minutes, then decrease the temperature to 350°F and bake for 40 minutes longer.

SODA BREAD

For days when time is short, soda bread — leavened only with baking soda — makes a fine alternative to slow-moving yeasted breads. The buttermilk lends a bright acidity, the baking soda a slight tang, and the sugar a gentle sweetness to round it all off. It is so delicious that I often wonder, as I greedily eat it in thick wedges, why I ever bother with yeast at all.

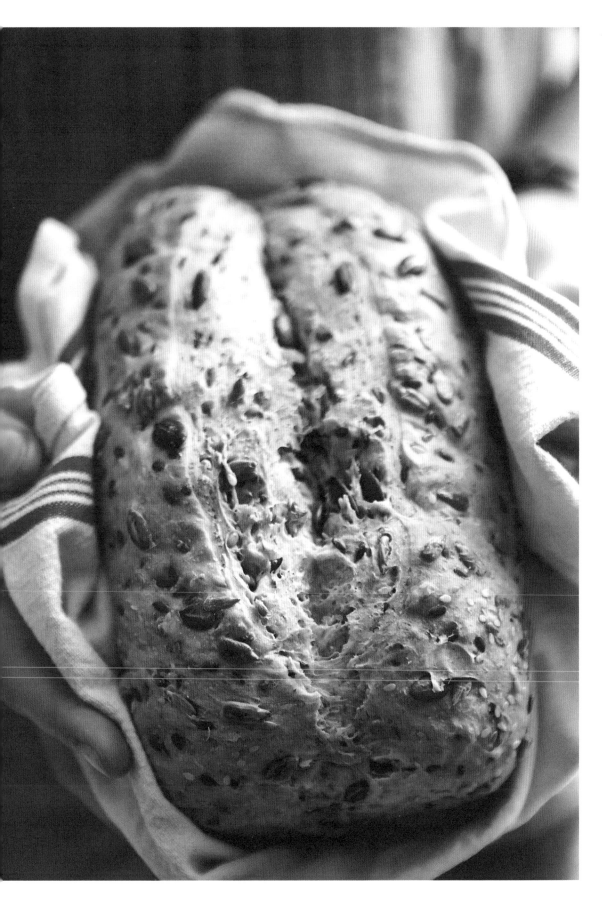

Makes 1 small loaf
330 grams (2¾ c) whole wheat flour
1 teaspoon baking soda
½ teaspoon salt

2 tablespoons dark brown sugar
1¼ cups buttermilk

 above

1   Preheat the oven to 350°F and dust a baking sheet with flour. Combine the flour,
    baking soda, salt, and sugar in a large bowl, then stir in the buttermilk. Knead the
    sticky dough very lightly, and then shape — dusting with plenty of flour — into a
    rough ball. Transfer to the floured baking sheet, score a deep cross into the top of
    the dough, and bake for 50 minutes. It couldn't be simpler.

THE WHOLE STORY

Not quite as easy to work with as white flour, but roughly ten thousand times more interesting, whole wheat flour is a miracle cure for all blandly anemic white loaves. Replacing as little as 10 percent of the white flour with whole wheat flour will begin to yield a more interesting, rounded flavor, while at amounts approaching half the bread will develop a deeply savory taste.

Because whole wheat flour contains all parts of the grain — endosperm, germ, and bran — it has a coarser texture than white flour and higher water absorbency. The percentage of fibrous bran in the flour also means it has less gluten than white flour. As such, loaves made with only whole wheat flour can tend to be heavy. I prefer to lighten the texture by using a blend of whole wheat and white flours.

WHOLE WHEAT WALNUT BREAD

Nutty whole wheat flour and a double dose of walnut are the secrets to this mellow, flavorful bread. It puts the lie to the old myth positioning austere, cardboard-like whole wheat opposite saintly sliced white. It has even seduced one of my most stubbornly whole wheat–phobic friends.

Once cut, this bread stales quickly, so I've called for baking two small loaves rather than one large loaf. Made this way, they can be relished one at a time. It also means a higher ratio of crust to crumb, which to my mind can't be a bad thing. If you'd rather make a single loaf, bake it for 45 to 50 minutes and be extra conscientious when shaping to ensure an even rise.

Makes 2 small boules
200 grams (1¾ c) coarsely
   chopped walnuts
250 grams (2 c) white bread flour
150 grams (1¼ c) whole wheat flour

2¼ teaspoons (1 packet) instant yeast
1 teaspoon salt
1 cup + 1 tablespoon lukewarm water
1 tablespoon honey
1 egg, lightly beaten, for glazing
   (optional)

1   Grind half of the walnuts in a food processor or coffee grinder. Stop as soon as the nuts resemble coarse sand, as over grinding will cause the nuts to release their natural oils, creating a greasy paste.

2   Mix the ground walnuts with the flours and yeast in a large bowl, then stir in the salt. Add the water and honey and combine. Let the dough rest for 20 minutes, then knead for 10 minutes. The kneaded dough won't become quite as smooth and elastic as you might be used to, due to the ground nuts and high proportion of whole wheat flour. Add the remaining walnuts, then knead them into the dough. Set aside in a large, covered bowl and let rise for about 1½ hours, until roughly 1½ times its original size.

3   Halve the dough and shape each piece into a small boule (see page 82 for tips on shaping) on a lightly floured work surface. Let proof on a baking sheet at room temperature for 45 to 60 minutes, until the loaves increase in size by half as much again. Meanwhile, preheat the oven to 350°F.

4   Brush the top of each loaf with the egg. With a very sharp knife, score each with a ½-inch-deep crisscross pattern, much like a tic-tac-toe grid (see page 84 for tips on scoring). Bake for 35 to 45 minutes, depending on how thick you'd like your crust.

Variation

It's not an innovative idea, but adding just a handful of raisins will make a big difference in these loaves. The toasted, slightly bitter taste of the walnuts will be balanced by the sweet raisins, and the bread will take on a slightly caramelized flavor. It makes a fine tea bread.

OLIVE & ORANGE CROWN

A happy glug of olive oil here is the secret to a rich, tender loaf. Orange and olive might not be an obvious pairing, but they strike a delicate balance, an echo of citrus playing off the punchy saltiness of the olives. Though I'm loath to descend into food snobbery, it has to be said: the quality of the olives really is paramount. Olive bread made with rubbery, briny, cheap olives really won't be the same. That said, olive bread is arguably — like pizza — good even when it's bad.

Makes 1 crown loaf
350 grams (2¾ c) white bread flour
1½ teaspoons instant yeast
¾ teaspoon salt
¼ cup olive oil

¾ cup cool water
Zest of 1 orange
100 grams (¾ c) Kalamata olives,
    chopped and patted dry

📷 page 99

1   Combine the flour and yeast in a large bowl, then stir in the salt. Add the oil, water, and orange zest and mix to combine. Knead for about 10 minutes. The dough will be wet and uncooperative to start with, but the high oil content should prevent it from sticking too much. Persevere until it is elastic and no longer sticky. Knead in the olives and set aside in a large, covered bowl at room temperature for 1½ to 2 hours, until doubled in size.

2   On a lightly floured work surface, divide the dough into 5 pieces and roll each into an oval shape — similar to a football. Arrange the portions in a circle on a large baking sheet, with each piece of dough very close to, but not quite touching, its neighbors (they will swell and join as they rise and bake). Let proof for 40 to 50 minutes at room temperature, until almost doubled in size. Meanwhile preheat the oven to 425°F.

3   Dust the risen dough with flour, score lightly along the length of each oval of dough (see page 84), and bake for 10 minutes. Decrease the temperature to 400°F and bake for 25 minutes longer.

SPELT FLOUR

Spelt, an ancient cousin of wheat, is an easy way to change up your bread baking. It brings with it a light nutty taste, slight sweetness, and moist texture. Its relation to wheat means that it's reasonably easy to substitute into most wheat bread recipes — there are just a couple of things to bear in mind.

Firstly, spelt, though reasonably high in gluten, is far less resilient than wheat flour. It needs to be handled sympathetically. When kneading all-spelt dough, it's crucial not to overdo it. After just a couple of minutes of kneading, you'll notice that the dough tightens and soon after it'll begin to tear. I find it best to knead spelt dough for only a minute or so, enlivening it without overworking it.

This weak gluten also means that spelt loaves run the risk of "flowing," even after shaping. The dough may seem flabby, and the loaf may spread apathetically across the baking sheet — it certainly won't stand as proud as the average loaf of white bread. However, there are things that can be done to combat this. Proper shaping technique will do wonders (see pages 80 through 83), as will preshaping. After the first rise, shape the dough into a ball as usual, then let it rest for 5 minutes and shape again. The dough will spread a little in the 5 minutes after preshaping but should hold better after the second shaping. It's also worth noting that small loaves will hold their shape better than very large, heavy ones.

But beyond that, there's little point trying to work against the grain. If spelt spreads, it spreads. Intricately shaped loaves may be out of the question, but you'll still be able to bake a fine boule or bâtard. So what if it's a little squat?

Secondly, and it's an important point, spelt flour ferments faster than wheat flour, putting your dough at great risk of over-proofing. To minimize the possibility of the dough exhausting itself, it's best to let shaped spelt loaves proof only as long as it takes for them to increase in size by half as much again. The loaf will quite quickly begin to feel fragile, so it's useful to have the oven preheated to a high temperature slightly in advance. That way you can transfer the loaf into the hot oven the moment it's proofed.

CHERRY SPELT LOAVES

Coffee gives this bread a subtle darkness against which the cherries taste all the more excitingly tart. If you can't find white spelt flour (it seems to be less easy to source than its whole-grain counterpart), you can use white bread flour instead.

As mentioned above, spelt flour has a far shorter window for baking than standard wheat flour; it'll very quickly go from oven-ready to over-proofed. For this reason, the rising times specified are a little shorter than for many of the other breads in this book. You'll also notice that the dough needs very little kneading.

Makes 2 small loaves
150 grams (1¼ c) whole grain spelt flour
360 grams white spelt flour (3 c) or white bread flour (2¾ c + 1 tbsp)
2¼ teaspoons (1 packet) instant yeast
1 teaspoon salt

2 tablespoons superfine or light brown sugar
1½ cups black coffee, lukewarm
100 to 150 grams (¾ c to 1 c + 2 tbsp) whole dried cherries

📷 page 101

1   Combine the flours and yeast in a large bowl, then stir in the salt and sugar. Pour in the coffee and work the dough with your hands until fully mixed. Lightly knead the cherries into the dough, working it for no longer than 1 minute. Put the dough in a clean bowl, cover, and let rise at room temperature for about 1 hour; it should be at least 1½ times its original size.

2   Divide the risen dough into 2 pieces and shape each into a neat boule or bâtard (see pages 80 through 83). Set them well apart on a large baking sheet (or use two baking sheets, if necessary — spelt dough tends to spread). It's important to shape tightly and neatly to ensure a decent rise from these fragile loaves. Let the loaves proof at room temperature in a draft-free spot for 30 to 40 minutes if using 100 percent spelt flour or up to 1 hour if you substituted white bread flour for a portion of the spelt. Meanwhile, preheat the oven to 475°F. The loaves are ready to bake as soon as they're 1½ times their original size; if you wait until they've doubled, the loaves may collapse.

3   Dust the risen breads with flour, score their tops (see page 84), and bake for 10 minutes. Decrease the temperature to 400°F and bake for 20 to 25 minutes longer, depending on how crusty you like your bread. Once completely cool, enjoy the loaves cut into slices no more than ⅜ inch thick, toasted and spread liberally with butter and a good cherry jam.

RYE FLOUR

Rye is one of the most exciting and difficult flours in the baker's arsenal. You can find dark, medium, and light varieties (corresponding to the varying percentages of bran and germ left in the flour) if you look hard enough, but the standard kind on supermarket shelves is dark rye, the most whole grain version. It's not thrilling to look at — grayish and speckled with dark, ashy flecks of bran — but rye bread is a pleasure to eat: sweeter than wheat, nutty, and very slightly sour.

Unfortunately, this remarkable flavor comes at a cost. Rye has little gluten, and the gluten it has is very weak, resulting in dense loaves. If this were the extent of rye's difficulties, I wouldn't much mind — there is, after all, something uniquely satisfying about a slim slice of heavy rye bread. But there are other problems to be overcome; chiefly, that enzyme overload in 100 percent rye breads can lead to something called (rather dramatically) starch attack. To take away the apocalyptic spin, this is what happens when enzymes break down rye flour, resulting in a slurry of sugars that will remain resolutely sticky, almost cement-like, even after baking.

There are ways to combat the decline and fall of rye breads, among them fostering a slightly more acidic environment in order to inhibit the overactive enzymes. Sometimes this might mean adding an acidic ingredient such as molasses or honey. Alternatively, sourdoughs naturally provide that sort of acidic microclimate, which is why you'll find that many rye breads are some days in the making. But you needn't be a martyr to your rye if you're savvy about combining flours. By using just a small proportion of dark rye flour in a loaf made primarily of bread flour, you can counter the self-destructive tendencies of rye while still enjoying its inimitable flavor.

SWEDISH CARAWAY RYE BREAD

In the UK, bread tends to be something of a wheat-fest; the mild climate is so perfect for cultivating wheat that it often means other grains are overlooked. Yet if we turn to northern Europe, with cooler climes where wheat struggles to grow, there's a rich culture of rye bread, from heavy German *vollkornbrot* to Danish *rugbrød* and crisp Norwegian *knekkebrød*.

Here's a chewy Swedish rye bread that carries on that tradition. I'm a big fan of its dark, grungy density. Grassy caraway, dark molasses, and rye mean that this is a bread that packs a punch — a good thing, as bread would be very dull indeed if it began and ended with airy sandwich loaves.

Using three different flours for one loaf might seem like overkill, but it's the key to a full-flavored bread that, though close-textured, isn't gummy. You can replace the whole wheat flour with an equal weight of white bread flour if you want, to increase the gluten levels and create a lighter, spongier texture.

Makes 2 small loaves
350 grams (2¾ c) white bread flour
125 grams (1 c + 1 tbsp) whole wheat flour
125 grams (1¼ c) dark rye flour
2¼ teaspoons (1 packet) instant yeast
1 teaspoon salt

1 tablespoon superfine or light brown sugar
1 teaspoon caraway or fennel seeds
Zest of 1 orange
¼ cup orange juice
1¼ cups lukewarm water
2 tablespoons dark molasses

📷 page 103

1 Combine the flours and yeast in a large bowl, then stir in the salt, sugar, and caraway seeds. In a separate bowl, beat together the orange zest and juice, water, and molasses. Add this to the flour mixture and stir to combine. Knead for 10 minutes, until the dough is stronger, stretchier, and no longer sticky.

2 Let the dough rise in a large, covered bowl at room temperature for 1 to 1½ hours, until just under double its original size.

3 Divide in half, shaping each half into a ball and then patting it down to a fat, round disk, about 2 inches thick. Place each loaf on a lightly floured baking sheet and let proof at room temperature for 45 to 60 minutes, until 1½ times the original size. Take care not to overproof the dough. Meanwhile, preheat the oven to 400°F.

4 Dust the tops of the loaves with a little flour, then score in any pattern you like, using swift, firm strokes and a very sharp knife (for tips on scoring see page 84).

5 Bake for 40 to 45 minutes. Let the loaves cool completely before slicing.

LEEK & CHEESE TART

This French tart, properly called *flamiche*, combines soft leeks and hard cheese in an enriched dough. Bread provides a far more substantial tart shell than the short crust pastry we're used to. It's an exceptional foil to the richness of the filling, too — when one is confronted, blissfully, with a forkful of quivering crème fraîche, cheese, and leek, a traditional, butter-heavy pastry crust can feel like overkill. Serve this with nothing more than a handful of peppery salad leaves.

You'd usually chill a brioche-type dough such as this prior to its second proof to set the butter and make shaping easier, but I'm not convinced it's necessary here; I've used less butter than in a standard brioche, yielding a dough that, though rich, acts in much the same way as a normal bread dough might.

The filling puffs up quite magnificently in the oven, so take care not to overfill the crust. The amounts here are just right for my deep pie pan at home, but should it be too much for your pan, just use less accordingly. Any leftover filling makes a fine sauce when tossed with linguine.

Serves 6

250 grams (2 c) white bread flour
1 teaspoon instant yeast
½ teaspoon salt
7½ tablespoons lukewarm water
1 large egg
3½ tablespoons unsalted butter, softened

1¼ cups crème fraîche
2 large eggs, lightly beaten
Pinch of nutmeg
150 grams (5.25 oz) Cheddar, Comté,
    or Gruyère cheese, coarsely grated
    (about 1⅓ c)
Salt and black pepper

Filling
3½ tablespoons unsalted butter
400 to 500 grams (14 to 18 oz) leeks,
    trimmed and sliced

1 egg, beaten, for glazing (optional)

**Large, deep pie or tart pan, 10 to
12 inches in diameter at the rim**

📷 page 105

1   Mix the flour and yeast in a bowl, then stir in the salt, followed by the water and egg. Mix with your hands to roughly combine, then knead for 5 to 10 minutes, until the dough is stronger and elastic. Once it has gained a little strength, knead in the butter until fully incorporated. Set aside to rise in a large, covered bowl at room temperature for 1 to 1½ hours, until doubled in size.

2   Meanwhile, start preparing the filling. Melt the butter in a large pan, add the leeks, and stir. Cover and cook over low heat for 25 minutes, stirring occasionally, until the leeks are meltingly tender. Set the leeks aside to cool.

3   When the dough has doubled in size, turn it out onto a lightly floured work surface and roll it out to form a large circle — big enough to line the bottom and sides of the pan. Let the dough relax for a minute or two after rolling; it'll shrink back slightly thanks to the gluten developed during kneading. Roll it out until it's the required size again, then transfer it to the pan, pressing the dough into the corners and pushing it up a little around the sides to create a slight overhang. Fold a little dough over the rim of the pan and tack it down against the outside by pressing firmly. This prevents the dough from sliding down inside the pan during proofing. Set aside to rise for 30 minutes. Preheat the oven to 400°F.

4   While the dough rises, finish making the filling. Stir the crème fraîche, eggs, nutmeg, and cheese into the leeks and season with salt and pepper. A generous hand with the pepper is crucial here to cut through the creamy richness of the filling. Once the dough has risen, spoon in the filling.

5   Brush the rim of the dough, which by now should be puffy, with the beaten egg. Bake for 40 minutes. The cooked tart should be mottled golden and brown on top and well risen. For an even more enticing tart, sprinkle on an extra 30 grams (1 oz) of grated cheese (about ¼ c) 10 minutes before the end of the baking time.

SMALL BITES & FLATBREADS

Bread is far too exciting to be limited to predictable slicing, buttering, and sandwiching. These next recipes show how varied the methods of shaping and serving bread can be. Some are leavened, others are not, and there are breads here to wrap, to split, or to eat in just one mouthful.

GARLIC DOUGH BALLS

Forget the greasy, half-baked dough balls that you find in cheap pizza chains and takeout boxes. Make these at home and revel in the chewy, unashamedly garlicky joy of them.

Makes 30 to 36
4 medium cloves garlic, unpeeled
¼ cup olive oil, plus a splash for roasting the garlic
1 cup + 1 tablespoon water
500 grams (4 c) white bread flour
2¼ teaspoons (1 packet) instant yeast

1 teaspoon salt
30 to 40 grams (½ to ⅔ c) parsley, finely chopped

2 large rimmed baking sheets

📷 page 108

1   Preheat the oven to 350°F.

2   In an ovenproof dish, roast the garlic cloves in their skins with a splash of olive oil for about 15 minutes, until soft and fragrant. Turn off the oven. Peel off the papery garlic skins and mash the pulp to a puree. Stir in the olive oil and water.

3   In a large bowl, combine the flour and yeast. Stir in the salt, followed by the garlic mixture and the parsley, until incorporated. Knead for 5 minutes or so, until the dough is just beginning to feel less sticky. There's no need to agonize about reaching windowpane stage with this dough; the balls are very small, so they don't need a perfectly developed, impressively elastic dough in order to rise and hold their shape.

4   Let the dough rise in a covered bowl at room temperature for about 1 hour, until doubled in size. Gently deflate the dough, divide it into 30 to 36 pieces, and roll each into a ball on an unfloured work surface. Oil the baking sheets generously, then spread the dough balls on the baking sheets. Proof for 30 minutes, during which time the balls will puff up slightly. Meanwhile, preheat the oven to 350°F.

5   Bake for 13 to 15 minutes, until well risen. The dough balls will still look a little anemic at this point, but they'll be cooked through nonetheless. Pile them into a bowl and eat while they're still warm. I like to drizzle them with a little melted butter, too. I can't officially recommend this for fear of reprisals from doctors and the health conscious, but what I will say is that it's buttery, garlicky ambrosia.

Variation

Forget the garlic and parsley, decrease the salt to ½ teaspoon, and knead in 150 grams (5.25 oz) grated Cheddar cheese (about 1¼ c) to make cheese dough balls. Dangerously addictive.

RYE CARAWAY BAGELS

Toasted then topped with cream cheese and smoked salmon, these bagels make an exceptional breakfast. But for more frugal days they're fantastic with just a slick of butter, too.

This recipe might seem a little laborious at first glance — individually shaping each one, boiling them in batches, and then baking — but these bagels merit the extra work. The shaping, though repetitive, is very simple and barely takes 10 minutes. The boiling is crucial for the bagel's characteristically chewy texture. The addition of baking soda to the boiling water helps to give a deeper color to the crust as the bagels bake (thanks to the Maillard reaction — see page 178), but it's by no means essential.

If you want to bake these in the morning for breakfast, prepare the dough the evening before and let it rise, covered, in the fridge overnight. In the morning, shape and let rise again, then proceed with the boiling and baking.

Makes 8
325 grams (2½ c + 1 tbsp) white bread flour
125 grams (1¼ c) dark rye flour
2¼ teaspoons (1 packet) instant yeast
1¼ teaspoons salt
1 tablespoon sugar
1 cup + 1 tablespoon lukewarm water
1 tablespoon oil
2 tablespoons caraway seeds

Flour or polenta, for dusting
2 tablespoons baking soda (optional)

Glaze & Topping
¼ cup water
½ teaspoon salt
35 grams (¼ c) poppy seeds (optional)

📷 page 110

1 Combine the flours and yeast in a large bowl, then stir in the salt and sugar, followed by the lukewarm water and oil. Using your hands, vigorously mix until the dough comes together into a ball, then knead for 10 minutes. It's a drier dough than most of the other breads here, so it will be tighter and less sticky. Gently knead in the caraway seeds. Cover the bowl with plastic wrap and let rise for about 1½ hours, until doubled in size.

2 Turn out the risen dough, divide it into 8 pieces, and shape into bagels. There are two ways of doing this. The first is to roll each lump of dough into a small ball, as you would for a bread roll, then push through the center with your finger. Twirl the dough around your finger, gradually widening the hole. The other method is to roll the dough into a long sausage shape, tapered so that it is thinner at each end. Slap the dough lightly against the work surface to allow it to shrink back a little, then let it rest for a minute. It needs to be 12 to 14 inches long once rested. Curve the dough around into a circle shape, twisting the tapered ends around

each other and pinching at the seams to secure. I prefer this second method, as the intertwined ends and asymmetry of the bagel are really very pretty.

3   Dust a baking sheet with flour, or to give the bagels a good crunch, polenta. Put the bagels on the baking sheet and proof at room temperature for 30 to 45 minutes, until puffy and almost 1½ times their original size. Meanwhile, preheat the oven to 350°F and bring a large pot of water to a boil. Generously oil two baking sheets.

4   Add the baking soda to the boiling water. Turn the heat down so that the water is simmering and boil the bagels in batches. They'll bob at the water's surface as they cook, half submerged. Let simmer for 60 seconds, then carefully turn them over and cook for 1 minute longer. It's important not to leave them in the water for too long, so be sure to have a watch or timer on hand for this. Remove with a slotted spoon and place on the oiled baking sheets.

5   To make the glaze and top the bagels, combine the ¼ cup of water and the salt. Stir until the salt is dissolved, then brush the bagels with this. Sprinkle the poppy seeds over the bagels. Bake for 25 minutes.

CHICKPEA & CUMIN SEED BUNS

Who says that a bun should play second fiddle to its burger? Traditionalists would have it that a bun is little more than a bland, cursory vessel. Toss that notion aside. These are suffused with a bold, earthy flavor, complementing even robust fillings. Try them with falafel, bean burgers, or even spiced lamb.

Makes 12
3 tablespoons olive oil
1 tablespoon cumin seeds
1½ cups (240 g) cooked, drained
    chickpeas

1¼ cups lukewarm water
3¾ cups white bread flour
2¼ teaspoons (1 packet) instant yeast
1 teaspoon salt

1   Heat the olive oil in a pan and fry the cumin seeds for barely 1 minute (any longer and they may become bitter). Put the chickpeas in a large bowl, add the oil and cumin seeds, and mash until no whole chickpeas remain. Beat in the water.

2   In a separate bowl, combine the flour and yeast, then stir in the salt. Add to the chickpea mixture, mix with your hands, then knead for 10 minutes, building elasticity and reducing stickiness in the dough. Let rise in a covered bowl at room temperature for approximately 1½ hours, until doubled in size.

3   Shape the dough into 12 buns (see page 82) and arrange them on a large baking sheet so that they're closely spaced (within ¾ inch of one another) but not touching. Let proof, preferably loosely covered with a piece of plastic wrap, for about 45 minutes, until at least 1½ times their original size and almost touching one another. Meanwhile, preheat the oven to 350°F.

4   Dust the risen rolls with flour and bake for 25 minutes.

SOCCA

These French chickpea flour flatbreads are arguably more pancake than bread, but I don't feel too conflicted about including them here. They're nutty, intensely savory, and versatile: think improvised pizza bases, wraps, and even — if cooked for a little longer — dipping chips and crackers. But I prefer them, partly in the name of simplicity and minimal washing up, eaten straight from the sizzling pan with just a grind of pepper.

In Nice and along stretches of the south coast of France, they are *socca*; further east and curving down the coastline into Italy, they're *farinata*. They're usually found on street corners at vendors' stalls, to be bought cheaply and eaten greedily while on the move. You may not have the pleasure of having a local *socca* vendor (although who knows where the street food movement will take us), but luckily these are easy, cheap, and quick to make at home. This is a simplified stove-top version, although thicker, more substantial oven-baked *socca* are also popular.

You can find gram flour (sometimes labeled chickpea or garbanzo bean flour) in the international sections of some larger supermarkets, at natural food stores, or in most Indian or Pakistani markets. Raw gram flour can have a bitter, astringent aftertaste, but this is remedied by toasting the flour first, which is what I've suggested here.

Makes 12
300 grams (2½ c) gram
   (chickpea or garbanzo) flour
Black pepper
½ teaspoon salt
2½ cups water
¼ cup olive oil

Additions (optional)
2 teaspoons paprika
or 1 onion, finely sliced and fried in oil
or 2 tablespoons rosemary, briefly
   fried in oil
or 2 tablespoons dried oregano or thyme
or 2 cloves garlic, finely chopped and
   gently fried in oil

📷 page 112

1   Toast the gram flour over medium heat in a large, dry pan, stirring continuously, for 5 to 10 minutes, until the flour has slightly darkened in color. It should begin to smell nutty and rich. Don't overcook the flour or let it sit unstirred; if it burns, it will slide back into exactly that bitterness that we're trying to lose. If it begins to look brown rather than just golden, whip it straight off the heat. Let it cool slightly before proceeding, using this time to prepare any desired additions.

2   Combine the flour, salt, and about half of the water in a bowl and stir to form a thick paste. Season with pepper. Add all but 7 tablespoons of the remaining water and the olive oil. The batter ought to be thick but not gloppy; add the remaining water as necessary to reach the right consistency. Stir in any additions that you're using at this point.

3   Preheat a small nonstick frying pan over medium-high heat, grease with olive oil, and pour in a ladle of batter — enough to form a roughly 6-inch circle. Cook for 1½ to 2 minutes, lifting the edges occasionally to prevent sticking, then carefully turn and cook for a minute or two longer. Repeat with the remaining batter, greasing the pan again each time.

CHORIZO & KALE FLATBREAD

Not one to be shoved to the sidelines, this bold flatbread combines spicy chorizo and iron-rich kale to become very much a meal in itself. Although hearty chorizo is the flavor powerhouse here, for me it's the kale that steals the show. It essentially fries in the oil from the meat, the once-virtuous greens growing crisp, salty, and delicious. This is a big flatbread — big enough to share, but I won't judge you if you don't.

Serves 2
250 grams (2 c) white bread flour
1 teaspoon instant yeast
½ teaspoon salt
¾ cup lukewarm water
5 tablespoons olive oil
100 grams (3.5 oz) chorizo, diced

125 grams (4.5 oz) kale or cavolo nero,
    stemmed and finely chopped

9 by 13-inch baking pan

📷 page 115

1   Combine the flour and yeast in a large bowl, stir in the salt, then add the water and 1 tablespoon of the olive oil. Mix with your hands until well combined, then turn out onto a clean surface and knead for 10 minutes, until the dough is elastic and less sticky. Let rise for 1 hour, until doubled in size.

2   While waiting for the dough to rise, bring a pot of water to a boil and add the kale. Boil for just 1 minute, then drain and rinse well with cold water. Once cool, gently press out any excess water.

3   Knead just under half of the kale into the risen dough. It'll be a little tricky due to the residual moisture on the leaves, but don't worry about it being perfect. Preheat the oven to 375°F.

4   On a floured surface, roll out the dough to about 8 inches in diameter. Use your hands to stretch the dough to approximately the size of the pan. It will shrink back a little as it rests, so keep on stretching it until it's about the size of the pan after shrinkage. Don't worry if some areas are a little thicker than others, and it's not a disaster if there are one or two holes in the bread — think of it as rustic. Coat the bottom of the pan with 2 tablespoons of the remaining olive oil and transfer the dough to the pan.

5   Let the dough proof at room temperature for 15 minutes, then sprinkle with the remaining kale and then the chorizo. Gently pat the toppings down, then dimple the dough using your fingertips. This is particularly useful here, as it helps to embed some of the topping, securing it to the dough.

6   Let proof for 5 minutes longer, then drizzle the final 2 tablespoons of olive oil over the top. Bake for 20 minutes.

Variations
You might wince at the idea of carb-upon-carb potato bread, but it is really very good. Just replace the chorizo with a few peeled, boiled, and diced potatoes. Lightly toasted cumin seeds work well with this, too, or even some crumbled goat cheese.

PARATHAS

These are soft, multipurpose flatbreads that — at around 20 minutes to make — are as close as bread comes to fast food. And what sets these apart from tortillas, pancakes, chapatis, or pita bread? Butter: melted, brushed lavishly on, and folded in, creates a flaky, golden bread. Some days, when baking spills over into the somber early morning hours, I wearily make a batch of these and eat one (or two, or more), plucked straight from the heat of the frying pan and slathered in raspberry jam. Let the purists protest.

You can make these less indulgent if you prefer: just forget the melted butter and don't fold the dough. Omitting this step will, granted, make these much less work. But without this characteristic layering of butter and dough, these are no longer *parathas*, and you won't achieve that same melting flakiness.

Makes 6
250 grams (2 c) all-purpose flour
¼ teaspoon salt

75 grams (⅓ c) salted butter
½ cup + 1 tablespoon water

1   Stir the flour and salt together in a medium bowl, then rub in 1 tablespoon of the butter until completely integrated. Add the water and very lightly knead for just a minute or so, until the dough is well combined. Set aside to rest for 15 minutes. During this time the flour will absorb more water, making it less sticky and therefore easier to roll out. The gluten will relax as the dough rests too, again aiding the rolling process. While the dough's having its break, melt the remaining butter.

2   Divide the dough into 6 pieces and roll each into a rough ball. Using a floured rolling pin on a well-floured work surface, roll the pieces out into circles about 8 inches in diameter. Brush lightly with the melted butter. There should be a little butter left over after this stage, to be used later when frying the *parathas*.

3   Fold the buttered dough into thirds as you would if you were folding a letter: bottom third folded up toward the middle, then top third folded down over this. Rotate the dough in front of you by 90 degrees (so that the folds are now running vertically) and fold again: bottom third up, top third down. You'll be left with small, square(ish) parcels of buttery dough. Roll these out again, flouring the surfaces as you go, until they're 6 to 8 inches in diameter. I find it easiest to go for roughly square *parathas*, although you could make circles of them if you're more artful with a rolling pin than I am.

4   To cook, brush one side of a *paratha* lightly with some of the remaining butter and fry over medium heat for 2 minutes, buttered side down. Brush the top with butter, flip and cook for another minute or two. Repeat with the remaining *parathas*. These are best eaten freshly cooked.

SLOW & STEADY

So far, the breads in this chapter have been the sort that can be made over the course of an afternoon, leisurely fitted around the odd hour of calm during a hectic day or even thrown from mixing bowl to griddle to plate in just a few minutes. The remaining breads are a little different. It's time that sets these apart: an unhurried rise leading coolly into deep flavor and a chewy texture. To rush these loaves would be to miss the point entirely.

THREE-CHEESE BRIOCHE

How grown-up (or otherwise) this bread turns out is dependent entirely on your choice of cheese. My combination lies at the less-sophisticated end of the spectrum: a cheesy but not overpowering bread, prettily flecked with red Leicester. For something a little more refined, try Gruyère, Taleggio, or Gouda.

The butter in this dough makes it a pleasure to knead and an even greater pleasure to eat. It'll be soft, extensible, and smooth as you work and shape it, and tender once baked. It pays to be patient, though; all the enrichments make the dough slower to rise than you might expect.

This can be made without the overnight stint in the fridge if you're in a hurry; it'll be trickier to shape, but it'll taste good nonetheless. Give the dough its first proof as usual, then skip straight to shaping and the second proof. The second proof will take far less time this way, starting as it does from room temperature.

Makes 1 large brioche, serving 8
400 grams (3c + 3 tbsp) white bread flour
2¼ teaspoons (1 packet) instant yeast
½ teaspoon salt
7 tablespoons milk
3 large eggs, lightly beaten
175 grams (¾ c) unsalted butter, softened
50 grams (1.75 oz) red Leicester,
   grated (about ½ c)

50 grams (1.75 oz) sharp Cheddar,
   grated (about ½ c)
50 grams (1.75 oz) Parmesan or
   Grana Padano, finely grated
   (about ½ c)

1 egg, lightly beaten, for glazing

**Deep 8- to 9-inch round cake pan
or 5 by 9-inch loaf pan**

1 Combine the flour and yeast in a large bowl, then stir in the salt. In a small pan over very low heat, warm the milk until barely lukewarm. Beat together the milk and eggs, add to the flour mixture, and knead for 10 minutes, until smooth and elastic.

2 Knead in the butter. This is a messy job. At the outset, the very different textures of the dough and the soft butter will have you believing that it's an impossible task, but I promise that after just a few minutes, it'll come together smoothly — scrunch, pummel, or squeeze the butter into the dough if need be. Once the butter is well incorporated, knead for 5 minutes longer, then knead in all the cheese.

3   Put the dough in a large bowl, cover, and let rise at room temperature until doubled in size, about 1½ hours. Once doubled, gently deflate, cover again, and place in the fridge for 8 to 10 hours (I usually leave it overnight).

4   Now for the shaping:
    — If using a deep 8- to 9-inch round pan with sides at least 2½ inches high, you can shape your dough rather impressively. Divide it into 7 equal pieces. Roll 5 pieces into balls, then space them evenly around the edges of the pan. Roll the remaining 2 pieces together into a larger ball and place this in the center.
    — Alternatively, if you're averse to unnecessary fussing around, shape all the dough into one large ball and pat this down to fill the tin.
    — There's really too much dough here for a 5 by 9-inch loaf pan (sometimes it just about works for me, but the swelling dough teeters precariously over the pan rim), so if you don't have a deep 8- to 9-inch round pan, shape three-quarters of the dough into a log, put it in a 5 by 9-inch loaf pan and mold the rest into little bun shapes to be baked separately. The buns will bake in 20 to 25 minutes, leaving you just enough time to enjoy them and clean up the crumbs before the big loaf emerges from the oven.

5   Let the shaped dough proof at room temperature until nearly doubled in size. This can take up to 2 hours for a large brioche, depending on the temperature of the room. Covering the pan loosely with plastic wrap will help prevent the dough's surface from drying during this time, although you'll have to watch out that the rising dough doesn't stick to it. Preheat the oven to 400°F.

6   Brush the risen brioche with the beaten egg glaze and bake for 40 minutes, whether in the round pan or the loaf pan. Thanks to the egg wash, it'll color quite deeply on top — this is not at all a problem, but if you're concerned that it might be coloring too much, try placing a foil tent over the bread for the remainder of the baking time.

WHAT IS A PRE-FERMENT?

A pre-ferment is a clever way of improving the taste and texture of bread. A small amount of dough — the pre-ferment — is made with just flour, water, and a tiny amount of yeast and allowed to ferment for 8 hours or more before being incorporated into the final dough. During this time, the yeast will work slowly on the flour, developing gluten and intensifying flavor.

The exact proportions of the pre-ferment will vary depending on its purpose, how long it's to be left to ferment, and the type of bread in which it will be used. A stiff pre-ferment, for example, can help to develop gluten strength in very wet dough, such as Ciabatta (page 120). A wetter pre-ferment, perhaps made with equal weights of water and flour, will develop a slight acidity over the course of a long fermentation, giving more flavor to even the simplest bread. It's a leap toward achieving some of the open texture, chewiness, and good flavor of a sourdough.

It's easier than it sounds, too: just a few minutes of mixing and then the pre-ferment can be left to its own devices for 8 to 16 hours until you're ready to make the bread.

FRENCH COUNTRY BREAD

This rustic, French-style loaf uses just a small amount of rye flour to add depth and balance to the white flour's sweetness. Between the rye, the pre-ferment, and the long proofing periods, this recipe yields a robust, full-flavored, crusty bread that will thoroughly trounce any flimsy sliced sandwich bread you might find at the store.

You only need a very small amount of yeast — ⅙ teaspoon — in this pre-ferment. The easiest way to measure such a small and unusual amount is by dissolving some yeast in water and using just a fraction of this yeast solution in the pre-ferment, as I've suggested below. Such fastidiousness isn't strictly necessary though, and if you can't be bothered (and I wouldn't blame you), a heaping ⅛ teaspoon of yeast will do just fine.

Makes 1 boule

Pre-ferment
½ teaspoon instant yeast
2 tablespoons lukewarm water
5 tablespoons cool water
100 grams (¾ c) white bread flour
50 grams (½ c) dark rye flour

Final dough
325 grams (2½ c + 1 tbsp) white
  bread flour
1 teaspoon instant yeast
1 teaspoon salt
1 cup + 1 tablespoon lukewarm water

1 To make the pre-ferment, sprinkle the ½ teaspoon of yeast into the 2 tablespoons of lukewarm water and stir well to dissolve.

2 Add 2 teaspoons of the yeast mixture to the cool water (the remaining yeast mixture can be discarded). Combine the flours, then stir in the liquid. It will form a reasonably stiff dough. Knead very lightly for just a few seconds to help integrate the ingredients, then place in a bowl, cover tightly with plastic wrap, and let rest at room temperature for 12 to 16 hours. If, toward the end of this time, you're not

yet ready to make the final dough, you can put the pre-ferment in the fridge for a few hours until you're ready. The pre-ferment is ready when it is 2 to 3 times its original volume and the surface is pockmarked with little holes.

3   To make the final dough, combine the flour and yeast in a large bowl, then stir in the salt. Pour in the water and mix to form a loose dough. Knead in the pre-ferment — this can be a little tricky as the pre-ferment and the new dough are so different in consistency, but it shouldn't take long. Once basically combined, set the dough aside to rest for 20 minutes or so. This rest isn't crucial, but it is helpful; during the resting time the dough will absorb more water and the gluten will begin to develop, making kneading easier.

4   Knead the rested dough for at least 10 minutes, but preferably closer to 15 minutes. It's quite a wet dough, so don't be discouraged if it feels sticky, heavy, and lifeless to begin with, and don't be tempted to add more flour. I promise that as you continue to knead (I'd recommend the kneading technique for wetter doughs on page 80) the dough will become easier to handle, and by the time you've finished kneading it'll be virtually unrecognizable: silky, supple, and smooth.

5   Transfer to a large bowl, cover, and let rise until doubled in size. This will take a little longer than usual because there's a comparatively small amount of yeast in this dough — anywhere between 1½ to 2½ hours, depending on the room temperature. This slower rise will result in a more flavorful, chewy bread in the end, so don't worry too much if your dough is dragging its heels.

6   Shape the risen dough into a boule (see page 82) and let it proof again at room temperature in a draft-free spot for about 1 hour, until nearly doubled in size. Meanwhile, preheat the oven to 475°F.

7   Dust the risen dough with flour and, using a very sharp knife, score the top with a cross (see page 84). Bake for 15 minutes, then decrease the temperature to 400°F and bake for 35 to 40 minutes longer. For an even crisper finish, put a little water in a rimmed baking sheet on a low shelf in the oven for the first 10 minutes of the bake. The resulting steam will, counterintuitively perhaps, create a wonderful crust.

CIABATTA

After recipes using a variety of flours, as well as nuts, spices, herbs, fruits, and seeds, I'll conclude with this simple and spectacular bread. I can't think of a better illustration of the shape-shifting versatility, chemistry, or alchemy of that magic four: flour, yeast, salt, and water.

In the French Country Bread recipe (page 119), the pre-ferment is included to add flavor. Its primary function here, however, is structural. The stiff pre-ferment develops strong networks of gluten over the course of its 10- to 12-hour rest. When kneaded into the final dough, this gluten lends strength and resistance to an otherwise very, very wet dough. It is then further developed by the long period of kneading and the subsequent stretches and folds during the first rise. The result: one of the most impossibly light loaves you'll ever eat.

Admittedly, this is a high-maintenance loaf. It needs a good 10-hour head start, 20 minutes of vigorous kneading, attention throughout the first rise, and a vigilant eye cast over it as it bubbles up precariously during its second proof. That said, as a chronically lazy baker I can reassure you that I wouldn't dream of going through this ciabatta saga if the results were anything less than sublime.

Makes 2 ciabatta loaves

Pre-ferment
¼ teaspoon instant yeast
150 grams (1 c + 3 tbsp) white
   bread flour
⅓ cup cool water

Final dough
300 grams (2⅓ c) white bread flour
1 teaspoon instant yeast
1 teaspoon salt
1 cup + 3 tablespoons lukewarm water

📷 page 123

1   To make the pre-ferment, mix the ¼ teaspoon of yeast with the 150 grams (1c + 3 tbsp) of flour in a bowl, then add the water. Stir and knead very briefly just to combine. You should be left with a stiff dough. Let rest in a small, covered bowl at room temperature for 10 to 12 hours. After this time the pre-ferment should be well risen, with bubbles pockmarking its surface.

2   To make the final dough, combine the flour and yeast in a large bowl, then stir in the salt. Add ¾ cup plus 2 tablespoons of the water, mix, then knead for 5 minutes. Work in the pre-ferment and knead for a couple more minutes. Now's time to add the remaining 5 tablespoons of water: return the dough to the bowl, work in the water with your hands, and then knead in the bowl for a full 15 minutes. It'll be far too wet to knead normally — instead, use a stretching and slapping motion, repeatedly pulling the dough upward and slapping it back down, folding it over itself. As you continue to stretch the dough, you'll notice it become gradually stronger and more elastic. Fifteen minutes will feel like a long time to be kneading, but it's essential for proper gluten development. The kneaded dough will still be sticky but should be supple, shiny, and strong. Whatever you do, resist the temptation to add any more flour; this dough is supposed to be very wet.

3   Divide the dough in half and put each piece in a large, lightly oiled bowl. (It's far kinder to the dough to divide it at this point, prior to rising, than to butcher it later and risk deflating it.) Cover the bowls and let the dough rise at room temperature. After 30 minutes, give the dough its first stretch. Lightly oil your hands, slide them underneath one of the pieces of dough, and pull to stretch the dough outward horizontally. Fold one stretched side back into the center, then the other one over. Rotate the bowl 90 degrees and repeat once. Do the same with the other piece of dough. Repeat this process after 30 more minutes, and then let rest again for 45 minutes. By this point the dough will have risen for a total of 1¾ hours, with stretches at 30 minutes and 1 hour.

4   Generously dust two baking sheets with flour. With lightly oiled hands, carefully scoop one of the pieces of dough out of its bowl and stretch it out to about 12 inches long. The aim here is to interfere with the dough's structure as little

as possible, so don't fold or squeeze the dough; just stretch it gently and lay it on the baking sheet. Repeat with the other piece. The dough won't be perfectly neat and it will spread a little but this isn't a problem.

5   Let the loaves proof for about 1 hour at room temperature in a draft-free spot, preheating the oven to 475°F in the meantime with a rimmed baking sheet on the lower shelf. The loaves will be tremulous and visibly bigger after the hour has elapsed. Sprinkle with flour, then put the risen loaves in the hot oven, adding a little water to the rimmed baking sheet (creating steam for a better rise). Bake for 10 minutes, then decrease the temperature to 375°F and bake for 20 minutes longer. Have a bowl of olive oil and balsamic vinegar at the ready. As soon as the loaves are cool, tear into chunks, dip, and enjoy.

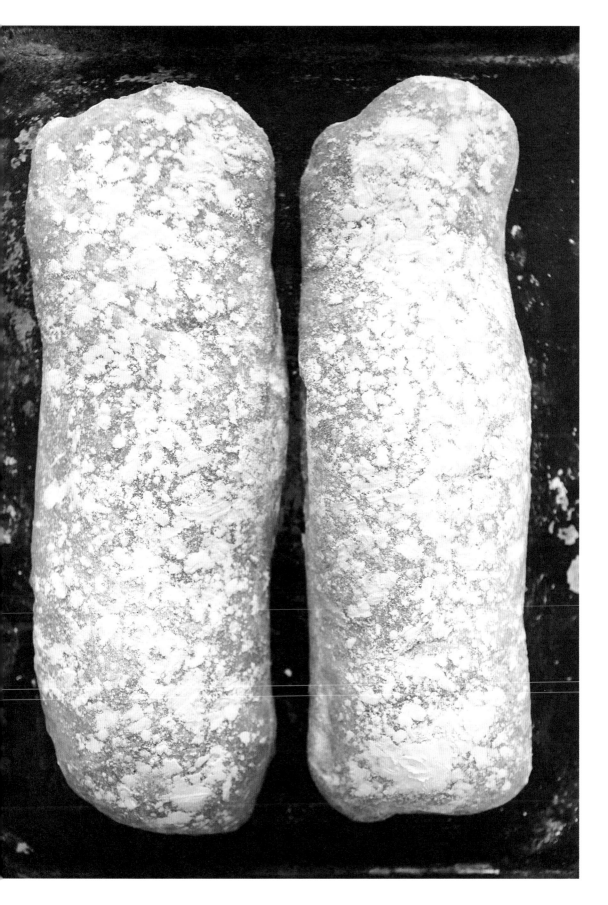

SWEET DOUGH

BUNS

BASIC SWEET DOUGH

THUNDER & LIGHTNING BUNS

SCANDINAVIAN ALMOND CREAM BUNS

BLUEBERRY SWIRLS • GLAZED SAFFRON BUNS

RASPBERRY MASCARPONE VATRUSHKAS

DOUGHNUTS

CUSTARD DOUGHNUTS • OLIEBOLLEN

GLAZED CAKE DOUGHNUTS

TO SHARE

COCONUT LIME LOAF • MONKEY BREAD

CRUMBLE-TOPPED PEAR & ALMOND COFFEE CAKE • BRIOCHE

CHERRY STOLLEN WITH PISTACHIO MARZIPAN

WHITE CHOCOLATE HAZELNUT COURONNE

Bread, but better. Sticky blueberry swirls, custard doughnuts, brioche, cream-filled buns, sweet coconut loaves, and golden saffron buns—this chapter is a hymn to sweet dough. These buns, often bulbous, messily iced, and generously proportioned, don't have the refinement of pastries or cakes, but there lies their appeal. Laced with butter, sugar, milk, and eggs to leave them sweet and tender, they're my favorite things to bake and to eat. And unlike more basic breads, these don't need any dressing up, spreads, or accompaniments — they're delicious just as they are.

BREAD WITH A DIFFERENCE

The recipes in this chapter use enriched versions of bread dough, so the techniques involved — mixing, kneading, rising, shaping, proofing, and baking — are the same as those in the Bread chapter (outlined on pages 77 through 79). The finished breads, however, are very different: because they're laced with milk, eggs, butter, and sugar, they're richer and more tender.

MILK

Milk is around 90 percent water, so it can be almost directly substituted for water in most bread recipes. It's the remaining 10 percent that makes the difference, though: in whole milk, this is a mixture of sugars, proteins, and fats. The sugars lend a slight sweetness, while the fats help to keep the bread tender and the crust soft. You'll also notice that breads made with milk rather than water tend to bake to a deeper color. Because 2% milk has half the fat of whole milk, it creates a marginally less delicate texture. As for skim milk, I never use it.

Milk can have a slight tightening effect on the structure of bread, due to proteins that interfere with gluten development. Some argue that this can be prevented by scalding the milk prior to use, breaking down these problematic proteins. However, I've made breads with both scalded and unscalded milk, and although the former produced a very slightly better texture, it won only by a hair's breadth. I'm not convinced that it's worth the time spent heating and cooling the milk. If you want to make prizewinning buns, by all means scald the milk first, but if you can't be bothered, don't worry. You can achieve a similar effect in a fraction of the time by simply increasing the amount of milk by a couple of tablespoons. (As discussed in the previous chapter, the wetter the dough, the more open the crumb.)

BUTTER

Butter is the secret to soft, rich bread. Quite aside from the fact that it lends a deep, buttery flavor, its fat plays an important structural role. Fat coats the flour particles and disrupts the formation of gluten, leaving enriched breads with a softer texture and crust than more basic flour-yeast-salt-water breads. It might seem self-defeating to undermine the gluten structure in this way, having so diligently developed it by kneading, but in truth it's a balancing act: a certain amount of gluten development is crucial for good structure, but fat is necessary for tenderness. Most of the time, you won't be adding enough fat to completely sabotage the gluten. But in very butter-heavy doughs, such as brioche, a compromise is reached by kneading before adding butter, to give the gluten a head start.

Butter also affects the way the dough feels and behaves during its preparation. Dough made with plenty of butter is a joy to handle: soft, supple, and less sticky. It is, however, far slower to rise and proof than other doughs, the enrichment slowing the action of the yeast. As such, you'll find that the breads in this chapter take a little longer to make than those without butter.

Even after the bread has been baked, butter continues to play an important role: breads made with added fats are slower to go stale.

EGGS

Eggs are complex cocktails of water, fats, and proteins, so their effects on bread are very similar to those of milk and butter. There are a couple of differences, however. Firstly, egg is very good at binding ingredients together, which means that breads made with egg will be less crumbly. Secondly, and more excitingly, the yolks give the bread a delightful yellow hue.

SUGAR

Obviously, adding sugar to a dough makes it sweet. Yeast will happily feed on sugars, so a small amount of sugar in dough can aid fermentation, making for a faster rise. You can, however, have too much of a good thing: very sweet doughs actually rise more slowly, as the excess sugar inhibits the yeast. This shouldn't be too much of a problem for the recipes here, however, as I've kept sugar to a minimum in the dough itself, instead adding sweetness in fillings and toppings.

SPICE & ZEST

Because spices can slow or even kill yeast, it's advisable to use them sparingly in yeast doughs. A small amount is usually unproblematic, but for a more intense hit of flavor, try adding spices separately, perhaps rolled up with the dough, as in cinnamon buns, or mixed into a glaze. The same goes for zest, although you shouldn't have to worry when including it in relatively modest quantities.

GLAZING

A matte, rugged finish can be appealing on top of a country loaf or a rustic bâtard, but for the more aesthetically aware breads and buns in this chapter, you'll probably want to aim for a more polished appearance. This needn't be anything difficult, costly, or time-consuming; more often than not, a simple lick of egg wash or milk is all it takes. Different glazes will leave breads with slightly different finishes. Milk will create a faint sheen; butter makes for a very tender crust; egg creates a richly colored, shiny finish; and a mixture of sugar and water will brown quickly on small buns, helping them to color during their short baking time. I usually suggest an egg glaze, but you can, of course, change or omit the glaze as you please.

SHAPING

There is no end to the ways you can shape sweet dough. Whichever shape you choose, whether traditional or off the top of your head, make sure you shape with conviction and consistency, sealing any seams, smoothing any wrinkles, and ensuring that the top of the dough is kept taut for an even rise.

BUNS

BASIC SWEET DOUGH

The following three recipes — Thunder & Lightning Buns (page 131), Scandinavian Almond Cream Buns (page 134), and Blueberry Swirls (page 136) — all use versions of this sweet dough recipe. That three such different baked goods can be made from one basic mixture only goes to show the versatility of sweet dough. It can metamorphose from sticky cinnamon rolls to behemoth Belgian buns with as little as a dusting of spice or a handful of dried fruit. Feel free to make your own additions, too.

Makes enough for 12 buns
500 grams (4 c) white bread flour
2¼ teaspoons (1 packet) instant yeast
1 teaspoon salt

2 tablespoons + 2 teaspoons
  superfine sugar
¾ cup + 1½ tablespoons whole milk
2 large eggs
60 grams (¼ c) unsalted butter, softened

1   In a large bowl, combine the flour, yeast, salt, and sugar. (Add any spices or zest at this point.)

2   Heat the milk very gently in a small pan over low heat until barely warm to the touch. It shouldn't be any warmer than tepid. Add the milk, eggs, and butter to the flour mixture and bring the dough together using your hands. There's really no way to avoid getting your hands dirty unless you're fortunate enough to own a stand mixer; you need to stretch, pummel, and squash the dough until the ingredients are all incorporated. Once combined, let the dough rest for about 15 minutes in the bowl, during which time the flour will absorb more of the liquid and begin to strengthen, becoming less sticky.

3   Knead the rested dough for 10 to 15 minutes. (There's some advice on kneading on page 80 if you need it.) It will feel sticky and heavy to begin with, but resist the temptation to add flour to the dough or to the work surface; I promise that the dough will become easier to handle the more you work it. It's particularly important to be thorough when kneading enriched dough such as this in order to counteract the weakening effects of the butter and sugar on the dough's structure. (Mix in any dried fruit or nuts you might be including once you've finished the main bulk of the kneading.)

4   Once the dough is elastic and smooth and has a slight shine, set it aside in a large bowl, cover, and let rise at room temperature until doubled in size. This could take anywhere between 1 and 2 hours, depending on the initial temperatures of the ingredients and the temperature in your kitchen.

5   Use the risen dough in one of the recipes on the following pages or invent one of your own. For a back-to-basics bun, just shape it into 12 small balls, let rise again at room temperature until doubled in size, and bake for 20 minutes at 350°F.

Is the boldly dark molasses the thunder and the bright cream the lightning? Or is it the other way round, with jagged streaks of molasses against the muffling heaviness of the cream? Either way, these traditional Cornish buns are spectacular. Unlike some recipes (Red Velvet Cake, I'm looking at you), their charm doesn't begin and end with the intrigue of their name, but instead carries through to the buns themselves, full of drama, contrast, and darkness.

The tradition of serving cream tea with sweet, yeasted buns is unfortunately one that doesn't seem to have taken hold beyond the southwestern tip of Britain. It's a shame; I find that the soft buns provide a far better counterpoint to the richness of clotted cream than scones do.

Makes 12

1 recipe of Basic Sweet Dough
  (page 130)
1 egg, lightly beaten, for glazing

Filling
¼ cup light corn syrup
2 tablespoons dark molasses
225 grams (8 oz) clotted cream

page 132

1   Prepare the dough as instructed in steps 1 through 4 on page 130, letting it rise until doubled in size. Line a large baking sheet or roasting pan with parchment paper.

2   Turn the risen dough out of its bowl and divide into 12 pieces. Shape each piece into a small ball (for more information on good shaping technique, see page 82). Arrange the balls on the lined baking sheet, spacing them about 1 inch apart. As the buns proof and bake, they'll grow enough to bridge this gap, fusing together in the oven to produce soft-sided, fluffy rolls to be torn apart.

3   Let proof for 45 to 60 minutes, or until approximately doubled in size. Meanwhile, preheat the oven to 350°F.

4   Brush the tops with beaten egg, then bake for 20 to 25 minutes, until golden brown and well risen. Transfer to a wire rack and let cool completely before splitting and filling.

5   To make the filling, mix the corn syrup and molasses in a small bowl. Tear the buns apart and make a very deep incision into the top of each one, from end to end, almost but not quite reaching down to the bottom of the bun — you want to split them, not bisect them. Open each bun along this split and dollop a tablespoon of clotted cream into it. Drizzle with the molasses mixture to give a shock of black against the bright cream.

Variations
If you're dubious about forgoing the more traditional jam for molasses and corn syrup, use a good-quality strawberry jam instead or — my favorite — sharp black currant compote. (But I'd encourage you to give the molasses a go — balanced with the corn syrup, it becomes sweeter and less bitter.)

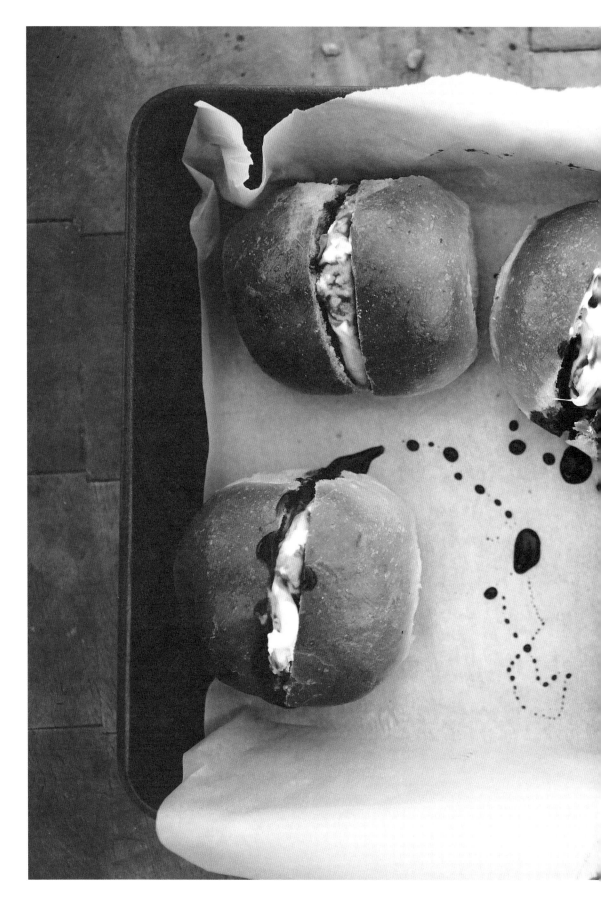

These buns differ slightly from authentic Swedish *semlor* or Norwegian *fastelavnsboller*, but they do share the same basic concept: sweet, cardamom-scented dough, cream, and almond filling. If you don't like cardamom you can leave it out, but its citrusy fragrance really does offset the sweetness of the almond cream.

Makes 12

1 recipe of Basic Sweet Dough
   (page 130)
8 cardamom pods, seeds only,
   finely crushed

Filling

150 grams (1⅔ c) sliced almonds
   (or 1½ c + 1 tbsp ground almonds —
   see step 4)
150 grams (⅔ c) unsalted butter, very soft
150 grams (⅔ c) superfine sugar
1¼ cups heavy cream

📷 page 135

1   Prepare the dough as instructed in steps 1 through 4 on page 130, adding the cardamom to the flour along with the yeast, salt, and sugar and letting the dough rise until doubled in size — about 1½ hours. Line a large, deep baking sheet or roasting pan (about 8 x 12 inches) with parchment paper.

2   Gently deflate the dough, turn it out of its bowl, and divide into 12 pieces. Shape each piece into a ball, rolling it in circles under a cupped palm on a clean surface (for more in-depth guidance on shaping, see page 82). Arrange on the lined baking sheet so that each bun sits a little apart from its neighbors.

3   Let the buns proof at room temperature for 45 to 60 minutes, until nearly twice their original size. Preheat the oven to 350°F. Once the buns have risen, bake for 20 to 25 minutes.

4   While the buns are baking, make the filling. Toast the almonds on a baking sheet on another oven shelf for 10 minutes, until light golden. Let cool briefly. Grind the almonds in a coffee grinder or food processor. (If you have neither of these, use almond meal instead, but add ¼ teaspoon of almond extract for more flavor.)

5   Beat the butter and sugar together, then stir in the almonds. In a separate bowl, whip the cream until soft peaks form. Loosen the almond mixture a little by beating in a couple of tablespoons of the cream, then fold in one-quarter of the remaining cream.

6   Once the buns are cool, halve them horizontally. Spread the bottom half with almond cream, spoon in some whipped cream, sandwich with the top half of the bun, and enjoy.

Slide out of the winter rut of heavy, hibernation foods and make these pastries — full of bright, fruity blueberries, delicate pistachios, and orange zest — at the first stirrings of spring. Granted, they're hardly light, but we can't be expected to just snap lithely into shape at the turn of the spring equinox. Consider these a transitional treat, somewhere between heavyweight stollen and light summer salads.

Makes 12

1 recipe of Basic Sweet Dough
   (page 130)
Zest of 1 orange

Filling
80 grams (5 tbsp + 2 tsp) unsalted
   butter, softened

120 grams (½ c + 1½ tbsp) light
   brown sugar
Zest of 1 orange
150 to 200 grams (1 to 1⅓ c) blueberries
100 grams (¾ c + 1 tbsp) pistachios,
   coarsely chopped

1 egg, beaten, for glazing

1   Prepare the dough as instructed in steps 1 through 4 on page 130, adding the orange zest to the flour along with the yeast, salt, and sugar and letting the dough rise until doubled in size — about 1½ hours.

2   Gently deflate the dough and, on a lightly floured surface, roll out to a rectangle measuring about 12 by 20 inches. Thanks to the gluten developed during the kneading and rising stages, the dough will tend to shrink back as you roll it. This elasticity can be annoying, but with patience and persistent rolling you should be able to get the dough to a point where it's the required size even after shrinkage.

3   To make the filling, beat together the butter, sugar, and orange zest and spread this mixture carefully over the rectangle of dough, taking care not to tear it. The filling needn't be perfectly even — it will level itself as the dough is rolled up and during baking. Scatter the blueberries and pistachios over the butter mixture, pressing down very gently to lodge them in the dough.

4   Roll up the rectangle of dough from long edge to long edge — that is, to make a roll about 20 inches long. Roll reasonably tightly and don't be afraid to slightly squeeze the dough as you go to ensure a uniform thickness. When you've nearly finished the rolling, tack the loose long edge to the work surface using a slightly dampened finger. Smear the dough downward and outward at the very edge so that when the dough log is rolled over on to that edge, it will stick to itself (see the upper right photo on page 164). Leaving the roll seam side down, trim the ends as needed to even them up, then cut the roll into 12 equal slices.

5   Line a large baking sheet or roasting pan with parchment paper. Lay the slices, cut sides facing up, so that they're close but not touching one another. Let proof for 45 to 60 minutes at room temperature, until almost doubled in size. If you have rolled tightly and tacked the dough to itself, the pastries shouldn't unroll, but if any do begin to unfurl during the proofing time, just gently press them back into shape. Preheat the oven to 350°F.

6   Once proofed, the swirls should be almost touching each other and visibly puffier. Brush the tops with the beaten egg and bake for 20 to 25 minutes.

Variations

Spread a few tablespoons of lemon curd over the dough instead of the butter filling, then drizzle the baked pastries with water icing flecked with lemon zest (see page 320) for easy lemon swirls. Alternatively, for something a little more autumnal, you could, of course, make more traditional cinnamon buns, adding 1 to 2 teaspoons of cinnamon when you beat the butter, sugar, and zest, and omitting the blueberries and pistachios.

GLAZED SAFFRON BUNS

Saffron is at once heinously expensive and ambrosially delicious. At around $150 per ounce, it's hardly a budget ingredient. Fortunately, a little goes a long way: a pinch is enough to dye an entire batch of dough a glorious yellow and infuse it with a fragrant, honeyed taste. It works equally well in custards, rice puddings, and almond cakes.

To show the saffron in its best light, I've avoided adding too much butter to this dough — such richness would mask the delicate flavor of the spice.

Makes 20 small or 12 large buns
1¼ cups + 2 tablespoons whole milk
2 to 3 pinches of saffron threads (no more than ½ teaspoon)
500 grams (4 c) white bread flour
2¼ teaspoons (1 packet) instant yeast
1 teaspoon salt
2 tablespoons superfine sugar

3½ tablespoons unsalted butter, softened

Glaze
2 tablespoons water
150 grams (1 c + 3 tbsp) confectioners' sugar

page 138

1   In a small pan, heat the milk and saffron together until the milk is scalding. As soon as the saffron threads hit the milk, you'll notice them bleeding an ocher color into the pale milk. Before long, the milk will have turned first creamy and then barely yellow, before finally settling on a color close to the golden hue of a block of good butter. You can squeeze even more color from the saffron by pressing it against the pan with the back of a spoon, as you might wring the flavor from a tea bag. Set the mixture aside to cool until tepid. If you taste the infused liquid at this point, you'll be able to detect the saffron flavor: nuanced, faintly metallic, and very slightly bitter.

2   In a large bowl, combine the flour, yeast, salt, and sugar. Add the tepid milk and the butter, combine using your hands, and then knead for 10 minutes, until smoother, less sticky, and elastic. Let rise in a large, covered bowl for 1 to 1½ hours, until doubled in size.

3   Line a large baking sheet with parchment paper. Roll out the risen dough to a rectangle measuring about 12 by 20 inches, lightly flouring the work surface as you go. Cut into strips of equal width, each 12 inches long, cutting 20 strips if making small buns or 12 wider strips for larger buns. One by one, roll the strips up

from the bottom to their midpoint, then flip and roll the top down to the middle, creating an S shape. Let the shaped buns to proof on the baking sheet for 45 to 60 minutes, or until almost doubled in size. Preheat the oven to 400°F.

4   Bake for 12 to 15 minutes for small buns or about 20 minutes for bigger ones, rotating the baking sheet halfway through the baking. Prepare the glaze by adding the water to the confectioners' sugar a little at a time, until smooth and thick, but loose enough that it will run from a spoon. Once the buns are cooked and while they're still hot, use a pastry brush to coat them all over with the glaze. Let cool on a wire rack.

Variations
A handful of dried currants could be kneaded into the dough. Saffron also goes very well with almonds: chopped almonds kneaded into the dough, sliced almonds sprinkled on top, or even a little marzipan grated over the rolled-out dough before shaping.

RASPBERRY MASCARPONE VATRUSHKAS

These Russian buns are fat disks with hollow centers heaped with sweetened mascarpone and topped with raspberries. The traditional versions use quark instead of the far richer mascarpone, but I find that this version better balances the brightness of the fruit. Use blackberries, blueberries, or black currants if you prefer.

There's mascarpone in both the dough and the filling of these *vatrushkas*, ensuring that the buns are tender without any of the greasiness that butter can bring. A mixture of all-purpose and bread flours makes the texture of these pastries particularly soft.

Makes 6

125 grams (1 c) white bread flour
125 grams (1 c) all-purpose flour
1½ teaspoons instant yeast
½ teaspoon salt
2 tablespoons superfine sugar
100 grams (3.5 oz) mascarpone
½ cup whole milk

Filling

150 grams (5.25 oz) mascarpone
1 large egg yolk
2 tablespoons + 2 teaspoons superfine
   sugar
1 tablespoon cornstarch
1 teaspoon vanilla extract
100 to 125 grams (¾ to 1 c) raspberries

1 large egg, lightly beaten, for glazing

page 141

1   Combine the flours and yeast, then add the salt and sugar. In a separate bowl, beat the 100 grams (3.5 oz) of mascarpone until smooth. Heat the milk in a pan over low heat until lukewarm, then whisk it, a little at a time, into the mascarpone. Once combined, add this to the flour mixture and mix with your hands.

2   Knead the dough for 10 minutes, or until smoother and more elastic. Don't add extra flour to the dough or the work surface — just have a spatula on hand to scrape up any dough that sticks to your hands or the surface, and knead with

speed and conviction. This dough might not feel quite as robust as some others, due to the amount of lower-gluten all-purpose flour in it, but it will grow supple nonetheless. Transfer to a large bowl, cover, and let to rise at room temperature for 1½ to 2 hours, or until doubled in size. It may take less time than this if your kitchen is particularly warm.

3   Line a large baking sheet with parchment paper. Divide the risen dough into 6 pieces and roll each into a ball. One by one, use a rolling pin to flatten the balls into disks about ⅜ inch thick, then use your hands to stretch them until they're around 5 inches in diameter. Stretch the centers quite a bit thinner than the edges to leave a rim of dough around the perimeter.

4   Transfer to the lined baking sheet (you may need to use two baking sheets if yours aren't very big) and proof for about 45 minutes, until visibly puffy and risen. While they rise, preheat the oven to 350°F. Prepare the filling by beating the mascarpone until smooth, then stirring in the egg yolk, sugar, cornstarch, and vanilla extract.

5   Once the rounds of dough have risen, neaten their shape by very gently pressing down the center to define the indentation and ensure that the rim is well above the level of the hollow. Fill each hollow with a spoonful of the mascarpone mixture, then press in a few raspberries.

6   Brush all over the buns with the beaten egg. This will be easy on the dough rims, but you'll have to be very gentle when brushing the surface of the filling and raspberries. Bake for 20 minutes. Let cool to room temperature, still on the baking sheet, before eating. The centers will only be softly set even when completely cooled, but this rich, quivering custard is precisely what makes these pastries special.

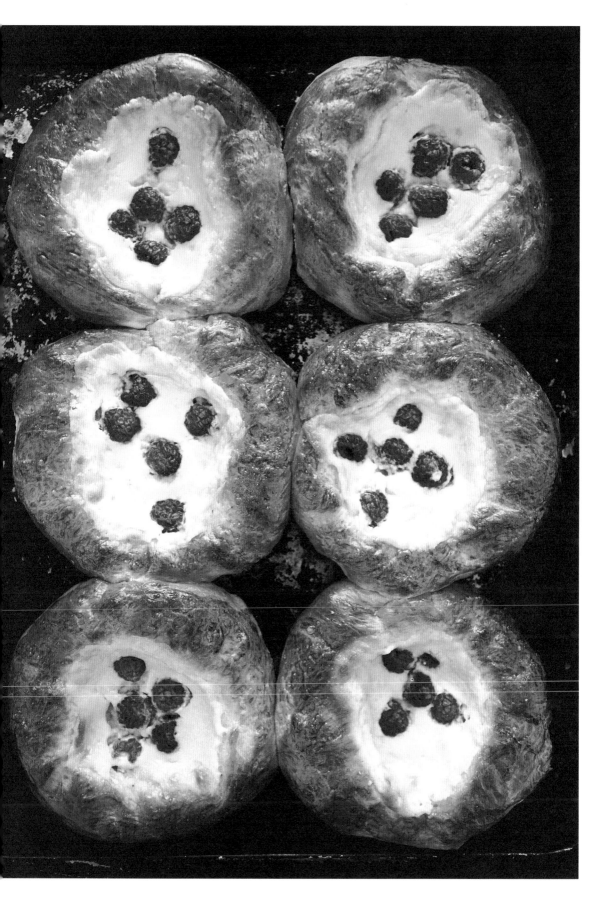

DOUGHNUTS

I don't imagine that it will come as a surprise to anyone to learn that doughnuts are bad for your health. These recipes are deep-fried, glazed, filled, frosted, and sugared, but it's precisely these health hazards that make the doughnuts taste so sublimely good. There are some who suggest baking doughnuts for a healthier alternative, but I think that misses the point entirely: what makes a doughnut a doughnut — instead of a bun or a cake — is the frying process, yielding a uniquely crisp, deeply colored crust and moist texture.

A FRYING START

Frying is a very different means of cooking than baking, and it's important to understand the process before you get started.

— Preparing the oil is something you'll need to allow time for, as it can take up to 15 minutes to come up to temperature. This is particularly important with time-sensitive items such as yeasted doughnuts, which will need to be fried as soon as they're proofed. Always use a large pan — one large enough to allow for at least 3¼ inches of oil in the pan yet still with plenty of room to spare. An overfilled pan could be incredibly dangerous should the oil foam up, splash, or spatter. And I wouldn't recommend a nonstick pan for deep-frying: stainless steel or cast-iron is better. I usually use sunflower oil, which has a neutral flavor and is safe to very high temperatures. Corn oil and peanut oil make suitable alternatives.

— Monitoring the temperature of the oil is crucial. When dough hits the intense heat of the oil, the moisture near its surface rapidly heats, then evaporates and is released as tiny bubbles of steam — hence the sizzling when a doughnut first enters the pan. Importantly, the outward rush of steam bars an inward rush of oil, preventing the doughnut from absorbing too much fat. As a result, if the temperature is too low, the doughnut will soak up the oil, leaving it greasy and heavy. But overly high temperatures present their own problems, browning the exterior of the doughnut too quickly while leaving the inside uncooked.

   The ideal temperature for deep-frying doughnuts is 350°F. There's no need to worry about a variation of a few degrees, but it's important to be in the 340°F to 375°F range. There is only one fail-safe method of measuring this, and that is with a candy thermometer. It's a small, inexpensive piece of kitchen equipment, but it will prove invaluable when frying dough. The other option is to test the oil's temperature using a cube of bread: if the bread browns all over in 60 seconds, the oil is approximately the right temperature. But this second method is unreliable and difficult to judge, so my loyalties lie with the candy thermometer.

— It's important to continue checking the temperature of the oil throughout the frying process, especially before frying each new batch. With a candy thermometer, this is as simple as keeping it hooked onto the side of the pan as you work. Although you'll need high heat to bring the oil up to 350°F in the first place, you won't need to continue with such fierce heat once you start frying.

Turn the heat down to medium-low, increasing it only if the oil temperature begins to drop.

— Frying the doughnuts is the exciting part. Drop one in: the oil, until now deceptively placid, will suddenly fizz, bubble, and hiss around the dough. The doughnut will sink slightly, then rise back through the amber oil, bobbing on the surface. It will begin to swell and bronze. You'll then flip it over, leaving it belly up for another minute or two before fishing it out, patting it dry, and letting it cool.

I've given frying times for each of the following recipes. Do stick to these, and use a timer rather than just guessing as the minutes roll by. A doughnut cooked too long will grow greasy, while one not cooked long enough will remain raw at its center, even if the outside has a promising hue.

A NOTE ON SAFETY

Hot oil is dangerous. Please be careful, focused, and organized when frying.

— Children and pets should be kept well clear of the kitchen.

— Don't leave hot oil unattended, even for an instant.

— Keep a close eye on the oil's temperature. If it exceeds 375°F, turn down the heat; if it begins to foam, spit, or smoke, turn the heat off immediately.

— Tempting as it will be, don't eat the doughnuts straight from the hot oil, as their interiors will still be very hot.

— Have a sink of cold water ready to plunge your hand into in case of burns.

— As long as you're vigilant, it's highly unlikely that the oil will catch fire, but in the event that it does happen, do not use water on the burning oil. Put a heavy metal lid over the pan to suffocate the flame and use a kitchen fire extinguisher.

This is a recipe for those who must always have the biggest, most indulgent, least modest thing on the menu: a sugar-crusted doughnut — soft-textured, plump with custard, and as big as your fist.

Prepare the pastry cream for this filling in advance: it will need a spell in the fridge before it's thick enough to use. If you're nervous about making custard, you can buy a good ready-made one, although it will be thinner than homemade, so it may ooze out of the doughnuts. Whatever you do, don't debase these doughnuts with the canary-yellow kind made from a powdered mix.

Makes 12

500 grams (4 c) white bread flour
2¼ teaspoons (1 packet) instant yeast
1 teaspoon salt
2 tablespoons superfine sugar
¾ cup + 2½ tablespoons milk
2 large eggs
3½ tablespoons unsalted butter, softened

About 6½ cups sunflower or corn oil, for frying

75 grams (⅓ c) superfine sugar, for coating

Filling
1 recipe of Pastry Cream (page 312)

page 146

1   Combine the flour, yeast, salt, and 2 tablespoons of sugar in a large bowl, taking care to ensure that the yeast and salt don't come into direct contact prior to mixing. Heat the milk gently until just lukewarm, then whisk in the eggs. Add to the flour mixture along with the butter, then work with your hands to combine. Knead for 10 minutes. The dough will become smoother and elastic. Set aside to proof in a large, covered bowl at room temperature for 1 to 1½ hours, until doubled in size.

2   Divide the risen dough into 12 roughly equal pieces (my inner pedant likes to weigh the pieces to make sure that they're even, but I won't advocate that sort of painstaking accuracy here). On a surface dusted with flour, roll each piece into a ball, gathering any excess dough underneath and rolling under a cupped palm to create a smooth surface (see page 82). Pat down slightly to create a flattened shape.

3   Cut 12 squares of parchment paper or foil measuring about 5 inches square, although the specific dimensions aren't important, so don't worry about getting the ruler out. Lightly flour each of these squares and lay a piece of dough on each. This is to allow for easy transfer of the fragile, risen doughnuts to the oil a bit later. Let the doughnuts proof for 45 to 60 minutes at room temperature, until they're at least 1½ times their original size.

4   It should take the oil 10 to 15 minutes to reach the required temperature, so start heating it well before the end of the proofing period. Pour the oil into a large pan (the oil needs to be at least 3¼ inches deep but nowhere near the top of the pan) and heat fiercely until it reaches 350°F. Then turn the heat down to medium-low while cooking to maintain the oil at this temperature. See page 142 for more guidance on frying temperatures and method.

5   Transfer the doughnuts to the pan using their squares of parchment as gurneys and carefully sliding them off into the oil, watching out for any splashes. You should be able to fit in 3 or 4 doughnuts at once. Fry for 2 minutes on each side, then lift out using a slotted spoon. Pat dry with paper towels, then roll in the 75 grams (⅓ c) sugar and let cool. Repeat the frying process with the remaining doughnuts.

You should notice a pale ring around their middles, a few shades lighter than their tops and bottoms. This characteristic "tan line" could be mistaken for a flaw, but it's actually the mark of a perfectly proofed and carefully fried doughnut.

6   Once completely cooled, use a butter knife to poke a hole in the side of each doughnut, deep into the center. Wiggle the knife around to create a hollow to accommodate the pastry cream. Using a pastry syringe or a piping bag with a wide nozzle, pipe some pastry cream into each doughnut. Don't just perch the nozzle at the edge of the doughnut when you do this; otherwise you'll end up with a tiny pocket of custard on one side of the doughnut. Press the nozzle right into the hollow you created and pipe generously. Repeat with the remaining doughnuts. (If you don't have a piping bag or nozzle, just make a small incision in the doughnut's side, pry it open with your fingers, and spoon the filling in.)

7   Let the doughnuts set for 10 minutes or so, propping them with the piping hole upward if the custard is leaking. Eat soon after, with napkins at the ready for cleaning up custard-smothered lips, chins, and fingers.

Variations

A chocolate glaze on top might just tip these from hedonism to lethality, but that's a risk I'm happy to take. The result is a sort of Boston cream doughnut, a riff on the Boston cream pie (incongruously, not an actual pie), with its trademark clever combination of custard and dark chocolate ganache. Forgo the stage where you roll the doughnuts in sugar; instead, after filling the fried doughnuts, dip their tops in warm Spreadable Ganache (page 321).

If you're not keen on custard, jam makes a fine substitution — particularly a vibrant one such as rhubarb. I once even used lemon curd and crème fraîche — an unexpected triumph, cutting cleanly through the sweetness.

BATTER DOUGHS

Some enriched doughs have such a high ratio of water to flour that they cease to be a recognizable dough at all, resembling a batter instead. When the liquid content is this high, it's impossible to knead the dough on the work surface as you might usually do. Instead, gluten needs to be developed by beating the mixture in its bowl.

Although it's hard work doing this by hand (you can of course use a mixer with a dough hook if you have one), it's well worth attempting it at least once to get a feel for the dough. Roll up your sleeves, put on some music, and, cradling the bowl in one arm, beat rapidly with the other hand. The motion you use doesn't particularly matter: a circular movement will work well, as will repeatedly stretching the dough up then slapping it back down into the bowl — whatever works for you.

At first, the dough will be very wet and heavy, but as you beat it you will notice strands of gluten forming, helping the dough to come away from the sides of the bowl. The lifeless mass will transform into something more elastic, stronger, and (sorry!) progressively more difficult to mix. After about 5 minutes (these may feel like the longest 5 minutes of your life), the dough will be firm rather than flabby, more alive, and more resistant. It's a workout for both you and the dough.

However, this hard work is not for nothing. When beating the batter, you're not only strengthening the gluten, which gives the bread or pastry its structure, but also incorporating countless tiny air bubbles into the batter. These air bubbles will expand as the yeast gets to work, creating a light, airy bread or pastry.

OLIEBOLLEN

These little Dutch doughnuts are traditionally New Year's Eve treats, but I see no harm in making them whenever you please. Because they need only one rise, you can whip up a batch quickly, whenever the craving takes hold. I make these far smaller than a conventional-sized doughnut, which not only means they are easier to cook, but also eases the guilt of having eaten one, two, or a bowlful.

Makes 20 to 25
350 grams (2¾ c) white bread flour
2¼ teaspoons (1 packet) instant yeast
¾ teaspoon salt
2 tablespoons + 2 teaspoons superfine
  sugar
1½ cups milk
Zest of 1 lemon
1 apple, peeled and diced small
  (less than ¼ inch)

100 grams (⅔ c) dried currants
100 grams (¾ c) mixed candied
  citrus peel
About 6½ cups sunflower or corn oil,
  for frying

60 grams (½ c) confectioners' sugar,
  for dusting

📷 page 149

1 Combine the flour and yeast, then stir in the salt and superfine sugar. Heat the milk over low heat until tepid, then stir in the lemon zest. Add to the flour mixture and stir to combine. Let the dough sit for 10 minutes.

2   If you have a mixer with a dough hook attachment, now is the time to feel smug. If not, roll up your sleeves. This very wet dough needs to be vigorously beaten for at least 5 minutes in its bowl to build up the gluten's strength. It's ready when it's more elastic, stringy, and resistant.

3   Incorporate the apple, currants, and candied citrus peel, then cover the bowl with plastic wrap and let rise at room temperature for about 1 hour. Once the hour is up, start heating the oil in a large pan, taking care not to fill the pan more than two-thirds full. The oil needs to reach 350°F, which is best gauged using a candy thermometer; otherwise, test by dropping a cube of bread in the hot oil — if it turns golden brown in 60 seconds, the oil is hot enough.

4   Using two tablespoons, scoop smallish balls of the batter into the oil, three or four at a time. Let fry for 1½ minutes, then turn and cook the other side for 1½ minutes. Carefully remove using a slotted spoon. Pour the confectioners' sugar onto a wide, rimmed plate or shallow bowl. Roll each doughnut in the sugar. Fry in batches, checking the temperature of the oil between each batch. I did entertain the idea of eating these, still warm, with some lemon gelato. It might be too great an indulgence for some, but I'll leave you to make up your own mind on that.

When I was growing up, the best bit of the summer holidays was always doughnuts. Not jam doughnuts, but cinnamon-coated cake doughnuts, fresh from the fryer at the fair, the beach, and festivals. On tiptoes, you might just be able to see the doughnuts plop into the oil and inch along the long conveyor, sizzling and spitting all the way, before being thrown headlong into a bucket of cinnamon sugar and heaped into grease-stained paper bags. Much of my childhood was spent like this, forehead pressed to the plastic window of the doughnut stall while the amusement park clamored on without me.

GLAZED CAKE DOUGHNUTS

All the fun of the fair, in a mouthful. If malt is in vogue at the moment, I can only wonder why it hasn't always been so. It's a fantastic flavor, particularly good at adding depth to vanilla and to chocolate. Here the malt comes in powdered form — by which I mean malted milk powder. This is easier to come by and less full-bodied than dark, syrupy, liquid malt extract, such as the one used in the Date Malt Loaf (page 38).

Because these doughnuts are leavened with baking powder, which works instantly upon contact with the hot oil, they're far quicker to make than the other doughnuts in this chapter. They have a very different feel, too: a fine-textured, soft interior, and a crisp, terracotta-colored crust.

Makes 10 to 12

2 tablespoons + 2 teaspoons unsalted butter
¼ cup whole milk
3 tablespoons superfine sugar
60 grams (8½ tbsp) malted milk powder
2 large eggs, lightly beaten
1½ teaspoons vanilla extract
2 teaspoons baking powder
¼ teaspoon salt
Pinch of ground cinnamon

300 grams (2⅓ c) all-purpose flour
About 6½ cups sunflower or corn oil, for frying

Icing
200 grams (1⅔ c) confectioners' sugar
40 grams (5½ tbsp) malted milk powder
2½ to 3 tablespoons water
1 teaspoon vanilla extract

page 151

1   In a small pan, melt the butter over low heat, then add the milk. In a large bowl, combine the sugar and malted milk powder, then gradually add the milk mixture, whisking constantly to prevent any lumps from forming. Add the eggs and vanilla extract and stir to combine.

2   Mix the baking powder, salt, cinnamon, and flour in a separate bowl, then add to the milk mixture, stirring the sticky ingredients together into a cohesive mass. Cover the bowl with plastic wrap and refrigerate for 1 hour.

3   Once chilled, the dough should be just firm enough to roll out, but if not, work in a little more flour. Lightly flour a work surface and roll out the dough to a thickness just shy of ¼ inch. Cut out ring shapes using a 3¼- to 4-inch circle cutter for the

outside, and a ¾- to 1½-inch cutter for the holes. If you don't have the right size cutters, you can cut free-form doughnuts using a sharp knife or improvise using any circle-shaped item in your kitchen. I use the bottom of a spice jar as a guide. Reroll any scraps and cut out more doughnuts.

4   Cut 10 to 12 squares of parchment paper or foil, lightly oil them and carefully transfer one doughnut to each. This might seem like a fussy step, but it really does help when it comes to transferring the doughnuts to the hot oil safely.

5   Heat the oil in a large, deep pan (not nonstick) over high heat — the oil needs to reach 350°F. See page 142 for guidelines on frying.

6   Once the oil is hot, pick a doughnut up by its parchment paper cradle and slide it into the oil. Be very careful not to drop it from too great a height, or the oil may splash. You should be able to fit 3 or 4 doughnuts in the pan at once. Fry for 60 seconds, then turn the doughnuts over and fry for another 60 seconds. Remove with a slotted spoon and pat with paper towels to remove excess oil. Repeat in batches until all of the doughnuts have been cooked, making sure that the oil remains at about 350°F throughout.

7   Once the doughnuts are cool, they can be iced. To make the icing, combine the confectioners' sugar and malted milk powder in a bowl, then slowly add the water and vanilla extract, stirring continuously to make a smooth, thick icing. It's important to make it thicker than you might expect: even a few drops too much water will create an icing that runs straight off the doughnuts rather than sitting proudly on top of them.

8   Dip the tops of the doughnuts in the icing, then set the doughnuts, icing side up, on a wire rack. These are best eaten soon after frying.

COCONUT LIME LOAF

After the excesses of doughnuts, this gentle loaf might be a relief. It's a mild, coconut-flavored dough flecked with lime zest and baked in a loaf pan. Because coconut milk is relatively high in fat, no extra butter or eggs are necessary to make it soft and tender.

Makes 1 large loaf, enough for
12 to 14 thick slices, serving 8

400 grams (3 c + 3 tbsp) white bread flour
2¼ teaspoons (1 packet) instant yeast
1 teaspoon salt
3 tablespoons superfine sugar

1¼ cups full-fat coconut milk
Zest of 2 limes

Milk or beaten egg, for glazing (optional)

5 by 9-inch loaf pan

1   In a large bowl, combine the flour and yeast. Stir in the salt and sugar. Heat the coconut milk over low heat until tepid, stirring well until smooth (coconut milk can tend to separate in the can, with the fat forming a thick layer on top). Add most of the coconut milk and zest to the flour mixture and stir to combine. If the dough feels dry and rubbery, add the remaining coconut milk (better that the dough is slightly too sticky than too stiff). Knead for 10 minutes, until stretchy and smooth. Set aside in a large, covered bowl to rise at room temperature for about 1½ hours, until doubled in size.

2   Shape the risen dough into a rough football shape approximately the size of the loaf pan, folding it over on itself to collect any loose dough underneath and leave a tight skin on top (see page 82). This careful shaping will help to ensure an even rise. Line the bottom of the pan with parchment paper and transfer the dough to the pan. Let proof for 1 hour. Meanwhile, preheat the oven to 350°F.

3   Brush the top of the loaf with milk or egg and score deeply along the length of the dough with a sharp knife (see page 84). Bake for 40 minutes, until the bread sounds hollow when tapped underneath. Let cool completely on a wire rack before serving with lime curd (adapt from the Lemon Curd recipe on page 324) or, if you fancy it, chocolate spread.

Variations
I've deliberately left this loaf very plain — I like the reassuring simplicity of it. If you want a more bells-and-whistles type of bread, however, it can certainly be adapted. Packed with golden raisins, candied citrus peels, and chopped dried pineapple, mango, and apple, it will become a sort of tropical tea loaf.

The origins of the name of this tear-and-share bread are anybody's guess. There's been plenty of speculation: perhaps it's a reference to the free-for-all serving style or the monkeying around involved in piecing it together. One person, perhaps hallucinating, suggested that it's because the bread resembles "a bunch of monkeys jumbled together." Forget the name, though; despite the whimsy, this really is a very good bread, cinnamon-spiced and stickily caramelized all over.

Makes 1 loaf, serving 8 to 10

400 grams (3 c + 3 tbsp) white bread flour
2¼ teaspoons (1 packet) instant yeast
1 teaspoon salt
1 cup + 1 tablespoon whole milk
2 tablespoons unsalted butter, softened

Coating
75 grams (⅓ c) unsalted butter

2 teaspoons ground cinnamon
100 grams (½ c) light brown sugar

9 to 10½-inch diameter Bundt pan or deep 8-inch round cake pan

page 155

1 Mix the flour and yeast in a large bowl, then stir in the salt. Warm the milk over very low heat until just tepid, then add to the flour mixture along with the 2 tablespoons of butter. Combine, then knead for 10 minutes, until the dough is elastic and smooth and has a light sheen. Let rise in a large, covered bowl at room temperature for about 1 hour, until roughly twice its original size, though the yeast may act more slowly if your kitchen is particularly cold.

2 To prepare the coating, melt the butter in a small pan over low heat. Brush the inside of the pan liberally with some of the butter, then set the rest aside. In a separate bowl, combine the cinnamon and sugar.

3 Break the risen dough into small chunks, each no bigger than a ping-pong ball, and roll into rough spheres. Dip each ball in the melted butter and then in the cinnamon mixture to coat. Pile the coated dough balls in the buttered pan. (There's no need to overthink the arrangement; just stack the balls in messy layers until you've used all of the dough.) Don't press the balls down to neaten the arrangement; they'll expand to fit snugly as they rise and bake. Let proof at room temperature for about 1 hour, preheating the oven to 350°F in the meantime.

4 When the dough has risen, bake for 30 minutes, then turn the bread out of the pan as soon as it's out of the oven. It should slide out easily as long as the tin was well greased. Once it's been inverted onto a plate, you'll be able to see the pattern of interlocking buns held together with a buttery, caramel glaze. Pick off a bun with your fingers and enjoy while still warm.

Variation
Sprinkle a small handful of chopped nuts (any will do) between the layers as you stack the dough balls in the pan.

This treat combines succulent pears with honey, almonds, and a crumble topping. It's best eaten at breakfast time, with strong coffee.

Serves 8
300 grams (2⅓ c) white bread flour
1½ teaspoons instant yeast
½ teaspoon salt
2 tablespoons honey
¾ cup + 1 tablespoon milk

Pear Topping
4 firm eating pears, such as Bartlett, Comice, or Bosc
2 tablespoons unsalted butter
¼ cup honey

¼ teaspoon ground allspice
70 grams (¾ c) sliced almonds

Crumble Topping
3½ tablespoons unsalted butter, at room temperature
50 grams (6½ tbsp) white flour (preferably all-purpose, but bread flour will do)
3 tablespoons light brown sugar
30 grams (⅓ c) sliced almonds, finely chopped

1   Combine the bread flour and yeast in a large bowl, then stir in the salt. Combine the 2 tablespoons of honey and the milk in a small pan over low heat, heating until tepid and the honey is dissolved, then add to the flour mixture. Combine, then knead for 5 to 10 minutes, until less sticky and more elastic. Set aside in a large bowl and cover loosely with plastic wrap. Let rise at room temperature for 1 hour, until approximately doubled in size.

2   While the dough rises, prepare the pear topping. Peel, core, and slice the pears about ¼ inch thick. Melt the butter with the honey and allspice in a large pan over low heat, then add the pears. Increase the heat to medium and cook, stirring regularly, for 5 minutes. The pears should slightly soften and caramelize, but remove from the heat if the slices begin to disintegrate. Add the sliced almonds and stir to combine. Let cool.

3   Prepare the crumble topping by rubbing the butter into the flour and sugar with your fingertips until the mixture comes together in small clumps. Add the almonds and stir to combine. Chill in the refrigerator until ready to use.

4   Turn the risen dough out onto a lightly floured surface and roll out to about 8 by 12 inches, pausing after rolling to allow the dough to shrink back a little, then rerolling until it stays at the desired size. Transfer to a large baking sheet lined with parchment paper and let proof for 30 to 45 minutes. Preheat the oven to 400°F.

5   Arrange the honey-coated, almond-encrusted pear slices over the risen dough, leaving a border of about ¾ inch around the edges. Sprinkle the crumble mixture over the pears. Brush the dough border with any remaining juices from the pear mixture. Bake for 10 minutes, then decrease the temperature to 350°F and bake for 20 minutes longer.

The amount of butter used in this brioche looks heinous on paper, but it's really important not to skimp: a low-fat brioche is no brioche at all. And as long as you're thorough when kneading and patient during the rise, the bread will emerge from the oven airily light in spite of its richness. This isn't a quick recipe — the bread needs a couple of long rises and an overnight spell in the fridge — but it's this slow fermentation that gives the brioche a soft texture and helps this heavily enriched dough rise.

Makes 1 large brioche, serving 6 to 8

450 grams (3½ c) white bread flour
1 tablespoon instant yeast
1 teaspoon salt
3 tablespoons superfine sugar
½ cup + 2 teaspoons milk
4 large eggs

250 grams (1 c + 2 tbsp) unsalted butter, softened
1 large egg, lightly beaten, for glazing

Deep 8-inch round cake pan, or if you're lucky enough to own one, a large brioche mold

page 158

1   Combine the flour and yeast in a large bowl, then stir in the salt and sugar. Very slightly heat the milk over low heat until barely lukewarm. This is particularly important if the milk is fridge-cold; the yeast already has to battle with a block of butter before it can get to work, so it needs a little warmth to help it along. Whisk the slightly warmed milk together with the eggs and add to the dry flour mixture. Mix well.

2   Knead the dough for 10 minutes, until smooth and elastic. The aim here is to develop the gluten and strengthen the dough before adding the butter. (Once the butter is incorporated, fat will coat the flour and inhibit gluten formation, so this period of kneading gives the gluten a head start.)

3   Once the dough has been kneaded, work in the butter. This won't be a case of just stirring it in, as the butter and dough have very different consistencies. Put the dough back in the bowl and add the butter one-third at a time, squeezing it in with your hands. It will feel like trying to mix oil and water at first, but after some mixing (which, with the slippery, supple dough, is surprisingly therapeutic), you'll find that the dough comes smoothly together. Once all the butter has been worked in, turn the dough out of its bowl and knead for 5 minutes. By this point the dough will feel unlike any other: cool, satiny, and elastic — it's a pleasure to work with.

4   Put the dough in a large bowl, cover, and let rise at room temperature for about 2 hours, until doubled in size. Gently press down the risen dough to deflate, cover the bowl very tightly, and let rest in the fridge for at least 6 hours or as long as 18 hours. During this time the dough will rise slightly due to the residual warmth from its initial rise, but as soon as it reaches fridge temperature the yeast will effectively become dormant and the rising will cease. This spell in the fridge is therefore more about flavor and practicality than about the rise itself: at cooler

temperatures, more nuanced flavors will develop in the dough, and the cooling will set the butter and allow for far easier shaping. One thing to bear in mind is that the fridge will have a drying effect on the dough if the bowl isn't securely covered, so use a couple of layers of plastic wrap or foil.

5   After chilling, pry the dough from its bowl. By now it should be almost puttylike in its plasticity. Shape into a large ball, then press down until it's about 8 inches in diameter. Grease the bottom and sides of the pan and, if the pan isn't loose-bottomed or springform, line the bottom with a circle of parchment paper. Put the dough in the tin. You could also shape it more intricately if you'd prefer, as in the Three Cheese Brioche recipe (page 117).

6   Cover the pan loosely with plastic wrap and let the dough to proof at room temperature for up to 2½ hours, until almost doubled in size. This proofing period is a good deal lengthier than for most other breads because the dough is both highly enriched and still cool from the fridge. Toward the end of the proofing time, preheat the oven to 400°F.

7   Brush the top of the brioche with egg to glaze it and bake for 15 minutes. Decrease the temperature to 350°F and bake for 25 minutes longer. The crust should be a deep color thanks to the browning effect of the egg glaze, and the loaf should be well risen. Let it cool for a short while in the pan before unmolding and cooling completely on a wire rack.

MARZIPAN

I love marzipan. I like to painstakingly peel it from Battenberg cake and eat it in one long strip, or to uncover, with joy, a log of the stuff nestled inside the buttery dough of a stollen. Every year, great slabs of Christmas cake are left, marzipan-less, around the house. There are even finger-shaped gouges in the block of marzipan in the kitchen cupboard. For all its sweetness and lurid yellow coloring, I'm very fond of the store-bought variety, although if you prefer your marzipan with a little more delicacy of flavor, making your own is very easy to do (see page 319). The pistachio marzipan in the stollen recipe below is a more grown-up version of the traditional type. Feel free to add a couple of drops of vanilla extract or even rose water to taste. A little orange zest can work well, too. This is one for even the most stubborn of marzipan-phobes.

CHERRY STOLLEN WITH PISTACHIO MARZIPAN

Stollen is archetypal Christmas fodder. In this stollen variation, sour cherries partner with citrusy cardamom and pistachios. Unlike cheap supermarket versions, which have a heavy, cakey feel and a taste that lies somewhere between cloves and cardboard, homemade stollen is a joy to eat. This is not the time to scrimp and save — generosity is key, so stud it with as much fruit and candied citrus peel as it will hold, brush liberally with melted butter, and dust with a thick crust of confectioners' sugar. More really is more here.

Makes 1 large stollen, serving 8
250 grams (2 c) white bread flour
5 cardamom pods, seeds only, crushed
½ teaspoon ground cinnamon
2 cloves, crushed, or 2 large pinches of
    ground cloves
2¼ teaspoons (1 packet) instant yeast
4 teaspoons superfine sugar
½ teaspoon salt
150 grams (⅔ c) unsalted butter
7 tablespoons + 2 teaspoons milk
1 large egg, lightly beaten
1 teaspoon vanilla extract
Zest of 1 orange
125 grams (¾ c + 2 tbsp) dried cherries,
    coarsely chopped

75 grams (½ c + 1 tbsp) mixed candied
    citrus peel

Pistachio Marzipan
150 grams (1¼ c) pistachios
130 grams (1 c) confectioners' sugar
Pinch of salt
30 grams egg white (about ⅔ of the white
    from a large egg)
A couple of drops of vanilla extract
    or rose water

30 grams (¼ c) confectioners' sugar,
    for dusting

page 161

1   Combine the flour, cardamom, cinnamon, cloves, yeast, and sugar in a large bowl.
    Stir in the salt.

2   Melt half of the butter in a small pan, then stir in the milk, egg, vanilla extract,
    and orange zest. The mixture should be lukewarm from the residual heat in the
    pan, but if it's not quite tepid, heat it very, very gently over low heat, just enough to
    make it slightly warm to the touch. Take care not to heat it too much — if it feels
    very warm, let it cool a bit.

3   Add the milk mixture to the flour mixture. Once everything's thoroughly combined
    in the bowl, turn it out onto a clean work surface and knead. Prepare to get your
    hands dirty: the dough needs to be kneaded for a good 10 minutes. It may start out
    a little wet, but due to the high butter content you'll find that it's less annoyingly
    sticky than some doughs. It will soon begin to feel smoother and more elastic
    (although it'll never reach the sort of silkiness you might expect in a basic bread
    dough). After 10 minutes, you can add the dried cherries and candied citrus peel.

4   Put the dough back in a large, clean bowl, cover with plastic wrap, and let proof
    for 1½ to 2 hours, until doubled in size. It rises quite slowly, but don't put it in too
    warm a spot to speed it up — normal room temperature is perfect for the yeast.

5   While the dough is rising, make the pistachio marzipan. Grind the pistachios
    in a food processor or, working in batches, in a coffee grinder. Alternatively, you
    could finely chop them then pound them using a pestle and mortar. Transfer to
    a medium bowl, add the confectioners' sugar and salt, and stir to combine. Sift
    the mixture into another bowl. Add the egg white (the quantity may seem fiddly,
    but adding even slightly too much risks making the mixture wet and sticky, so do
    weigh the egg white if possible). Combine the egg with the pistachio mixture by
    stirring and mashing it with the back of a fork. It might look too dry to start with,
    but it will come together. Once it's integrated, you can use your hands to very
    lightly work the paste into a smooth mixture. If it's too dry to come together, add
    a few more drops of egg white, or some vanilla extract if you prefer.

6   Turn the risen dough out onto a work surface dusted with flour and roll it out to a rectangle measuring about 8 by 12 inches. It doesn't matter if the dough is still slightly sticky — just flour the surface with extra flour as necessary. Roll the marzipan into a rough log shape about 12 inches long and lay it along the middle of the dough. Roll the dough around the marzipan and, with the seam downward, fold the ends of the log underneath. Gently pat into a more squat, slightly flattened shape. Let rise for about 1 hour, until increased in size by half. Preheat the oven to 350°F toward the end of the rising time.

7   Bake for 40 minutes. Toward the end of the baking time, melt the remaining 75 grams (⅓ c) of butter over low heat. As soon as the stollen emerges from the oven, brush it all over (even underneath) with the melted butter. It seems like an extravagance, but this is what will create a meltingly soft crust and the sort of richness that really makes you think twice before eating a second slice. Once cool, dust generously with confectioners' sugar. Because it's almost mummified in butter and sugar, this bread keeps surprisingly well. Wrap it in greaseproof paper or foil and continue to indulge, at your leisure, over the Christmas period.

Variations
Stollen is too good to have just once a year. Swap the cloves for a pinch of nutmeg or perhaps ginger for a less Christmassy-tasting bread. Even better, add a handful of dark chocolate chips to the dough and use a traditional almond marzipan.

WHITE CHOCOLATE HAZELNUT COURONNE

Why go for the jewel in the crown when you can have the crown itself? This *couronne*, or crown, is rolled, layered, swirled, cut, woven, twisted, and sealed to create a bread fit for a queen. The shaping might look difficult at first glance, but it helps to skim through the basic steps before starting and to look at the photos to give yourself an idea of the end goal.

Makes 1 large couronne, serving 8 to 10
300 grams (2⅓ c) white bread flour
1½ teaspoons instant yeast
½ teaspoon salt
2 tablespoons superfine sugar
¾ cup + 1½ tablespoons milk
¼ teaspoon almond extract
2 tablespoons unsalted butter, softened
Zest of 1 lemon

Filling
60 grams (¼ c) unsalted butter, softened
3 tablespoons light brown sugar
1 teaspoon vanilla extract
100 grams (¾ c) blanched hazelnuts
100 grams (3.5 oz) white chocolate, coarsely chopped

1 large egg, lightly beaten, for glazing

📷 pages 163 & 164

1   Combine the flour and yeast in a large bowl, then stir in the salt and sugar. Warm the milk and almond extract over low heat until tepid, then add to the flour mixture, along with the butter and lemon zest. Mix well to combine, then knead for 5 minutes or so to develop the gluten. Put the dough in a large bowl, cover, and let rise at room temperature for 1 to 1½ hours, until doubled in size.

2   Prepare the filling components: Beat together the butter, sugar, and vanilla extract until smooth and spreadable. If the hazelnuts aren't pre-roasted, preheat the oven to 350°F, then roast the hazelnuts for about 10 minutes, just until golden brown. Finely chop the hazelnuts.

3   Roll out the risen dough into a rectangle measuring about 8 by 18 inches. You'll need to lightly flour the work surface and the dough. It will keep shrinking back as you roll it, but you should find that with some perseverance and a firm hand, the dough will eventually reach the desired size and stay there.

4   Spread the filling mixture evenly over the dough, then scatter the hazelnuts and white chocolate on top. Roll up tightly from long edge to long edge, to create a roll about 18 inches long. Tack the remaining long edge to the work surface using a slightly dampened finger, then smear it outward so that when the log is rolled onto it, it will stick to itself (see the upper right picture, opposite).

5   This next stage is tricky, and it can be invaluable to have another pair of helping hands at this point to support the dough as you twist it. Line a large baking sheet with parchment paper and transfer the dough to the lined baking sheet. It's far easier to put it in place now than after it has been woven into a fragile crown shape.

   Using a sharp knife, cut all the way through the dough along the length of the roll, almost completely halving it but stopping just before the end to leave the two halves barely attached. Keeping the cut sides of the dough strands facing upward at all times, cross the strands over each other, starting at the end where they join. Next, cross them over each other again, with the strand that went underneath the first time going over the top. Repeat until the two strands are twisted together along their entire length. Curve this "braid" around into a circle. Don't worry if the strands splay open a little as you work — just keep pressing them back into shape.

   Cut through the end where the two strands were still joined and attach to the other end of the loop, pressing gently to secure the dough into one continuous circle. If there are any chunks of white chocolate protruding from the surface, lightly press them back down into the dough to prevent them from burning as the bread bakes.

6   Let proof at room temperature for 45 to 60 minutes, until around 1½ times its original size. Preheat the oven to 350°F while you wait.

7   Brush the risen dough with the egg wash and bake for 30 minutes. It should be well risen, with intertwined layers of rich, golden-brown dough.

Variation

For a festive *couronne*, replace the filling with a 200-gram (7 oz) can of sweetened chestnut spread mixed with some dried currants, a couple of tablespoons of cornstarch, a capful of brandy, and some orange zest.

COOKIES & CRACKERS

CRUNCH

GINGER COOKIES · GINGER LIME SANDWICH COOKIES

DARK CHOCOLATE ORANGE BOURBONS

BISCOTTI

CHEW

ROSE & BURNT HONEY FLORENTINES

ORANGE LEMON COCONUT COOKIES · PECAN COOKIES

HAZELNUT DARK CHOCOLATE COOKIES · SPICED OAT THINS

CRUMBLE

SHORTBREAD · RYE OAT COOKIES

TAHINI LEMON COOKIES

SNAP

CINNAMON ORANGE TUILES · FENNEL SEED & CHILE CRACKERS

STILTON & POPPY SEED CRACKERS

I used to think that baking cookies was more hassle than it was worth. The pleasures of the cookie jar, full of worthy rich tea biscuits, custard creams, and hobnob after hobnob after hobnob (because one is never enough) weren't to be complicated or tampered with. But one day I made a buttery shortbread and finally realized what I'd been missing. You can prepare a batch of florentines, chocolate hazelnut cookies, or fennel seed crackers in about the time it takes to trudge to the store for a package of cookies, and the taste is incomparable. If you want your cookies neatly dimpled, crimped and stamped, rippled with chocolate, or jammily grinning back at you — buy them. But if you want cookies with oomph — heavily spiced, packed with chunks of chocolate and nuts, or bursting with citrus — you'd better turn the oven on.

SHAPING

In this chapter you'll find cookies and crackers of every shape and size. One is thinly spread with a spatula and a steady hand — a hair's breadth between success and broken shards. Some are neatly rolled and stamped into shapes as simple or as artful as you like. But for others, the magic doesn't happen until after the cookies are in the oven and out of your hands, with dough dolloped haphazardly on baking sheets emerging from the oven as fat, craggy, chewy disks.

How a cookie or cracker ought to be shaped depends entirely on the type of dough in question. Both the initial consistency of the dough and the way in which it behaves when heated will have a bearing on the shaping methods suitable. The former is easy enough to gauge, but the latter is less straightforward. Chilled cookie dough, for instance, can be rolled thin and cut into neat circles but spreads a great deal as it bakes, so if you start off with just a thin layer of the stuff, you'll end up with a potato chip. Don't worry too much, though; I've tried to be clear about shaping in these recipes, and the more cookies or crackers you make, the more you'll get a feel for the dough.

LEAVENING

Many cookies use baking powder or baking soda to give them a little lift in the oven. Even if the rise itself is only marginal, it has a significant impact on the texture: the tiny air pockets expanded by leavening agents lighten the cookie, providing a better crunch. Plus, the more a cookie grows vertically, the less it'll spread outward. This honeycomb structure isn't the only benefit of using a leavening agent, though. Baking soda brings with it a whole set of benefits for flavor and color, too, which I've explained on page 178. Some crackers even use yeast for a rounder flavor and good snap.

CHILLING OUT

Not all cookie and cracker doughs need to be chilled, but a spell in the refrigerator can be useful for those particularly high in fat, firming the dough and helping the cookies or crackers retain their shape while baking. A rolled-and-cut-out cookie or cracker will benefit from being briefly chilled *before* being shaped, making the dough easier to handle. A balance does need to be struck, though. If dough is allowed to chill completely prior to being rolled, it will tend to crumble and crack, so give it 10 minutes or so at room temperature to very slightly soften before shaping.

You can also freeze most doughs. Wrap in parchment paper and then seal in a freezer bag. Defrost the dough overnight in the fridge when you're ready to use it.

A NOTE ON BAKING

Because cookies are small and have high sugar content and low hydration, they bake very quickly, with only a few minutes separating raw dough from burnt cookies. To avoid blowing it all at this last hurdle, time them accurately in the oven and keep a close eye on them. Most are ready when their edges have deepened to a golden-brown color.

The type of baking sheet you use will have a greater impact on cookies and crackers than most other baked goods. A heavy-duty one will conduct heat more slowly than a thin one, so you might find that cookies and crackers baked on the latter will spread less and bake faster.

A common error is to bake cookies and crackers for too long, mistaking their softness when they first come out of the oven for rawness. Most will be chewy when freshly baked, firming only as they cool. Even the crunchiest cookie or cracker will be a little limp while it's still hot. The cooling period here is therefore every bit as important as the oven time. Remember that you can always return a batch of slightly underdone cookies or crackers to the oven for a few minutes if they're still soft after cooling, but there's no salvaging overbaked, rock-hard ones.

TEXTURE

I've arranged the recipes in this chapter by texture: crunch, chew, crumble, and snap. It's not a rigorous categorizing scheme, but it does a fair job of dividing these baked goods by preference, I think. A cookie with crunch is fine with tea, but one that's chewy provides a comfort all its own. A crumbly, butter-rich cookie is an exercise in indulgence, while a crisp cracker is a simpler pleasure.

CRUNCH

GINGER COOKIES

There are always ginger snaps left in the cookie jar once the more exciting ones have long since been pilfered. Not even the lengthiest soak in a mug of tea can soften them. I'm convinced that they would be the last cookies standing after a nuclear apocalypse.

This version, however, bears little resemblance to those rock-hard disks. These are spicily gingery and dark with molasses. With a little luck you'll bake them just right, leaving the centers densely chewy while the edges set to a crunch.

Makes 28 to 32

125 grams (½ c + 1 tbsp) unsalted
  butter, cubed
250 grams (2 c) all-purpose flour
5 teaspoons ground ginger

½ teaspoon baking soda
200 grams superfine sugar (¾ c + 2 tbsp)
  or granulated sugar (1 cup)
1 large egg
5 tablespoons dark molasses

1   In a large bowl, rub the butter into the flour using your fingertips until only very small visible flakes of butter remain. Stir in the ginger, baking soda, and sugar. Whisk together the egg and molasses and add to the flour mixture. Use the back of a fork to mash the ingredients until the dough comes smoothly together.

2   Refrigerate the dough for 30 minutes, meanwhile preheating the oven to 350°F. Line two baking sheets with parchment paper.

3   Break off pieces of the chilled dough, each about the size of a brussels sprout, and roll into balls, spacing them at least 2 inches apart across the baking sheets. You should be able to fit 8 to 12 on each baking sheet. Whatever dough is left over can be put back in the fridge until ready to be baked in a second batch.

4   Bake for 15 to 17 minutes, rotating the baking sheets and swapping oven shelves halfway through the baking time. The cookies will seem very soft when they first come out of the oven, but please don't be tempted to bake them longer, as they set firmer when they cool. Transfer to a wire rack and let cool until completely set.

5   Repeat shaping and baking in batches until all the dough has been used.

Variations
Try adding 1 teaspoon of cinnamon and ¼ teaspoon of ground cloves for a more Christmassy cookie, similar to German *lebkuchen*. Alternatively, you could add the bright zest of an orange to kick the cookie out of its languid toffee sweetness and into life.

GINGER LIME SANDWICH COOKIES

A slick of buttercream can transform a cookie. Make your Ginger Cookies (page 171) and prepare this buttercream while they cool.

Makes 14 to 16
60 grams (¼ c) unsalted butter
Zest and juice of 2 limes

1¼ cups confectioners' sugar
28 to 32 Ginger Cookies (page 171)

Beat the butter until smooth, then add the lime zest. Beat in the sugar a little at a time and add a splash of lime juice to taste. Sandwich pairs of cooled ginger cookies together with a dollop of this buttercream.

DARK CHOCOLATE ORANGE BOURBONS

The key to a good bourbon cookie is the contrast between the mild cocoa wafer and the chocolate kick inside. This version stirs things up with a peppering of orange zest.

   The cookies will lose some of their crispness after several hours, so if you won't be eating them all at once (although I can't imagine why anyone wouldn't), reserve some of the cookie halves and buttercream and fill them when you're ready. The buttercream should be kept in the fridge in the meantime, but bring it up to room temperature before using.

Makes 16 to 20
240 grams (1¾ + 3 tbsp) all-purpose flour
¼ cup cocoa powder
140 grams (½ c + 2 tbsp) unsalted butter, cubed
100 grams (7 tbsp) superfine sugar
Zest of 1 orange
2 tablespoons milk or water

Buttercream
100 grams (7 tbsp) unsalted butter, softened
2 tablespoons cocoa powder
Zest of 1 orange
150 grams (1 c + 3 tbsp) confectioners' sugar

📷 page 172

1   Sift the flour and ¼ cup of cocoa powder together into a large bowl. (I rarely advocate sifting, but here it helps to incorporate the cocoa powder, which has a tendency to clump.) Rub in the 140 grams (½ c + 2 tbsp) of butter using your fingertips, working lightly and speedily until no visible flakes of butter remain. Stir in the superfine sugar and orange zest, then sprinkle on the milk. Use a butter knife or something similar to cut through the mixture, blending the liquid with the dry ingredients until the dough begins to come together in small clusters.

2   Press the dough into one piece, wrap in plastic wrap, and refrigerate for at least 30 minutes. Meanwhile, preheat the oven to 350°F and line a large baking sheet with parchment paper.

3   Depending on how chilled the dough is after its time in the fridge, you may need to let it soften just slightly before rolling. If the dough is too hard, it'll crack as you roll; if it's too soft, it'll stick. It should feel cool to the touch and just firm. Roll out on a lightly floured work surface to about 10 by 12 inches. Cut into rectangles measuring about 1¼ by 3¼ inches, although the precise dimensions don't matter as long as all of the rectangles are more or less the same size. You can stack and reroll any scraps, but doing this more than once could result in the dough toughening.

4   Transfer the cut dough to the lined baking sheet and bake for 12 minutes. Transfer to a wire rack and let cool completely.

5   While the cookies are baking and cooling, prepare the buttercream. Beat the butter, cocoa powder, and orange zest until smooth, then beat in the sugar a little at a time. The mixture should be smooth and soft enough to spread or pipe.

6   Spread or pipe a generous layer of buttercream onto half of the cooled cookies, then sandwich with the remaining cookies. Chill in the fridge for 10 minutes if they need any extra help setting.

BISCOTTI

The word *biscotti* has etymological roots in old French for "twice cooked." Biscotti are cooked first as a log of dough, and again later in slices to dry them, taking them to their trademark state of desiccation.
    These keep well when stored in an airtight container at room temperature, so you can double or even triple the quantities given here to make a larger batch.

Makes 12 to 16
125 grams (1 c) all-purpose flour
1 teaspoon baking powder
Pinch of salt
¼ teaspoon ground cinnamon
85 grams (6 tbsp) superfine sugar
Zest of ½ lemon

50 grams blanched almonds (⅓ c) or
    pistachios (6½ tbsp), coarsely chopped
50 grams (⅓ c) dried currants
1 large egg, lightly beaten
1 tablespoon milk

📷 page 175

1   Preheat the oven to 350°F and line a baking sheet with parchment paper.

2   In a large bowl, combine the flour, baking powder, salt, cinnamon, and sugar. Add the lemon zest, almonds, and currants and toss to combine. Add the egg and milk, first stirring, then cutting through the mixture to combine. You should be left with a reasonably sticky, heavy dough.

3   Lightly flour your hands and the dough and shape it into a rough log, 8 to 10 inches long. It doesn't matter if it's not completely even. Position it in the middle of the lined baking sheet.

4   Bake for 35 minutes, then, while it's still hot, cut into slices about ¾ inch thick using a sharp, serrated knife and a gentle sawing motion.

Cookies & Crackers

5   Decrease the oven temperature to 300°F. Lay the slices across a large baking sheet
    (or two, if necessary) and bake for 10 minutes, then turn the slices over and bake
    for 10 minutes longer. Let cool completely before serving with — of course — strong
    coffee for dunking.

Variations

This is a versatile recipe, so feel free to adapt it to your tastes. You could add a
teaspoon of ground ginger, some sour cherries, or a handful of chocolate chips.
One particularly good variation includes ground fennel seeds, added to taste.

CHEW

ROSE & BURNT HONEY FLORENTINES

I'd usually cringe at the thought of using something as cutesy as rose petals but they're actually lovely to eat as well as to look at. You can find them online, in some specialty baking shops, and in some of the more upscale supermarkets. Just make sure you buy the kind sold as edible rose petals — nobody wants potpourri florentines. But if you can't find (or be bothered to find) rose petals, it's really no tragedy.

Cooked for a few minutes until it darkens and sizzles, honey takes on a far mellower flavor. The intense sweetness is subdued and toasted, and toffee notes come to the fore. It's an easy way of making a little honey go a long way.

Makes 8 to 10
2½ tablespoons honey
3½ tablespoons superfine sugar
3½ tablespoons unsalted butter
1 tablespoon half-and-half
1 teaspoon rose water
2 tablespoons all-purpose flour

50 grams (½ c) sliced almonds
50 grams (⅓ c) golden or regular raisins
50 grams (¼ c) candied cherries,
   coarsely chopped
¼ cup dried rose petals (optional)
150 grams (5.25 oz) dark chocolate

📷 page 176

1   Preheat the oven to 350°F and line a large baking sheet with parchment paper.

2   Put the honey in a medium pan over low heat. After a couple of minutes it'll begin to bubble. Let it simmer, stirring often, for 1 to 2 minutes, until the honey is fragrant and has darkened by a couple of shades.

3   Add the sugar, butter, half-and-half, and rose water, stir to combine, and then bring to a boil. Immediately turn off the heat and add the flour, beating to combine. Stir in the almonds, raisins, cherries, and rose petals.

4   Spoon into small mounds spaced 4 to 6 inches apart on the lined baking sheet (they'll spread a lot while baking — don't underestimate them). You may need to use two baking sheets to lessen the likelihood of a conjoined monster florentine emerging from the oven later.

5   Bake for 15 to 17 minutes. The florentines will spread to form wide disks, and their edges will become lacy and golden brown. Once they're baked but still hot, gently nudge their outer edges inward using a spoon, pushing them back into a neatly circular shape. Let cool on the baking sheet until firm, then transfer to a wire rack.

6   Melt the chocolate in a heatproof bowl suspended over a pan of simmering water or, very carefully and in short bursts, in the microwave. Using a pastry brush, coat the underside of each florentine with a layer of chocolate and let set, in the fridge if necessary. If you have extra chocolate, you can drizzle it on top.

ORANGE LEMON COCONUT COOKIES

Coconut has a tendency to be blandly sweet, but lifted by orange, lemon, and cardamom, these cookies are a far cry from standard, terminally beige coconut cookies. They're bright, light, and chewy.

Makes 20

110 grams (½ c) unsalted butter, softened
175 grams (¾ c) superfine sugar
1 large egg
Zest of 1 orange
Zest of 1 lemon
150 grams (1 c + 3 tbsp) all-purpose flour
½ teaspoon baking soda

¼ teaspoon salt
8 cardamom pods, seeds only, ground or crushed*
100 grams (½ c) unsweetened dried coconut

* I grind the seeds in a coffee grinder, although crushing with a mortar and pestle will work just as well.

1   Preheat the oven to 350°F and line two baking sheets with parchment paper.

2   Cream the butter and sugar together in a large bowl, beat in the egg, then stir in the orange and lemon zest.

3   In a separate bowl, combine the flour, baking soda, salt, and ground cardamom. Stir this into the butter mixture, then fold in the dried coconut.

4   Use two teaspoons to heap little mounds of batter onto the lined baking sheets, spacing them 2 to 3 inches apart because they'll spread as they bake. You may have to bake them in a couple of batches.

5   Bake for 12 to 14 minutes, until barely golden. Let firm slightly on the baking sheets before transferring to a wire rack to cool completely.

GOLDEN BROWN: BAKING SODA & THE MAILLARD REACTION

There's more to baking soda than rising power. In the next two recipes, it helps to give the cookies their hallmark golden-brown color and lightly caramelized flavor. The chemistry at work here is complex and comprises many individual reactions, but to sum up, when sugar is strongly heated in the presence of certain proteins, the Maillard reaction occurs. This involves the browning of the outside of the food and the development of a set of unique flavors. It's what happens to the outside of a steak as it sears on the griddle, to the crust of a baking loaf, to deep amber dulce de leche and to sizzling French fries.

The Maillard reaction works best in quite alkaline environments, and this is where baking soda, which is an alkali itself, comes in. When a food that contains proteins, sugar, and baking soda is cooked at a high heat, the Maillard reaction will occur particularly quickly. For this reason, when cookies are leavened with baking soda, the result is a golden, caramel-flavored treat — despite the short baking time. It's an exciting bit of kitchen chemistry. It's also what gives bagels (page 109) their perfectly browned crust.

PECAN COOKIES

Walnuts are bitter, almonds sweet, hazelnuts stridently autumnal, and fat macadamia nuts buttery. Pecans, however, perch somewhere in between: sweet, nutty, delicate, rich, and woody all at once. It's this balance which, in my opinion, makes pecans the finest and most versatile of the lot.

Makes 14 to 16

150 grams (1⅓ c) coarsely chopped pecans
140 grams (½ c + 2 tbsp) unsalted butter
60 grams (5 tbsp) light brown sugar
100 grams superfine sugar (7 tbsp) or granulated sugar (½ c)

1 large egg
1½ teaspoons vanilla extract
200 grams (1½ c + 1½ tbsp) all-purpose flour
¼ teaspoon baking soda
¼ teaspoon salt

1   Preheat the oven to 350°F. Line a large baking sheet with parchment paper.

2   Put the pecans on a baking sheet and toast for 8 to 10 minutes, until they just begin to darken. They should smell sweet and nutty. Set aside to cool, leaving the oven on for the cookies.

3   Melt the butter either in the microwave or in a pan over low heat. Set aside to cool slightly, then add the sugars and beat vigorously for 1 minute. Stir in the egg and vanilla extract. In a separate bowl, combine the flour, baking soda, and salt. Add this to the butter mixture, stirring only until just combined. Stir in the pecans.

4   Using a couple of tablespoons, scoop out walnut-sized balls of dough and space them 2 to 3 inches apart on the lined baking sheet, reserving some dough for a second batch if they won't all fit. Bake for 13 to 15 minutes, until just turning golden brown at the edges. The cookies will firm as they cool, so don't worry if they feel soft right after baking. As for the eating, there's no need for preciousness: dunk unceremoniously in a glass of cold milk.

LET IT REST

If you can bear to wait, try wrapping your next batch of raw cookie dough tightly in plastic wrap and refrigerating for 24 to 48 hours before baking. During this time some of the starches in the flour will begin to break down into sugars. The result: cookies that are chewier and more deeply colored, with a toffee taste.

HAZELNUT DARK CHOCOLATE COOKIES

These cookies are vegan, but you could be forgiven for not realizing it. They're laden with chocolate and nuts, densely chewy at their center, and have caramelized, gold-brown edges. There's nothing about them that feels lacking. I made these regularly when I was living in university dorms, and they were always stolen from my cupboard. I would have been annoyed, but it was a bittersweet victory, seeing the pilferers — vocally, obnoxiously antivegetarian and antivegan — unwittingly eating their words.

Where most cookies use butter for tenderness and taste, these use nut oils. I like to use hazelnut oil to complement the hazelnut in the dough, but almond oil also works very well (and is far cheaper) for a gentler, sweeter flavor. You ought to be able to find both almond and hazelnut oil in most large supermarkets. You could swap the nut oil for corn oil or peanut oil in a pinch — the texture will still be good, but the flavor will be compromised, so add a tad more vanilla extract if you do so.

You can buy vegan chocolate for these cookies if you want, but you'll find that most good-quality dark chocolate is vegan anyway, especially those with a high percentage of cocoa solids. But do check the ingredients first: all sorts of dairy-derived products, among them butterfat and milk powder, can be smuggled into cheaper brands. If you're not worried about making these cookies vegan, it won't matter what dark chocolate you use, and you can also use dairy milk in place of the soy milk.

Makes 14 to 16

100 grams (½ c) light brown sugar
100 grams (7 tbsp) superfine sugar
7 tablespoons hazelnut or almond oil
¼ cup soy milk
1 teaspoon vanilla extract
200 grams (1½ c + 1½ tbsp) all-purpose
    flour

¼ teaspoon baking soda
¼ teaspoon salt
75 grams (2.5 oz) dark chocolate,
    chopped into small chunks
75 grams (⅔ c) coarsely chopped
    hazelnuts

page 181

1   Preheat the oven to 350°F and line a large baking sheet with parchment paper.

2   In a large bowl, beat the sugars, oil, and milk vigorously for 1 minute; this helps to incorporate air and emulsify the mixture. Stir in the vanilla extract. In a separate bowl, combine the flour, baking soda, and salt. Add to the sugar mixture, stirring for only as long as is necessary to achieve a smooth mixture. Fold in the chocolate and hazelnuts.

3   Using a couple of teaspoons, space heaping spoonfuls of the cookie dough 2 to 3 inches apart on the lined baking sheet. The cookies probably won't all fit on one baking sheet, so bake in batches if necessary.

4   Bake for 15 to 17 minutes, just until the edges begin to lightly brown. Steal a couple while they're still soft and warm, sandwich a scoop of ice cream between them, and eat without shame or restraint.

SPICED OAT THINS

These oatmeal cookies might boast an ingredient list as long as your arm, but it's comprised mostly of spices that you probably already have in your cupboard. Some of the flavors here are baking regulars, while others are less commonplace. Fiery black pepper and earthy celery salt, for instance, lift these cookies out of the generic holiday-spice rut and push them in a different direction altogether.

Makes 18

100 grams (7 tbsp) unsalted butter
100 grams (½ c) dark muscovado or
    dark brown sugar
2 tablespoons light corn syrup
Pinch of ground cloves
½ teaspoon ground cinnamon

¼ teaspoon ground allspice
½ teaspoon ground ginger
½ teaspoon ground black pepper
¼ teaspoon celery salt (or table salt)
120 grams (1½ c) regular rolled oats
90 grams (⅔ c + 1 tbsp) all-purpose flour

1   Preheat the oven to 350°F and line a large baking sheet with parchment paper.

2   Gently heat the butter, sugar, and corn syrup together until the butter has melted. Remove from the heat and stir in the cloves, cinnamon, allspice, ginger, pepper, and celery salt, then stir in the rolled oats and flour.

3   Using two teaspoons, spoon small mounds of the mixture roughly 4 inches apart on the baking sheet (they'll spread quite substantially during baking). I managed to fit only 6 on my baking sheet, so you will probably have to bake in batches. Bake for 10 minutes, then let cool completely before peeling off the parchment. Because these are so robustly flavored, I find it best not to serve them with anything that might vie for attention; complement them simply with a pot of black tea.

CRUMBLE

A SHORT STORY

In baking, *short* refers to a dough or pastry that is rich, crumbly, and tender. That is exactly what these next cookies are. The following recipes all differ slightly in their means for achieving this "shortness," but the aim is the same: minimize gluten formation. Gluten in flour is responsible for elasticity and a strong structure. Such properties play a crucial role in other areas of baking (most notably in bread, where gluten is positively courted), but they're antithetical to a crumbly cookie.

And bad news for the health conscious: fat is the key to subduing gluten — the more butter, the better. Gluten cannot work without first being hydrated. Coating the flour generously with fat before adding the water therefore hinders gluten development. As such, you'll notice that the following recipes use a fairly high proportion of fat and as little water as possible.

Gluten is also encouraged to form by handling of the dough, which is why we knead bread so vigorously. For shortbread cookies, however, it's important to manipulate the dough as little as possible. The shortbread dough below, for instance, is simply pressed into its tin. For rolled cookies, roll the dough lightly and sympathetically, teasing it into shape and taking care not to stretch it. The cookies will usually survive one rerolling of the dough, to use up any scraps, but any further rolls will yield progressively tougher cookies. Resting the dough in the fridge prior to baking can help to remedy this, though.

Another option for a crumblier cookie is to use flour that is low in gluten or even gluten-free. The Rye Oat Cookies (page 184) are an example of this; the use of rye flour leaves them so delicate that they crumble under the slightest pressure.

SHORTBREAD

It would be wrong to talk about crumbly cookies without mentioning shortbread. It's all in the name, of course: shortbread, with a ratio of near equal parts butter and flour, is superlatively short. A bad one will be tough as hardtack and approximately as tasty, but good shortbread is delicate, light, and sweet. The key is a heavy hand with the butter and a light touch when handling the dough. Be sure to chill the dough thoroughly and bake slowly.

Semolina is crucial for achieving a slight grittiness and crunch, as shortbread made with flour alone tends to feel almost gummy.

Makes 8 to 10 wedges

140 grams (½ c + 2 tbsp) unsalted
   butter, softened
75 grams superfine sugar (⅓ c)
   or granulated sugar (6 tbsp)

70 grams (7 tbsp) semolina
Generous pinch of salt
130 grams (1 c + 2 tsp) all-purpose flour

**8-inch round cake pan, preferably
loose-bottomed or springform**

1   Beat the butter in a large bowl for about 1 minute, until completely smooth. Add 60 grams of the sugar (¼ c of superfine sugar, or 5 tbsp of granulated) and stir to combine. Mix in the semolina and salt. Add the flour and stir lightly but firmly. It'll likely seem quite dry and lumpy, but with a little perseverance you'll soon see the mixture come together — try mashing it gently under the back of the spoon. Just take care not to overmix, as this will toughen the dough and leave the cookies chewy rather than with the desired delicacy.

2   Line the bottom of the pan with parchment paper. Pat the dough down into the pan, molding it to the pan's shape without too much rough handling. Refrigerate for 1 hour, preheating the oven to 325°F during the tail end of this chilling period.

3   Sprinkle the remaining sugar on top of the chilled dough and lightly pat it into the surface. Bake for 50 to 60 minutes, until just the palest golden color and sandy on top. Let cool completely before cutting into fat wedges.

RYE OAT COOKIES

In Britain, a type of cookie know as digestives, akin to graham crackers, are a perennial favorite. In this recipe, they're made with dark rye flour for a rounder whole grain taste. You might question the point of making these at home when you can buy a package of graham crackers so cheaply from the corner store. To that I say (almost sacrilegiously) that this homemade cookie is immeasurably better. They're packed with oats, soothingly sweet, rubbly, and faintly nutty. I'm not advocating cookie puritanism here, and I firmly believe that for most tea breaks, midmorning pick-me-ups, and furtive snacks, a store-bought cookie will do just fine. But when a real treat is in order, try a batch of these.

Makes 16 to 20
80 grams (1 c) regular rolled oats
100 grams (1 c) dark rye flour
1 teaspoon baking powder
Generous pinch of salt

80 grams (5 tbsp + 2 tsp) unsalted butter, cubed
3 tablespoons soft light brown sugar
1 to 2 tablespoons milk

📷 page 185

1   Preheat the oven to 350°F and line a large baking sheet with parchment paper.

2   Grind the oats in a food processor or coffee grinder until no whole oats remain, but stop before it becomes powdery — the oats should just be broken down into smaller fragments. If you don't have a food processor or grinder, just buy cheap quick oats instead. Unlike good-quality rolled oats, cheaper versions tend to be composed of broken or partly powdered oats in the first place.

3   In a large bowl, combine the rye flour, baking powder, and salt. Using your fingertips, rub the butter into the flour mixture until no visible flakes of butter remain. Add the oats and sugar and toss to combine. Drizzle in the milk and cut through the mixture using a butter knife to incorporate the milk. It will begin to clump and will soon be moist enough that it can be squeezed together into one mass.

4   There's no need to chill this dough before baking, although you can do so if you
     want to prepare it in advance. I roll the dough out right away on a well-floured
     work surface to a thickness just shy of ¼ inch. Thanks to the whole grain, low-
     gluten rye flour and the high proportion of oats, it's a crumbly, difficult dough
     to roll, but you should find that it holds its shape a little better once compacted
     under the weight of the rolling pin. If the dough does crack as it's rolled, don't
     worry; just piece together the broken bits and pinch to seal.

5   Cut into whatever shape you want; I go for simple squares so that I don't have to bother with rerolling the scraps. Carefully transfer to the lined baking sheet and bake for 15 minutes, until the edges are beginning to brown. Let cool on the baking sheet for a few minutes to firm up before transferring to a wire rack to cool completely. Serve them in the only way they ought to be served: with a mug of no-frills, perfectly brewed English breakfast tea.

Variations

If you can't get ahold of dark rye flour, a more pantry-friendly version of these cookies can be made using whole wheat flour instead. You could even dip the tops in melted chocolate, although whether it should be milk or dark chocolate is a surprisingly divisive issue — and a choice that only you can make.

TAHINI LEMON COOKIES

Tahini, a paste made from sesame seeds, has a powerful flavor; it's reminiscent of peanut butter but far more bitter. Yet lightened with lemon zest and well sweetened, it mellows to a gentler nuttiness. The result is a delicate cookie, as tender as shortbread but without the heaviness. You'll find tahini in the international or natural food section of most supermarkets, and in Middle Eastern grocery stores and natural food stores.

Makes about 24

120 grams (8½ tbsp) unsalted butter, softened
120 grams (½ c) tahini
120 grams superfine sugar (8½ tbsp) or granulated sugar (½ c + 1½ tbsp)

Zest of 2 lemons
240 grams (1¾ c + 3 tbsp) all-purpose flour
1 teaspoon baking powder

📷 page 187

1   Preheat the oven to 350°F and line a large baking sheet with parchment paper.

2   Cream the butter, tahini, and sugar together until pale and fluffy, then mix in the lemon zest. In a separate bowl, combine the flour and baking powder. Stir the flour mixture into the butter mixture, mashing gently under the back of a spoon to combine.

3   Roll out about 24 chestnut-sized balls from the mixture and space them apart on the baking sheet. Pat each ball down to a flattish disk about ⅜ inch thick. It doesn't matter in the slightest if the cookies have little cracks around the edge. You can use a fork at this point to make lines or a crosshatch pattern on the top of the cookies.

4   Bake for 12 to 15 minutes, until the edges are golden brown. The cookies will be very crumbly when first baked, but leave them on the baking sheet and they will become firmer as they cool.

SNAP

SNAP JUDGMENTS

The next three recipes are for very thin, crisp cookies and crackers. With these, it's not so much the mixing that's important but rather the baking. Timing is everything: for wafers less than $\frac{1}{16}$ inch thick, an extra 30 seconds can mean the difference between doughy and perfectly cooked, and another minute could leave them bitter and burnt. A cookie that snaps cleanly and crisply needs to be watched, carefully timed and impeccably judged. Use a timer rather than guesstimating and have oven mitts at the ready.

CINNAMON ORANGE TUILES

Whether these are strictly cookies is open to debate. They certainly don't fall into line with the traditional idea of a cookie: something comforting, butter-rich, and robust enough to be dunked with impunity into a mug of tea. Instead, they are wafer-thin and — with some careful baking — perfectly crisp.

    Why, then, include them here among the heavyweight shortbreads, biscotti, and cookies? Firstly, they look very much at home in a cookie jar. Secondly, there's something very addictive about them at any time of day — with coffee, after dinner, at snack times, and huddled in bed — which means they rarely stay safe in that cookie jar for very long at all. It's hardly the comprehensive criteria of cookiehood, but it's enough to make these tuiles honorary cookies, at least in my eyes.

Makes about 16
30 grams (2 tbsp) unsalted butter
30 grams (¼ c) flour
½ teaspoon ground cinnamon
30 grams (¼ c) confectioners' sugar

Zest of ½ orange
1 large egg white, lightly beaten
50 grams (1.75 oz) dark chocolate,
   coarsely chopped

📷 page 188

1   Preheat the oven to 350°F and line a large baking sheet with parchment paper.

2   Melt the butter over low heat, then set aside to cool a little. In a medium bowl, combine the flour, cinnamon, sugar, and orange zest. Whisk in the egg white and melted butter to form a smooth, thick batter.

3   There's a tidy way of doing this next step . . . and then there's the way I do it. The proper way is to cut a circle out of an old ice cream tub lid or something similar, discard the circle, and use what remains as a tuile template. Lay the template over the lined baking sheet, then dollop a small amount of batter into the center of the circle. Using a frosting spatula or something similar, spread the batter very thinly across the cut-out area. Peel the template away to reveal a crisp-edged, neat circle of batter. Repeat until there's no space left on the baking sheet (these will have to be baked in batches). My easier, though less polished, tuiles are shaped as follows:

place about a teaspoonful of batter onto the parchment paper and spread it thinly using a spatula until you've got a uniform smear of batter about 2 by 4 inches in size. The resulting ragged-edged cookies aren't the most professional, but they are very quick. The most important thing is to spread the batter thinly and evenly, as varying thicknesses will yield a cookie that's alternately chewy and burnt. Don't worry if the first ones aren't perfect — there's enough batter here that you'll need to bake in batches, so you can improve your spreading technique as you go.

4   Bake for 6 to 7 minutes, until golden and just beginning to brown at the edges. In the meantime, have a rolling pin on hand to mold the baked tuiles.

5   This next step must be done quickly, while the tuiles are still fresh from the oven and malleable. They will, of course, be hot, so do be careful. If the duck-bill curve of a molded tuile isn't, to your mind, worth the risk of burnt fingers, no problem. It's only aesthetic, after all. If you do decide to mold them, lay each tuile across the rolling pin and gently wrap it to the curve. You should be able to fit a row of them along the length of the pin. After a minute or so they'll cool and harden. Those gifted with asbestos fingers may be able to go further, hand rolling the tuiles into delicate cigar shapes, cones, and other cookie origami. It's up to you.

6   Repeat the spreading and baking in batches until all the batter has been used.

7   Melt the chocolate either in short bursts in the microwave or in a heatproof bowl suspended over a pan of simmering water. Dip the ends or rims of the tuiles into the chocolate and set aside to cool. These are good enough to eat by themselves, but they excel as a crisp, smart counterpoint to a bowl of chocolate ice cream.

FENNEL SEED & CHILE CRACKERS

Good cheese deserves a good cracker. These very thin, crisp ones are flavored with fennel and laced with chile flakes. If you're not keen on spice, use just ¼ teaspoon of chile flakes, but even with the full ½ teaspoon, these crackers aren't excessively hot.

Makes 20 to 25
200 grams (1½ c + 1½ tbsp) all-purpose
    flour
¼ teaspoon salt
1 teaspoon superfine sugar
1 teaspoon fennel seeds

½ teaspoon dried chile flakes
Generous grind of black pepper
2 tablespoons olive oil
4½ tablespoons water
Sea salt flakes (optional)

📷 page 191

1   Preheat the oven to 400°F. Lightly grease a large baking sheet or line it with parchment paper.

2   In a large bowl, combine the flour, salt, sugar, fennel seeds, chile flakes, and pepper, then stir in the oil and water. Knead lightly for a minute just to bring the dough together. If it's too dry to come together, sprinkle in a bit more water — barely a teaspoonful at a time — until no loose flour remains.

3   Let the dough rest for about 15 minutes to allow the gluten to relax. Working on a lightly floured surface, roll it out into a circle as thin you can. It should stretch to 14 to 18 inches in diameter and about ⅛ inch thick.

4   Cut into whatever shapes you want. I use a sharp knife to cut free-form rectangles measuring about 2 by 3 inches. The only thing to bear in mind is that very small shapes will take less time to cook. Sprinkle with sea salt flakes.

5   Bake for 10 minutes. Serve with a good, soft cheese — perhaps Camembert. Alternatively, these go surprisingly well with curry in place of traditional *papadums*.

STILTON & POPPY SEED CRACKERS

I was put off cheese snacks for a long time by the only kind that I knew: the sort that leaves you with bright orange fingertips and contains (probably) no real cheese. But these crackers are a different story altogether: crisp, salty-sharp, and quite good enough to eat by themselves.
   You can replace the Stilton if you're not keen on blue cheese, but I want to reassure you that the Stilton flavor here is quite mellow. If you do swap cheeses, be sure to choose a strongly flavored, hard cheese, as a softer cheese will add too much water to the mix, resulting in unacceptably chewy crackers.

Makes 24 to 32
100 grams (7 tbsp) unsalted butter, cubed
200 grams (1⅔ c) whole wheat flour
Pinch of salt
100 grams (3.5 oz) Stilton

3½ tablespoons poppy seeds
1 to 2 tablespoons cold water

📷 page 192

1   In a large bowl, rub the butter into the flour and salt. Crumble in the cheese and lightly rub this in, too, stopping when there are no longer any large chunks. Stir in the poppy seeds, then drizzle the water over the mixture. Using a small knife, cut through the mixture repeatedly to incorporate the water. The flour should all be moistened and coming together in clumps. If there's still dry flour, add more water one drop at a time.

2   Press the dough into one lump, wrap in plastic wrap and refrigerate for about 15 minutes, until firmer but not rock solid. If chilling longer, give the dough a little time at room temperature afterward to make it slightly more manageable to roll. Meanwhile, preheat the oven to 400°F and line a large baking sheet with parchment paper.

3   On a lightly floured work surface, roll out the dough to a thickness of about ⅛ inch. It'll be slightly crumbly thanks to the whole wheat flour and poppy seeds, but just patch any breakages with more dough. Cut into slim rectangles, perhaps about 1 by 4 inches, and arrange on the lined baking sheet.

4   Bake for 10 to 12 minutes, until just beginning to deepen to a golden-brown color at the edges.

DECADENT DESSERTS

CHEESECAKE

INDIVIDUAL PASSION FRUIT CHEESECAKES

RASPBERRY, WHISKEY & OAT CHEESECAKE

BLACKBERRY RICOTTA CHEESECAKE

195

MERINGUES & CUSTARDS

AUTUMN BERRY PAVLOVA · LEMON MERINGUE ROULADE

BAY & BLACK CURRANT CRÈME BRÛLÉE · BLUEBERRY CLAFOUTI

SPONGE PUDDINGS

RASPBERRY CHOCOLATE FONDANTS

MAPLE PECAN SPONGE PUDDINGS · STICKY TOFFEE PUDDING

STEAMED ORANGE & GINGER PUDDING

LIGHTER CHRISTMAS PUDDING · ORANGE & SAFFRON SPOTTED DICK

RHUBARB JAM ROLY-POLY

I can't help but be suspicious of those who are happy to leave their meal on a savory note: for me, there has to be a dessert of sorts, even if it's as simple as a plate of perfectly ripe figs, otherwise the dinner just isn't complete.

Most of the desserts in this chapter — slivers of cheesecake, fruit-laden pavlovas, and snowy lemon roulades — are about lightness, brightness, and elegance. They're designed to sate a sweet tooth without being inelegantly hearty or rich. But I have also included a selection of my favorite puddings. British puddings lumber at the opposite end of the spectrum and are the sort of food served in school cafeterias and on cold winter nights. Christmas pudding, spotted dick, and jam roly-poly don't seduce you as much as challenge you to take them on and finish them right up. Even the word *pudding* has a heavy, clumsy quality to it. I love it.

CHEESECAKE

There is a cheesecake for just about everyone: New York-style baked cheesecake with the tang of sour cream; unbaked ones so tremulously soft that they melt in the mouth; fruit-topped versions; or imported adaptations using ricotta, quark, or mascarpone. I prefer to keep things simple, perhaps adding some fruit or zest, or maybe a swirl of chocolate. Anything else is just gilding the lily.

In terms of method, there are three basic types of cheesecake. The first is baked, adding eggs to the filling to set in the heat of the oven. The second is set with gelatin. I'm loath to mess around with setting agents like gelatin unless it's absolutely necessary, and as it happens, it's not: the third type of cheesecake — unbaked, with firmly whipped cream folded into it — will set perfectly well in the fridge without any gelatin at all. The type you choose will depend on your personal tastes, the flavors to be included, and the time available to you. Baked cheesecakes tend to be slightly firmer, with a mellower flavor. No-bake cheesecakes have a brighter taste but, especially when set with whipped cream, can verge on cloying. They need fruit or zest to cut through the creaminess.

There's no mystery to no-bake cheesecakes, as you'll see in the recipe for Passion Fruit Cheesecakes (page 199). But baked cheesecakes require a little more care if they're to be excellent rather than merely good. It is attention to detail that will make all the difference.

THE CRUST

It is possible to make a cheesecake crust with pastry, but for me much of the joy of cheesecake lies in the crumbly cookie crust. The type of cookie is an open question: ginger snaps go well with lemon, lime, or passion fruit; graham crackers are a good all-around choice; I've used oatcakes in the Raspberry, Whiskey & Oat Cheesecake (page 201); and the more adventurous will use Oreos, shortbread rounds, or amaretti. But regardless of which cookie you use, it's important to prebake or chill the crust. This will give it a chance to set before the wet filling goes in, preventing (or at least minimizing) any sogginess.

MIXING

It really does help to have all of the filling ingredients at room temperature before you start mixing. Mix eggs straight into a block of cold cream cheese and you'll end up with an infuriatingly lumpy mixture that you'll then have to strain. Always beat the cheese until smooth before adding the other ingredients, and then do so gradually. Take care not to beat too much air into the mix, however: this is one of the rare instances in baking where density is a virtue.

BAKING

Baking is the most crucial stage. Bake too quickly at too high a temperature, and the cheesecake will puff up, brown on top, and develop a grainy, almost chalky, texture. Patience pays off here, and I say that as a chronically impatient person. Cheesecake bakes best at very low temperatures: the slower it cooks, the smoother it sets. For most baked cheesecakes, 230°F to 265°F is about right.

WATER BATHS

Some insist that cheesecake must be cooked in a water bath for a perfectly smooth set. Because water (in its liquid state, at least) can't reach temperatures higher than 212°F, it protects the dessert from the fierce heat of the oven. This helps the cheesecake to cook evenly (reducing the appearance of puffy edges and a sunken middle) and creates a creamy texture. But, although I concede that it does make for a velvety texture, I'm not convinced that it's really necessary. You can achieve the same result by baking the cheesecake at a lower temperature for a longer time. Plus, half-submerging a cheesecake in a pan of sloshing water is a fraught kitchen experience, and even the most carefully foil-swaddled pan can leak, leaving the filling curdled and the crust sodden. Avoid it if you can.

COOLING

Sometimes a cheesecake will develop a large crack across its center as it cools — usually just as you proudly usher everyone into the kitchen to show them how fabulous it looks. You can't always predict or prevent this, but it'll certainly be less likely to happen if you bake at a low temperature. Another solution is to gently loosen the edges of the cheesecake from the tin after baking. The cheesecake will shrink slightly as it cools, but if the sides are free to fold inward a little, it'll be less likely to tear. And importantly, cool the cheesecake slowly. You could turn off the oven slightly before the cheesecake is set and let it cool in the oven; otherwise, cool completely to room temperature before transferring to the fridge to chill.

INDIVIDUAL PASSION FRUIT CHEESECAKES

You could make this as one large cheesecake, but I think it's best served in individual ramekins: it's far quicker than making a "real" cheesecake, you don't have to worry about it setting perfectly firm, and you get the selfish pleasure of having something to eat that is all yours — no need to share with anyone else.

Because this cheesecake isn't baked, it has a softer set than the other two in this chapter. It uses heavy cream, whipped to firm peaks, for its structure. The result is a creamy texture and rich flavor, offset by the brightness of the fruit.

Makes 6

6 passion fruits, plus 1 for the topping (optional)
200 grams (7 oz) full-fat cream cheese
80 grams (5 tbsp + 2 tsp) superfine sugar
½ cup + 2 tablespoons heavy cream
120 grams (4.25 oz) ginger snaps

6 small glasses or ramekins

1   Halve the 6 passion fruits, scoop out their pulp and seeds, and strain through a fine-mesh sieve. Spend a bit of time pressing the pulp into the sieve to extract as much juice as possible.

2   Beat the cream cheese in a bowl until smooth. Add the passion fruit juice and stir to combine. In a separate bowl, whisk the sugar with the cream until the mixture is firm and just about holds stiff peaks. Fold the whipped cream into the cream cheese mixture, cutting through with the spoon or spatula to gently combine the two. The mixture should be unctuous and smooth. Taste it: if it needs a touch more passion fruit juice or sugar, add it now.

3   Crush the ginger snaps in a large bowl with the end of a heavy wooden rolling pin or, more efficiently, in a food processor if you have one. Divide the crumbs between the glasses, spreading an even layer across the bottom of each and pressing down firmly. Spoon in the cream cheese mixture, level the top with the back of the spoon, and refrigerate for at least 2 hours to firm up.

4   Just before serving, scoop a little passion fruit pulp over the top of each cheesecake. The black seeds and bright orange juice will look striking against the creamy cheesecake, but it's not an essential addition.

RASPBERRY, WHISKEY & OAT CHEESECAKE

Here, the building blocks of Scottish *cranachan* are brought together in a different guise, layered into an alternately crisp, creamy, and fruity cheesecake. It's not as rustically simple as the dessert that inspired it, but it does, I think, stay true to *cranachan*'s ingredient-centric ethos, with honey, raspberries, whiskey, and oats in perfect balance.

Serves 8, generously

Crust
150 grams (5.25 oz) oatcakes
25 grams (5 tbsp) regular rolled oats
1 tablespoon + 2 teaspoons superfine sugar
100 grams (7 tbsp) unsalted butter

Filling
400 grams (14 oz) full-fat cream cheese
½ cup + 2 tablespoons sour cream
¼ cup honey

100 grams (7 tbsp) superfine sugar
1 teaspoon vanilla extract
2 to 3 tablespoons whiskey
3 large eggs
200 to 300 grams (1½ to 2½ c) fresh raspberries

8-inch round loose-bottomed or springform pan

📷 page 200

1   Preheat the oven to 350°F.

2   To make the crust, crush the oatcakes with a rolling pin or in a food processor until sandy and no chunks remain. Stir in the rolled oats and sugar. Melt the butter over low heat in a small pan, then add it to the crushed oatcakes and stir to combine. Add a bit more butter if the mixture feels dry; it needs to be moist enough to hold together in small clumps. Spoon it into the pan and press firmly with the back of a spoon. Bake for 10 to 15 minutes, until just set (it will firm as it cools). Set aside while you prepare the filling. Turn the oven down to 250°F.

3   To make the filling, beat the cream cheese in a large bowl until smooth. Add the sour cream and stir to combine, then add the honey, sugar, and vanilla extract. Stir in the whiskey to taste. (You can add a little extra, or none at all, if you prefer.) Lightly whisk the eggs in a separate bowl, then gradually add them to the cream cheese mixture while stirring continuously to prevent lumps from forming. The mixture should be thick and smooth.

4   Pour the filling over the pre-baked crust. Bake for about 1½ hours, until the filling is set and has just the slightest wobble in the center. Because it's baked at such a low temperature, it should be barely colored, just deepening to a light gold. Let cool to room temperature in the pan, then unmold and chill.

5   Shortly before serving, arrange the raspberries on top of the cheesecake, fat ends down and tapered bottoms upward. You can cover with the raspberries earlier, but there's a risk that, if they're particularly ripe, their juices will seep into the creamy cheesecake.

BLACKBERRY RICOTTA CHEESECAKE

I love the swirls of deep purple berries against this creamy cheesecake. Ricotta produces a less smooth texture than the heavier cream cheese, but the taste is cleaner, allowing the fruit to really shine.

Serves 8 to 10

Crust
150 grams (5.25 oz) graham crackers
75 grams (⅓ c) unsalted butter

Blackberry Swirl
150 grams (1 c) blackberries
2 tablespoons superfine sugar
Juice of ½ lemon
1 teaspoon cornstarch (optional)

Filling
500 grams (17.5 oz) ricotta cheese

2 tablespoons cornstarch
½ cup + 2 tablespoons heavy cream
125 grams (½ cup + 1 tbsp) superfine sugar
2 large eggs, plus 1 large yolk
Zest of 1 lemon
1½ teaspoons vanilla extract

8-inch round loose-bottomed or springform pan

📷 page 203

1   Preheat the oven to 350°F.

2   To make the crust, crush the graham crackers with a rolling pin or in a food processor, until sandy. Melt the butter over low heat, then mix it with the graham cracker crumbs. The crumbs need to be moist enough that they'll hold together in clumps if squeezed, so add a bit more butter at this point if necessary.

3   Spread the mixture over the bottom of the pan and press down firmly all over. Bake for 10 minutes, then remove and let cool slightly. Decrease the oven temperature to 250°F.

4   Next, make the blackberry swirl. In a small pan, heat the blackberries, sugar, and lemon juice over low heat, stirring occasionally, until the blackberries soften. Crush with the back of a fork until no whole berries remain, then set aside to cool. If the blackberries release a lot of juice, add the teaspoon of cornstarch while the pan's still on the heat and stir for another minute or two, until thickened.

5   To make the filling, beat the ricotta and cornstarch together in a large bowl until smooth, then stir in the cream. Once combined, beat in the sugar, followed by the eggs and yolk (one at a time), lemon zest, and vanilla extract.

6   Pour the filling onto the baked crust. Dollop spoonfuls of the blackberries on top and gently swirl through the filling using a spoon. Bake for 1¾ to 2 hours, until the filling has no more than a slight wobble in the center. The cooked cheesecake should be quite firm all over except for the blackberry swirls, which will now be slightly sunken, jammy, and a deep purple color.

7   Let the cheesecake cool completely in the pan before unmolding. Then, for a firmer texture, chill in the fridge before serving.

MERINGUES & CUSTARDS

Like a lot of home cooks, I'm both intrigued and terrified by meringue. It's the building block of some of the most impressively extravagant desserts in the baker's repertoire, but it can seem intimidatingly tricky. It doesn't deserve this reputation, though. Once you've become familiar with a few basic dos and don'ts, you'll find a billowing meringue every bit as simple to whip up as a Victoria sponge cake.

There are three main types of meringue: French, Italian, and Swiss. Each has slightly different characteristics and methods, but the one I use in these next recipes is the most basic — a French meringue.

GETTING STARTED WITH MERINGUE

First things first: Use a very, very clean bowl and whisk. Even the slightest residue or grease will interfere with the meringue's development as it's whisked, leaving it flat and flabby. Plastic bowls are unsuitable for meringues for that very reason, because they often retain a film of dirt and oil after even the most thorough scrubbing. Glass or stainless steel bowls are the best options, and make sure that you use a large bowl, as the meringue will expand a lot when it's whisked.

THE INGREDIENTS

Meringue is, quite simply, egg white and sugar. That something so strange and delicious can come from two such unremarkable ingredients is part of its charm.

Reasonably fresh eggs make the best meringues. You'll notice that older eggs have runnier whites — a sign that their proteins, responsible for structure in the meringue, are breaking down, so the resulting dessert will be less voluminous. If your eggs are a little older, you can add a pinch of cream of tartar or a drop of lemon juice (roughly ¼ teaspoon per 2 large whites) to the egg before you begin to whisk. This touch of acidity will help to strengthen the meringue. The temperature matters, too: fridge-cold eggs will whip up more slowly than those at room temperature.

As for the sugar, use superfine. Granulated sugar will take far longer to dissolve and could lead to "weeping" in the finished meringue, when tiny droplets appear on the surface of the meringue after it's been baked. The amount of sugar depends on the sort of meringue you're aiming for. A crisp, firm meringue will need up to 60 grams (¼ c) of sugar per egg white, whereas a softer version, such as that heaping on top of a meringue pie or baked Alaska, can work with just a couple of tablespoons of sugar.

SEPARATING THE EGGS

Yolk is bad news for meringue — as little as a speck of golden yolk in the egg whites can stop a meringue from gaining the volume that it should. This leaves the whole process of separating the eggs quite fraught, given that the building blocks for your meringue are nestled snugly alongside its nemesis. Just work slowly and, if you're not a confident egg breaker (I still get eggshell in my cakes), separate the whites over a small bowl one at a time, decanting each into the larger mixing bowl as you go.

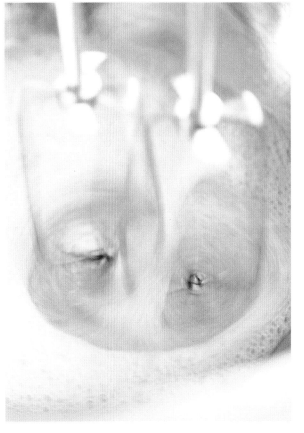 

WHISKING

The first step is to whisk the egg whites (with the cream of tartar or lemon juice, if using) until they're completely foamy. This stage is crucial, but it's important not to overdo it: the eggs need a head start before the sugar is added; otherwise the meringue will be dense, but if they're overwhisked they could be weakened and collapse. Whisk only until the whites are thick enough that when a bit drops from the whisk, it sits happily on the foam's surface rather than sinking straight back in. The foamy whites should hold in crests and waves.

Next, add the sugar. This must be done slowly, giving the sugar time to dissolve into the whites. Adding too much at once will leave the meringue deflated and can cause weeping (see page 205) after baking. I usually pour the sugar in one-quarter at a time, whisking well after each addition.

As you continue to whisk the egg whites and sugar, you'll see the mixture transform. Air is beaten into the whites, and the vigorous whisking rearranges their proteins to form a dense foam. The result is that the whites — at first slimy and heavy — become thick, voluminous, and bright white. A well-whisked meringue should transform from merely foamy to almost creamy, with a glossy finish to it.

Unless otherwise specified, you'll have to keep whisking the meringue until stiff peaks form. This is the stage at which, when the whisk is lifted slowly from the meringue, it leaves a spike of the mixture behind it — bolt upright, not curling at its tip (if it does droop, it's only a soft peak, and you've got another few minutes of whisking to go).

Another, more theatrical, test is to hold the bowl upside down. If the meringue is stiff enough, it won't budge. Unfortunately, this is a bit of an all-or-nothing approach — if the meringue isn't ready, you'll have a big mess to clear up.

It does take a while for the meringue to reach the stiff peaks stage, but as long as the equipment is clean, the eggs aren't too old, and the sugar is added slowly, you ought to be able to whisk the whites up to volume in 10 to 15 minutes — and even quicker if you have an electric mixer. My electric mixer makes a din so terrible that I'm always forced to make meringues by hand, and it really isn't too much of a chore.

BAKING

How you bake a meringue can determine whether it's crisp, chewy, or soft. A long, very cool bake (sometimes for as long as overnight in a barely hot oven) will produce very dry, crisp meringues — the sort that maintain a snowy white glow and break into thick sugar shards as you eat them. Baking for an hour or so in a medium oven, such as in the Autumn Berry Pavlova recipe (page 208), will yield a meringue that's crisp outside and chewy inside — for me, by far the best type. A short time in a moderate oven will cause the meringue to brown slightly but won't allow it time to dry out, leaving it with a just-set exterior and mousse-like interior. You'll have to take the sugar content (see page 205) into account too, though, as this will also have a bearing on texture.

AUTUMN BERRY PAVLOVA

The only difficult thing about this pavlova is saying no to second and even third helpings. It's a good way to familiarize yourself with basic meringue, too, if you've never made it before.

You can use just about any berry or soft fruit for a pavlova, but I like to choose something bold enough to stand its ground in the face of mountains of meringue and cream. Raspberries, with their hint of acidity, are perfect. So are sharp black currants and red currants and inky blackberries. Sour Morello cherries are fantastic, but their easier-to-find sweet cousins are unfortunately less punchy. And then, of course, there are strawberries, for the classic summer pavlova.

Serves 8
Meringues
3 large egg whites
150 grams (⅔ c) superfine sugar

Filling
1¼ cups heavy cream

3½ tablespoons superfine sugar
1 teaspoon vanilla extract
300 grams (about 2 c) fresh berries

📷 page 209

1 Preheat the oven to 285°F and line a large baking sheet with parchment paper.

2 First, make the meringue. In a large, very clean, preferably glass or metal bowl, whisk the egg whites for a couple of minutes until they're whipped up into a dense foam. Add the sugar gradually — a couple of tablespoons at a time — and whisk well after each addition to give the sugar time to dissolve. Once all of the sugar has been added, continue whisking for about 5 minutes, until the mixture is very thick and glossy. It should hold stiff peaks when you slowly lift the whisk out.

3 Spoon the meringue in one big heap right onto the lined baking sheet, then gently spread it out, using the back of a spoon, to form a circle 9 to 10 inches in diameter. Make a slight hollow in the center, pushing the extra meringue toward the edges to create a wide, gently sloping rim. This "bowl" of meringue is what will hold the cream and fruit filling.

4 Bake for 1 hour. The meringue should be barely a shade darker and shouldn't have browned. If at any point during baking it appears to be browning or burning, turn the oven down a bit.

5 Leave the meringue on its baking sheet to cool for 15 to 20 minutes, then carefully peel off the parchment paper and transfer the meringue to a large paper serving plate or tray.

6 To make the filling, combine the cream, sugar, and vanilla extract in a large bowl and whisk until firm. Spoon this into the "bowl" of the meringue. Crush a few of the berries under the back of a fork (their bright juices will look amazing against the cream and meringue), then spoon all of the fruit over the cream. Enjoy soon after making, refrigerating the rest if you don't eat it all in one sitting.

LEMON MERINGUE ROULADE

In this dessert you have the bare bones of a lemon meringue pie — sharp, sunny lemon curd and voluminous meringue — without having to mess around with a pastry crust.

Store-bought lemon curd is okay in this filling, but homemade will have far more zing to it. There's a handily economical recipe for it on page 324, which uses all the yolks left over from making this meringue.

Serves 6 to 8
4 large egg whites
½ teaspoon lemon juice
200 grams (¾ c + 2 tbsp) superfine sugar
30 grams (¼ c) confectioners' sugar, for dusting

Filling
1¼ cups heavy cream
40 grams (⅓ c) confectioners' sugar
150 to 200 grams (5.25 to 7 oz) lemon curd

9 by 13-inch baking pan

📷 page 211

1   Preheat the oven to 325°F and line the pan with parchment paper.

2   In a very clean, dry bowl, whisk the egg whites with the lemon juice just until they're completely foamy and hold soft mounds as the whisk is lifted out. Add the superfine sugar a little at a time, whisking thoroughly after each addition. Adding the sugar all at once or before the previous addition has been incorporated may cause the meringue to collapse, so do be patient here.

3   Once all the superfine sugar has been added, keep whisking. You'll feel the meringue become thicker and see it grow glossy and smooth, but don't stop until the point when, as you slowly lift your whisk away from the meringue, the mixture holds a firm, well-defined, straight peak. Carefully spoon the meringue into the lined pan, level the top, and bake for 30 minutes.

4   Once the meringue is baked, dust another sheet of parchment paper with the 30 grams (¼ c) of confectioners' sugar and turn the meringue out onto it so that it's upside down. Peel away the parchment paper from the underside (now the top) and let the meringue cool.

5   To make the filling, whip the cream and confectioners' sugar until the cream holds soft peaks. Gently fold the lemon curd into the cream. Spread this lemony mixture over the cooled meringue, then, using the sugar-dusted parchment paper as an aid, roll the meringue up into a log, rolling from long edge to long edge to create a roll about 13 inches long. Don't worry if the meringue cracks or if some of the cream oozes out — this is a beautiful dessert but not one to get precious about.

 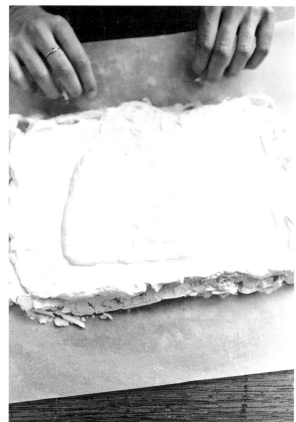

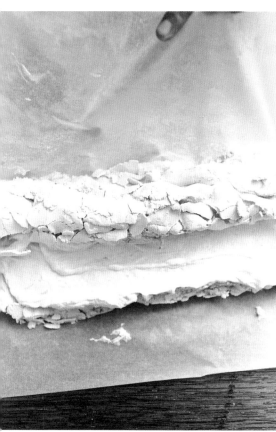 

BLACK CURRANTS

Black currants are an unrivaled joy when you can get them fresh, but even during their short season (primarily July and August) they can be difficult to find. A huge percentage of black currants grown in the UK are, woefully, turned into a syrupy base for beverages, so they rarely grace our produce aisles. But do keep an eye out over the summer for the occasional, fortuitous basket of the inky, jewel-like berries. They're mouth-puckeringly sharp when raw, but with the addition of heat and sugar they really come alive. If you can't find black currants for the crème brûlée below, try blackberries; or leave out the bay leaf and use red currants instead. Their flavor is shallower, but they have the tartness required to cut through the creamy custard.

BAY & BLACK CURRANT CRÈME BRÛLÉE

A whisper of licorice left on the tongue by a velvety bay-infused custard, and the dark warmth of black currants at the end of a spoonful is one of my favorite flavor combinations. Crème brûlée is an impressive way to end a meal, and if you have a blowtorch to caramelize the sugar on top, even better. People are rarely as thrilled as when their dessert comes with a side of pyrotechnics.

This recipe is a nutritionist's worst nightmare, but there's really no point in trying to devise a slimmed-down version of a dessert whose very essence is indulgence. Enjoy the crème brûlée in all its calorific glory; just don't make a habit of it.

If you can't find fresh bay leaves, dried bay leaves can be substituted, although the flavor may not be as strong.

Makes 2 to 4, depending on the size
  of your ramekins
3 large egg yolks
3 tablespoons superfine sugar
1¼ cups heavy cream
50 to 75 grams (½ to ⅔ c) black currants
2 to 4 fresh bay leaves

40 to 60 grams (3 to 5 tbsp) granulated
  sugar

**2 to 4 individual ceramic or glass
  ramekins**

📷 page 212

1   Preheat the oven to 300°F.

2   In a medium bowl, whisk the egg yolks and superfine sugar together until the mixture begins to lighten in color. Heat the cream in a small pan until almost boiling. Pour the cream slowly over the egg mixture, whisking all the while. Scatter a few black currants in each ramekin.

3   Divide the hot custard between the ramekins, then stand a bay leaf in each (it doesn't have to be fully submerged — if you leave it propped against the side of the dish, it will be easier to pull out later).

4   Put the ramekins into a small pan deep enough to accommodate hot water reaching two-thirds of the way up the ramekins. Bake until the custard is mostly firm but still barely wobbling in the center — this should take 30 to 45 minutes depending on the size of the ramekins, but do keep an eye on them and give them

more or less time as necessary. When they're ready, gently tease out the bay leaves. Let the custards cool to room temperature, then chill.

5   Sprinkle the granulated sugar generously over each custard. The caramelizing can be done either using a blowtorch or under a hot broiler — either way, be vigilant. If using a blowtorch, first make sure that the work surface is completely clear, then — giving it your full concentration — work the tip of the blue flame lightly over the sugar. The sugar will at first seem unchanged, but soon it will melt, then bubble, brown, and burn. If using a broiler, allow plenty of time for the broiler to heat up before you put the custards underneath: the sugar must be caramelized quickly to allow the top to set without melting the custard underneath.

6   Let cool at room temperature for 10 minutes or so before serving. Take a spoon in your hand and bring it firmly down onto the surface of the crème brûlée with a crack. It's a feeling to be relished. Enjoy.

BLUEBERRY CLAFOUTI

This dessert actually uses a batter similar to pancake batter, but because it's enriched with plenty of sugar and butter and baked to a slight wobble, it feels more like a thick custard, hence its inclusion here. It's usually made with cherries, but the floral fruitiness of blueberries works very well.

Serves 6
2 tablespoons unsalted butter, melted
90 grams (6 tbsp + 1 tsp) superfine sugar
2 large eggs
40 grams (1/3 c) all-purpose flour
1/4 teaspoon salt
Zest of 1 lemon
1/2 teaspoon vanilla extract
7 tablespoons milk

1/2 cup + 2 tablespoons half-and-half
400 grams (2 2/3 c) frozen or fresh
   blueberries
30 grams (1/4 c) confectioners' sugar,
   for dusting

9- to 10-inch pie pan or deep cake pan

📷 page 215

1   Preheat the oven to 350°F. Use a little of the melted butter to grease the pan. Sprinkle roughly 1 tablespoon of the superfine sugar evenly within the greased pan to coat.

2   Whisk the eggs with the remaining superfine sugar, then stir in the flour, salt, lemon zest, and vanilla extract. Slowly add the milk, half-and-half, and remaining melted butter.

3   Arrange the blueberries in the bottom of the prepared pan, then slowly pour in the batter. (If using frozen blueberries, use them straight from the freezer; otherwise they'll dye the batter an unappetizing shade of gray.) Bake for 30 to 40 minutes, until just set with only a bit of wobble in the center. If you've used frozen blueberries, it may take a little longer. The *clafouti* will have risen and turned golden brown in parts, and the blueberries will have burst their papery skins and melted down to pockets of fragrant blueberry juice. Let cool until just warm, dust liberally with confectioners' sugar, and dig in.

SPONGE PUDDINGS

These puddings are hearty winter fare. They can be made in individual portions or baked in one large, domed pudding basin. The sponge can be fluffy or dense, baked or steamed, zesty or dark. Some, such as the Maple Pecan Sponge Puddings (page 218), are soothingly sweet, whereas others — the dark chocolate fondants below and the ginger orange pudding (page 222) — are bolder. What they have in common, though, is that they should all be served steaming hot with plenty of ice cream, custard, cream, or sauce. A pudding served dry is no pudding at all, in my eyes.

RASPBERRY CHOCOLATE FONDANTS

As far as baked puddings go, these fondants sit at the more refined end of the spectrum. They're elegantly minimalist and, alongside a neat scoop of ice cream, nothing less than beautiful. It's not all about appearances, though: beneath the moist sponge exterior is (if you cook them just right) a molten chocolate core.

Chocolate fondants can sometimes be too rich, even for my taste, but the raspberry in the center of these helps to lift that darkness. If you don't have individual pudding molds, you can use a muffin tin instead. The fondants will be smaller, but that may not necessarily be a bad thing, considering how decadent they are.

Makes 4 large or 8 small fondants
110 grams (½ c) unsalted butter
100 grams (3.5 oz) dark chocolate,
   70% cocoa solids
2 large eggs
110 grams (½ c) superfine sugar

60 grams (½ c) all-purpose flour
75 grams (⅔ c) raspberries

4 individual pudding molds or
  a 12-cup muffin tin

📷 page 216

1   Preheat the oven to 400°F. Melt 2 tablespoons of the butter over low heat and use it to grease the pudding molds or eight cups in the muffin tin: brush the bottom and sides with a coat of butter, freeze for a couple of minutes to set, brush again with a second coat, then leave in the fridge to chill. This might seem fussy, but it's important if you want to be able to turn the cooked fondants out easily. The last thing you want is to end up having to heavy-handedly pry the delicate puddings out of their molds later.

2   Coarsely chop the chocolate and melt it in a large, heatproof bowl suspended over a pan of barely simmering water. Make sure that the bottom of the bowl doesn't touch the water. Once the chocolate has melted, turn off the heat, add the remaining 80 grams (6 tbsp) of butter and stir until fully combined. Set aside to cool slightly.

3   Whisk the eggs and sugar together for at least 5 minutes, until very, very thick and creamy. When the whisk is lifted from it, the mixture ought to fall in a ribbon that sits on the surface for a second or two before sinking back (see page 61).

4   Gently fold the chocolate mixture into the whisked eggs, cutting through the mixture to combine and digging right to the bottom of the bowl (the chocolate will tend to sink). Sift in the flour, then fold it in.

5   Divide the mixture between the molds or muffin cups, putting a spoonful in the bottom of each, followed by three raspberries (use just 1 or 2 raspberries if making the smaller, muffin-sized fondants), and then more batter on top of the raspberries.

6   At this point, you can chill the fondants to be baked later. Otherwise, bake for 10 to 12 minutes for large fondants, or 8 to 9 minutes for small ones. The baked fondants should be well-risen and have a crust. The trick is to cook them just long enough that they're hot through, but briefly enough that the centers remain liquid. You might want to sacrifice one if you're really not sure: using an oven mitt, unmold the pudding straight from the oven, cut in half, check for readiness, and eat, all in the name of testing. If you decide to chill the fondants to bake later, add a minute or two to the baking time.

The larger, individually molded puddings should be easy enough to turn out, but if you've baked a batch of smaller ones in a muffin tin, it takes a little more care to turn them out safely. Slide a clean baking sheet over the top of the muffin tin and, using oven mitts, deftly flip the whole lot over, leaving the muffin tin upside down on top, and the baking sheet underneath. When you tease up the muffin tin, you should be faced with 8 fondants in neat rows. Serve with cream or ice cream.

Variation
A couple of cubes of white chocolate in the center of each fondant can bring a welcome sweetness to this otherwise dark dessert.

MAPLE PECAN SPONGE PUDDINGS

This twist on traditional syrup sponge pudding uses maple syrup in place of the usual corn syrup. Once turned out of their molds, the puddings have sweet, maple-soaked tops and nutty cake underneath. If you don't have a coffee grinder or food processor for grinding the pecans, omit the ground pecans and the milk, and add a full 100 grams chopped pecans to the batter instead.

Makes 4 large or 8 smaller puddings
4 tablespoons maple syrup
100 grams (¾ c + 2 tbsp) coarsely
    chopped pecans
80 grams (⅔ c) all-purpose flour
1 teaspoon baking powder
Pinch of salt
80 grams (5 tbsp + 2 tsp) unsalted butter,
    softened

80 grams (6½ tbsp) light brown sugar
2 large eggs
1 teaspoon vanilla extract
1 tablespoon whole milk

**4 individual pudding molds or a
    12-cup muffin tin**

1   Preheat the oven to 350°F. Grease the pudding molds or 8 muffin cups and line the bottom of each with a small circle of parchment paper. Spoon 1 tablespoon of maple syrup into the bottom of each large mold, or 1½ teaspoons into each muffin cup.

2   Toast the pecans on a baking sheet for 8 to 10 minutes, keeping an eye on them to make sure they don't burn. They're done when they're barely a shade darker and becoming fragrant. Let cool slightly. Leave the oven on for the puddings.

3   Grind half of the toasted pecans in a food processor or coffee grinder until coarsely ground. Be careful not to process too much, as this will release the pecans' oils and the mixture will clump.

4   Combine the flour, ground pecans, baking powder, and salt in a medium bowl. In a large bowl, cream the butter and sugar together, then beat in the eggs and vanilla extract. Stir in the milk and a couple tablespoons of the flour mixture. Once mixed, add the remaining flour mixture and the chopped pecans and stir lightly to combine.

5   Spoon the mixture into the pudding molds until they're just over two-thirds full. Bake for about 25 minutes for large puddings, or 15 to 20 minutes for smaller puddings, until a knife inserted into the middle comes out clean. Loosen the puddings with a small knife and turn them out onto serving plates. If their tops are particularly domed, you may want to slice them off before turning out to give the puddings an even base. Serve immediately, with plenty of maple syrup and custard.

STICKY TOFFEE PUDDING

This is arguably the ultimate comfort food. Whenever I'm in need of something gratuitously indulgent to see me through a weepy film or a cold winter evening, I seek solace in caramel: cubes of chocolate-covered caramel; butter toffees to weld my mouth shut; dark, syrupy sponge cakes; and even, at lower ebbs, caramelized condensed milk (dulce de leche), spooned straight from the can. This pudding, however, has always been my favorite.

Dates have a natural toffee-like edge to them, and when added to this moist sponge pudding and flooded with caramel sauce, they become as stickily sweet and chewy as if they were chunks of fudge themselves.

Makes 1 large pudding, serving 6
200 grams (1⅓ c) coarsely chopped dates
1 teaspoon baking soda
¾ cup + 1½ tablespoons boiling water
75 grams (⅓ c) unsalted butter, softened
100 grams (½ c) light brown sugar
1 large egg, lightly beaten
1 teaspoon vanilla extract
150 grams (1 c + 3 tbsp) all-purpose flour
1½ teaspoons baking powder
2 teaspoons cocoa powder
100 grams (¾ c + 2 tbsp) coarsely chopped walnuts or pecans

Caramel Sauce
100 grams (½ c) light brown sugar
½ cup + 2 tablespoons heavy cream
75 grams (⅓ c) unsalted butter
1 tablespoon dark molasses
Generous pinch of salt

Baking pan, approximately 6 by 9 inches, although the precise dimensions aren't important

📷 page 220

1   Preheat the oven to 350°F. Grease the pan and line it with parchment paper.

2   Combine the dates and baking soda in a bowl, then pour in the boiling water. Set aside while you prepare the remaining ingredients. You'll find that the baking soda quickly softens the dates.

3   In a large bowl, cream together the butter and sugar. Add the egg and vanilla extract and stir to combine. In a separate bowl, mix the flour, baking powder, and cocoa powder. Add to the butter mixture, along with the date mixture (water and all) and whisk lightly to combine. Stir in the nuts.

4   Spoon the mixture into the prepared pan and bake for 30 to 35 minutes, until a knife inserted in the center emerges with only a crumb or two stuck to it.

5   While the pudding bakes, prepare the caramel sauce. In a small pan, heat the sugar, cream, butter, molasses, and salt over low heat, stirring occasionally, until combined. Increase the heat slightly and let bubble for a minute or two. Serve the pudding cut into generous portions (how else?) with a ladleful of sauce over each.

STEAMING

Steaming is a clever way of keeping a sponge pudding moist. This is particularly useful for large puddings, which — if baked in the dry heat of the oven — become tough on the outside before they have time to cook through. It's also crucial for suet puddings, discussed on page 226. This method of cooking is slightly more involved than plain baking, but the results are spectacular: the cakes end up spongy, soft, and moist.

The first step is to prepare the steamer. Fill the bottom of a steamer pan with an inch or so of water and perch the rack or steamer compartment over the top, ready to accommodate the pudding basin.

It's no tragedy if you don't have a specialized steamer, though; it's easy enough to create a makeshift one. Make a small stand or platform for the pudding inside a large, deep pan. For this, choose something that the pudding basin can rest on comfortably — perhaps a small can, a metal cookie cutter, a trivet, or a ramekin. This is just to raise the pudding up away from the intense heat of the pan itself, leaving the boiling water and steam to do the cooking. Make sure that you can still fit the lid onto the pan once the pudding basin has been lowered into it.

The pudding then needs to be wrapped or covered to shield it from the direct heat and moisture of the steam; it's one thing to have a slightly moist cake, and quite another if it ends up sodden. Cover the pudding basin with two layers of parchment paper, folding a wide pleat into the middle of each piece to allow the pudding room to expand as it cooks. Tie each consecutive layer securely around the rim of the pudding basin with a length of kitchen twine.

You can also make a twine handle at this point if you're worried that it might be tricky to lift the hot pudding out of the steaming pan. Just tie a piece of twine over the top of the pudding basin, securing it at each end to the lengths already securing the parchment paper.

The steaming itself is easy: bring about 1 inch of water to a boil in the steamer and add the wrapped pudding. If using an improvised steamer, the water shouldn't reach any further than about an inch up the sides of the basin. Put the lid on and steam. Steaming takes longer than baking the pudding, but the advantage is that it's far harder to overcook and almost impossible to burn. Just keep the water topped up throughout the cooking time, and test as you would any other cake, inserting a knife into the center and seeing that it emerges basically clean.

STEAMED ORANGE & GINGER PUDDING

There's a whole orange lurking inside this pudding. This is no gimmick, though: as the pudding steams, the orange releases juice and flavor into the surrounding cake, leaving the pudding fantastically moist, zesty, and tender. Serve with (lots of) ice cream.

Makes 1 medium pudding, serving 4 to 6
2 medium oranges
125 grams (½ c + 1 tbsp) unsalted butter, softened
125 grams (½ c + 2 tbsp) dark brown sugar
2 large eggs
2 to 3 inches fresh ginger, peeled and grated

1 tablespoon ground ginger
115 grams (½ c + 3 tbsp) coarsely chopped crystallized ginger
125 grams (1 c) all-purpose flour
1½ teaspoons baking powder

3½- to 5-cup pudding basin

📷 page 223

Decadent Desserts

1   Prepare a steamer using the instructions on page 221. Get out your parchment paper and a length of kitchen twine.

2   Bring a small pan of water to a boil. Zest both of the oranges and set the zest aside. Boil one of the oranges in the water for 10 minutes, then set aside to cool while you prepare the remaining ingredients.

3   In a large bowl, cream the butter and sugar together for a couple of minutes, then add the eggs and all the ginger (fresh, ground, and crystallized). In a separate bowl, combine the flour and baking powder, then add to the butter mixture, along with the zest, and stir to combine.

4   Grease the pudding basin generously with butter, then line the bottom with parchment paper (this will help with unmolding later). Cut one crosswise slice from near the middle of the unboiled orange and put it in the bottom of the basin. This will look impressive when the pudding is turned out and also serves to hide the top of the orange that you're going to put inside the pudding.

5   Half fill the basin with the batter. Pierce the boiled orange all over with a sharp knife or cocktail pick then press it into the batter, placing it centrally. Spoon the remaining batter around the orange. If its top is still peeking above the level of the batter at this point, don't worry; the pudding will rise to cover it as it bakes. You may not need all of the batter, depending on the precise size of your pudding bowl and of the orange inside it; only add enough to fill the basin to about 1 inch below the rim.

6   Cut two large squares of parchment paper, make a wide, crisply folded pleat down the middle of each, and lay them over the top of the pudding basin. The pleat will allow plenty of room for the pudding to expand. Secure the parchment paper with a length of twine tied tightly around the basin rim.

7   Place the pudding on the steamer rack (or makeshift steaming platform), make sure that there's at least 1 inch of water in the bottom of the pan, and put a lid on. Steam for 2 hours, topping up the water periodically.

8   When the pudding is ready, unwrap it, loosen the edges with a knife, and turn out onto a plate. Peel back the circle of parchment paper on top and slice proudly down the middle to reveal the whole orange inside. This is a dish best served hot.

LIGHTER CHRISTMAS PUDDING

This treat has all of the delicate flavors of panettone in a steamed sponge pudding. I know that the winter holidays offer a good excuse for gluttony (and I always seize such opportunities with both hands), but having a traditional, dark Christmas pudding after a day of feasting is sometimes a bit too much. The traditional version is a spectacular pudding — especially booze-soaked, lit, and brought to the table in a merry inferno — but I prefer something lighter to top off the Christmas meal.

This pudding strikes a fine balance between the sort of heaviness typical of a Christmas pudding and the lightness required if we're actually going to be able to stomach the thing. Because it's suet-free, it's far spongier than the old-fashioned types. It's not nearly as alcoholic either: just a splash of sweet white wine to soak the fruits (save the brandy for after-dinner drinking).

This won't keep for nearly as long as a traditional pudding, but it will cook far more quickly, so you won't lose an entire day to its preparation. Just soak the fruit on Christmas Eve, make the batter in a jiffy in the morning, and let the pudding quietly steam for a couple of hours while dinner's in the oven.

Makes 1 medium pudding, serving 4 to 6

Zest of 2 lemons
7 tablespoons sweet white wine, such as muscat
40 grams (¼ c) raisins
40 grams (¼ c) dried cranberries or cherries
40 grams (¼ c) dried coarsely chopped apricots
40 grams (¼ c) coarsely chopped prunes
50 grams (5 tbsp) coarsely chopped crystallized ginger
40 grams (¼ c) mixed candied citrus peel

125 grams (½ c + 1 tbsp) unsalted butter, softened
50 grams (¼ c) light brown sugar
75 grams (⅓ c) superfine sugar
2 large eggs
2 teaspoons vanilla extract
135 grams (1 c + 1 tbsp) all-purpose flour
1½ teaspoons baking powder
Pinch of salt

3½- to 5-cup pudding basin

📷 page 224

1   The day before you make the pudding, mix the lemon zest, wine, raisins, dried cranberries, dried apricots, and prunes in a bowl, cover with plastic wrap, and soak overnight at room temperature.

2   The following day, prepare the steamer, referring to the instructions on page 221. Prepare the pudding basin by lightly buttering the interior and lining the bottom with parchment paper to help with unmolding later. Have a couple of large pieces of parchment paper and some kitchen twine on hand, ready to cover the pudding.

3   Add the crystallized ginger and candied citrus peel to the soaked dried fruit mixture. In a large bowl, cream the butter and sugars until pale and fluffy, then mix in the eggs and vanilla extract. In a separate bowl, combine the flour, baking powder, and salt, then stir into the butter mixture. Add all of the soaked fruit and ginger, along with the soaking liquid. Stir lightly to combine.

4   Spoon the batter into the prepared pudding basin. Lay one sheet of the parchment paper over the top of the basin, fold a wide pleat into it (to allow the pudding to expand as it cooks), then tie a length of kitchen twine around the rim to secure it. Repeat with the second sheet of parchment paper. The cover should be secure but loose enough that it won't constrict the rising pudding.

5   Bring the water in the steamer to a boil, put the pudding in, cover with the lid, and steam for about 2 hours, until well risen and firm and a knife inserted into the center comes out clean. It's important that you keep an eye on the water level during this time, topping it up regularly so that the pan doesn't boil dry.

6   When it's ready, carefully unmold the steamed pudding, loosen around the edges, and invert onto a large plate. Serve with ice cream (homemade, spiked with a dash of sweet white wine, is particularly good) to finish the feast.

SUET

Suet is the last word in puddings, and in spite of the blight that is low-fat diets, it's still alive and well in British kitchens. It's actually had a resurgence lately, with the burgeoning national appetite for revival food, British culinary heritage, and so on. I can only hope suet is here to stay and not just a passing fad.

Traditionally, you might have used beef suet (that's the fat scraped from around the animal's kidneys), but I've called for a vegetarian version for these sweet puddings. Beef suet gives a slightly richer flavor, but I feel uneasy about sullying a jam roly-poly with animal fat, and vegetarian suet creates a perfectly good texture. By all means use the old-fashioned variety if you'd rather for authenticity's sake, but it's really not a deal breaker. You can still obtain fresh suet from some butchers, but by far the easiest form to use comes in a shelf-stable package; it's less messy and comes "shredded" — in small pellets ready to be stirred straight into the flour.

Suet contains more fat and less water than butter. And unlike butter, which melts with the slightest warmth, suet doesn't become liquid until it reaches about 115°F. This gives the surrounding dough time to set first, so as the pieces of suet melt, they leave tiny gaps behind. The upshot is that puddings and pastry crusts made with suet tend to have a fine, open texture when freshly baked.

But the problem is that as suet cools, it resolidifies to produce a pastry that — no matter how tender and light it was when it left the steamer — becomes waxy, solid, and dense. For this reason, suet puddings are always best eaten hot.

ORANGE & SAFFRON SPOTTED DICK

The name still brings chokes of laughter to our dinner table, but spotted dick is too perfect a pudding to forgo just because of the name. It's an old-fashioned pudding but has persisted for a reason, being instantly comforting and made from just a handful of ingredients.

The saffron and orange blossom water included here are good counterpoints to the pudding's characteristic heaviness. They balance earthiness with floral lightness, and the orange zest follows through with a kick. If you'd rather omit the saffron, that's no problem — just add a bit more zest or vanilla extract in its place.

The quantities here are slightly smaller than usual for a suet pudding, but I find that this amount fits comfortably in a medium steamer and is enough to satisfy a family of 6 in one sitting without leftovers. This really isn't something that should be left to cool once made. When fresh out of the steamer it's moist, light, and delicate, but once cool it gains the density and mouthfeel of a block of lead. Get it while it's hot.

This version of the pudding is steamed, but you could also bake it in a steamy oven if you'd prefer — follow the baking instructions for the jam roly-poly on page 229 but bake for about 1 hour.

Makes 1 medium pudding, serving 6
7 tablespoons + 2 teaspoons milk
Couple of pinches of saffron threads
Zest of 1 orange
1 teaspoon orange blossom water
½ teaspoon vanilla extract
150 grams (1 c + 3 tbsp) all-purpose flour

1½ teaspoons baking powder
75 grams (2.5 oz) vegetable suet
120 grams (¾ c + 1 tbsp) dried currants
75 grams (⅓ c) superfine sugar
¼ teaspoon salt

📷 page 228

1   Heat the milk and saffron over low heat until the milk is just scalding. Remove from the heat, stir in the zest, orange blossom water, and vanilla extract, and let cool. The milk will turn a sunny yellow hue as the saffron infuses.

2   In a large bowl, combine the flour, baking powder, suet, currants, sugar, and salt. Measure the cooled milk, and if there's any less than 7 tablespoons plus 2 teaspoons (some of it may have evaporated over the heat), top up with an extra splash, then stir into the flour mixture. The dough will be sticky, making it difficult to handle at this point but producing a far lighter pudding in the end. Let it sit for a few minutes.

3   You'll need a medium to large steamer or pan with a steaming rack (see page 221). Bring a kettle of water to boil. Cut two large, 14-inch squares of parchment paper and grease one side of one of them with butter.

4   Scoop the wet dough neatly into the middle of the greased piece of parchment paper to form a sausage shape about 8 inches long (or approximately the diameter of the steaming pan you're using). Wrap the parchment paper around it, folding a wide pleat into the paper on top of the dough to allow room for the pudding to expand as it cooks. Twist the ends of the paper and secure with two pieces of kitchen twine. Wrap this parcel in the other piece of parchment paper, pleating, twisting, and tying as before.

5   Pour about 1 inch boiling water into the pan or steamer and place the pudding on the steamer rack. Cover with the lid and steam for 1¼ to 1½ hours, topping the water up regularly so that the pan doesn't boil dry. The pudding should be golden and firm but springy, and a knife inserted into the center should come out clean.

6   Right after steaming, cut into thick slices, serve with ice cream, and loosen your belt a notch — what other way is there of eating a pudding like this?

RHUBARB JAM ROLY-POLY

Roly-poly is designed to be heavy and filling — the sort of sponge pudding that could sustain you through a long, cold winter — but it doesn't have to be sickly sweet. Roly-polys made with jams such as strawberry, raspberry, or (heaven forbid) apricot end up cloying and bland. It's crucial that there's some balance in the recipe — something acidic to balance the richness of the pastry and accompanying custard. This pudding uses rhubarb jam for that reason. You can make your own jam, following the recipe on page 323 if you have the time and if good, tender rhubarb is in season. Otherwise, buy good-quality rhubarb preserves.

Like all suet puddings, this is prone to drying as it cooks, so it should be baked over a pan of hot water and swaddled in parchment paper and foil to minimize the formation of a thick crust. You could also steam it on the stove top for an even more tender result. If you do, wrap and cook it as instructed for the Orange & Saffron Spotted Dick (page 227) and steam for about 1 hour.

Serves 4 generously
150 grams (1 c + 3 tbsp) all-purpose flour
1½ teaspoons baking powder
75 grams (2.5 oz) vegetable suet
2 tablespoons superfine sugar

Zest of 1 orange
7 tablespoons whole milk
150 grams rhubarb jam (about ½ c)

1   Preheat the oven to 350°F. Find a large roasting pan and set a steaming rack or wire cooling rack in it. There needs to be sufficient clearance between the rack and the bottom of the pan for about 1 inch of water, so prop the rack up on a couple of metal cookie cutters or something similar if necessary. Have a couple of large pieces of parchment paper and four 4-inch lengths of kitchen twine ready for wrapping the pudding. Boil a kettle full of water.

2   In a large bowl, combine the flour, baking powder, suet, sugar, and orange zest. Add the milk and stir to bring together in to a slightly sticky dough.

3   Dust a work surface with plenty of flour and roll the dough out to a rectangle measuring about 8 by 12 inches. Flour generously as you go; otherwise the dough will stick. Spread the jam over the dough, leaving a border of about ½ inch around the edges. Roll up from short edge to short edge to make a roll about 8 inchs long.

4   Grease one of the sheets of parchment paper with butter, transfer the roll to the center of the sheet, and wrap the paper around it, folding a wide pleat on top to give the pudding room to expand as it cooks. Twist the ends of the paper and secure with two pieces of the twine. Wrap again with the second piece of parchment paper, pleating and tying as before. Put the pudding in the center of the steamer rack.

5   Transfer the roasting pan with the rack and pudding in it to the oven, then carefully pour about 1 inch of boiling water into the pan. Bake for about 45 minutes, after which time the pudding should be cooked through. Serve as is only right for a rhubarb-swirled, suet pudding comfort food: with a pitcher of thick vanilla custard.

PIES & TARTS

SHORT-CRUST PASTRY

SPICED EGGPLANT & SWISS CHARD PIE

BROCCOLI & GORGONZOLA QUICHE

BUTTERNUT SQUASH & MOZZARELLA TARTLETS WITH HERB PASTRY

231

HOT WATER–CRUST PASTRY

SPICED PORK PIE • CAULIFLOWER GRUYÈRE PASTIES

QUICK PUFF PASTRY

QUICK PUFF PASTRY DOUGH • CHICKEN, PALE ALE & CHICORY PIE

FISH PIE • BANANA THYME TART

SWEET SHORT-CRUST PASTRY

PEAR, SESAME & CHOCOLATE TART • CHERRY PIE

LEMON & BASIL TART • ROSEMARY PECAN PIE

STEM GINGER TART • SPICED CHOCOLATE TART

There aren't many foods that don't taste better encased in a pastry crust. What good would baked, crimson cherries be if not sandwiched between two layers of short crust? Or chicken baked in a creamy sauce without flaky pastry draped on top? It's a shame, then, that pastry has such an unfair reputation for difficulty. We often reach unquestioningly for the premade stuff, concerned that homemade pastry will be too thick, crumbly, wet, tough, time-consuming, or fiddly. The term "soggy bottom" has given rise to a neurosis wherein a pie is declared a disaster if its pastry shell isn't perfectly crisp. These impossible standards might be how success is calibrated in patisseries and on TV shows, but they have no place in the home kitchen. I'd go so far as to say we should champion the soggy bottom. I can see nothing not to love about buttery pastry sodden with fruit juices, or custard, or rich gravy.

LINING A PIE OR TART PAN

There's no great secret to lining a pie or tart pan with pastry, although it is something that grows easier with practice. I've outlined the basic steps below for those who want the pastry to be even, neat, and symmetrical, but if you're not bothered about appearances, just dive in. The worst that can happen is that you'll end up with a slightly lopsided, rough-edged, undulating pie crust, bubbling through with syrup, or fruit juices, or gravy . . . and that really doesn't sound so bad.

1   Roll out the pastry to a circle that is big enough to cover the bottom and sides of the pan, making sure that you roll evenly and to a reasonable thickness — ⅛ inch to just shy of ¼ inch is about right. Too thick and the pastry will dominate; too thin and it risks tearing or leaking. I often roll on a sheet of lightly floured parchment paper. This not only prevents sticking, but also helps when transferring the pastry to the pan.

2   To move the pastry into position, either slide it off the parchment paper and into the pan or use your rolling pin to pick it up: roll one edge of the pastry over the pin and pick it up from this edge, draping the rest behind the rolling pin, sliding the pan underneath, and lowering the pastry into it (see photo, page 230). Don't worry if the pastry cracks a little — you can patch it up later.

3   Press the pastry into the pan, and neatly into the grooves if using a fluted pan. You could use a small piece of pastry to do this, thus avoiding excessively touching and warming the dough, but I've never found it necessary. As long as you don't fiddle around for too long, the pastry will be fine. Take care not to stretch the pastry; let it fall back under its own weight, and only gently tease it into shape. It helps to press the pastry up about ⅛ inch above the rim of the pan, too, to allow for any shrinkage as it cooks.

4   Chill the lined pan for at least half an hour in the fridge before baking.

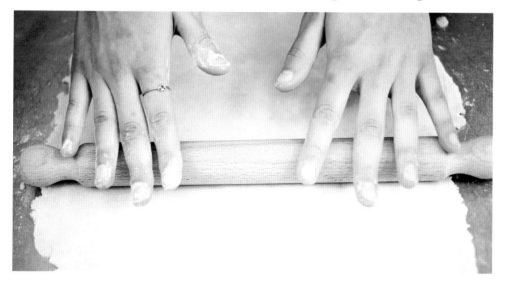

BLIND BAKING

Blind baking isn't as scary as it sounds. It's simply cooking a pie or tart shell prior to filling it to give the pastry a chance to set and crisp up. This is crucial when using liquid fillings, such as those in custard tarts and quiches, although it's a trick that can be used on more or less any pie or tart when you want to have a perfectly crisp, dry pastry shell. Most of the time, the pastry is subsequently returned to the oven with the filling to continue cooking, but if you bake blind for an extra 5 minutes or so, you can completely cook the shell. A fully blind-baked pastry shell can then be used as a vessel for pastry cream and fresh fruits, or even a chocolate ganache.

It's common to use baking weights to hold the pastry down while blind baking; otherwise it's liable to dome upward at its center and sink down at the sides. You'll find pie weights (little ceramic marbles) made specifically for this purpose in stores, but there's no need to shell out for them when uncooked rice or dried beans make perfectly effective, and far cheaper, substitutes.

To blind bake, first line the pan as described on page 233. Chill for 30 minutes or so while you preheat the oven to 400°F. Scrunch up a large piece of parchment paper, then roughly smooth it out again (this just makes it easier to fit the pastry contours). Lightly press it into the pastry-lined pan so that it covers the bottom and sides. Fill with a thick layer of pie weights, uncooked rice, or dried beans. Bake for 15 minutes, then carefully lift out the parchment parcel and weights and cook the pastry uncovered for 5 to 10 minutes longer, until firm and dry to the touch.

SHORT-CRUST PASTRY

Despite short crust so often being billed as a "basic" pastry, for a long time I found it to be one of the trickiest of them all. There are only four ingredients — flour, butter, water, and salt — leaving little margin for error and no place to hide. Too warm, cold, dry, wet, buttery, or lean, and it'll lack that crucial shortness. It's the Goldilocks of pastry, but with a little care and patience, you should have no trouble getting it right.

BEFORE YOU START

The butter should be firm, but not fridge-cold. If it's too hard, it'll prove difficult to rub into the flour; too soft, and it'll melt between your fingers, leaving the pastry greasy and tough. The water, however, should be chilled, so if it's a particularly warm day, have a few ice cubes ready to chill the water before adding it to the pastry.

MIXING

The mixing stage is a balancing act, but not an impossible feat: you'll need to mix thoroughly but avoid handling the pastry for too long. The key is keeping the mixture cool. Toss the cubes of butter with the flour. Then, using only your fingertips, work quickly and lightly to rub the butter into the flour, breaking it into smaller and smaller pieces until there are no visible chunks of butter remaining. In doing this, you coat the flour particles with fat. This layer of fat repels water and restricts the development of gluten (the protein responsible for making dough strong and elastic) so that the resulting pastry is as crumbly and tender as possible.

Once the butter has been incorporated, mix in the salt (and any sugar or spices), followed by the water (some sweet short-crust doughs use egg instead). Always use cold liquid and add it gradually — too much will leave the dough sticky and difficult to roll and, worse still, encourage the gluten development we're aiming to avoid. When mixing in the water, use a cutting motion: draw a small, sharp knife through the mixture again and again until the moisture is evenly distributed throughout the flour. This combines the dough without developing much gluten. As soon as the flour is moistened and beginning to come together in small clumps, the mixing is done.

Use your hands to lightly but firmly press the pastry into a ball. If it won't hold together, add a few more drops of water. Wrap the ball in plastic wrap and refrigerate for at least 30 minutes to give the butter a chance to chill and the dough time to relax.

ROLLING AND SHAPING

Roll gently, don't use excessive flour to dust the surface, and don't stretch the dough. After such careful mixing, it'd be a shame to overwork the pastry now. If the pastry begins to stick, let it chill a little more; if it's crumbly, let it warm for a few minutes at room temperature. As for rerolling any scraps, you can do it, but don't do so more than once, or the dough could become elastic, rather than crumbly or flaky.

RESTING

Once you've rolled the pastry and lined your pan (see page 233), it's crucial to let the pastry shell rest before baking. This should be done in the fridge for at least 30 minutes, or in the freezer for 15 minutes if you're short on time. During this resting period, the gluten in the pastry will relax, minimizing shrinkage during baking. It also affords you time to prepare the filling and preheat the oven.

BAKING

Depending on the type of pie or tart, you may have to blind bake your short-crust pastry shell separately before filling (see page 234). A well-baked short crust should be firm to the touch, sandy textured (a French version of sweet short-crust pastry is called *pâte sablée*, or "sandy pastry"), and no darker than a light golden brown. And in terms of texture, the crumblier, the better.

WHY IS MY SHORT-CRUST PASTRY . . .

Because its method is straightforward and its ingredient list short, it's usually easy to figure out where your short crust went wrong. Here are a few of the most common problems, and some suggestions for avoiding them in future.

. . . SHRUNKEN ONCE BAKED?

— Too much water. This encourages troublesome gluten to form, leaving the pastry elastic and prone to shrinking in the oven. Add the water gradually next time, and use only as much as is necessary to bring the pastry together.

— When short crust is handled too much or rerolled too many times, it'll lose that important fragility and become rubbery.

— If the pastry is stretched when lining the pan, it will spring back as it's cooking.

— Patience is a virtue. Short crust that has not rested for long enough after being rolled won't have had time to relax, and therefore will shrink.

— Using too much flour when rolling can also be a cause. Dust your work surface with just enough flour to prevent the pastry from sticking.

. . . TOUGH?

— Again, this may be a case of too much water or excessive handling or rerolling.

— It may also be that you used too much flour when rolling.

. . . TOO HARD AND CRUMBLY TO ROLL?

— Your pastry may actually be too cold. Let it rest at room temperature for a few minutes, then give rolling another shot.

— Your pastry may be too dry. Roll slowly and carefully, patching up any cracks as you go, and remember to add a little more water to the dough next time.

— Too much whole wheat flour or sugar can also create a pastry that crumbles when rolled.

...TOO STICKY TO ROLL?

— The dough might be too warm. Let it chill for another 10 minutes before attempting to roll it.

— If the pastry is tacky even after chilling, you might have used too much water.

...RAW UNDERNEATH?

— Sometimes pastry needs a head start if it's going to play host to a particularly wet filling, such as a custard or cream. On such occasions, the pastry needs to be blind baked (see page 234) before being filled.

— If the filling can tolerate a little extra time in the oven, it might just be that the pastry hasn't been baked for long enough. From raw, most short crusts will need at least 20 minutes to become crisp, and this could take much longer depending on the topping or filling.

— Try baking in a slightly hotter oven next time. If the oven is too cool, the pastry will end up greasy and soft. The temperature shouldn't be any lower than 350°F for short crust.

SPICED EGGPLANT & SWISS CHARD PIE

There's little to be gained from trying to make a vegetarian pie into an ersatz steak-and-kidney or second-rate "mince" and potato version. Meat-free pies should be exciting and different, not apologetic. They're all the more interesting for not relying on the usual meat-and-gravy formula. This one's all about showcasing the vegetables: eggplant, carrot, and Swiss chard, seasoned, spiced, and layered.

You could make this pie vegan by swapping the butter for vegetable shortening, in which case you might need an extra tablespoon or so of water to bring the dough together. The problem with vegetable shortening, however, is that it doesn't have much flavor. Consider adding a couple of teaspoons of spice — perhaps ground coriander or toasted cumin seeds — to make the pastry more interesting.

Makes 1 large pie, serving 8

Pastry
400 grams (3 c + 3 tbsp) all-purpose flour
200 grams (¾ c + 2 tbsp) unsalted butter, firm but not fridge-cold, cubed
¼ teaspoon salt
¼ cup cold water

Filling
4 large carrots, peeled and thickly sliced
3 cloves garlic, peeled
Juice of ½ lemon
50 grams (⅓ c) sesame seeds
Salt and black pepper

¼ cup olive oil
2 large onions, sliced
2 teaspoons ground coriander
2 teaspoons ground ginger
1 teaspoon paprika
200 grams (7 oz) Swiss chard, thickly sliced
1 eggplant

1 large egg, lightly beaten with a pinch of salt, for glazing (optional)

Deep 8-inch round springform or loose-bottomed cake pan

📷 page 241

1   First make the pastry. Rub the flour and butter together in a large bowl, working quickly and lightly to fully combine them without melting the butter. Add the salt and then the water, cutting through the pastry with a small knife until all of the flour is moistened and beginning to come together in clumps. Add an extra couple of teaspoons of water if the dough is too dry to hold together. Press into a disk, wrap in plastic wrap, and chill for at least 30 minutes.

2   To make the filling, bring a large pan of water to a boil, then add the carrots and garlic. Boil until the carrots are tender. Drain, then use a handheld blender or food processor to puree the carrots and garlic together until smooth. Stir in the lemon juice and sesame seeds. Season with salt and pepper, then set aside to cool.

3   Heat the oil in a large frying pan over medium-low heat, then gently cook the onions with a pinch of salt for 10 minutes or so, until soft and translucent. Add the coriander, ginger, and paprika and sauté for another minute or two, until fragrant. Add half of this to the carrot mixture and stir well to combine. Return the other half to the stove over low heat, add the Swiss chard, and cook, stirring gently, for a couple of minutes, until the chard has wilted. Season with salt and pepper, then let cool.

4 By this point the pastry should be well rested. On a lightly floured surface, roll out just over two-thirds of it to a circle roughly 10 inches in diameter. Forget what you might've heard about thinness and delicacy being the keys to a good pastry shell; this is a deep, hearty pie, and it needs a reasonably robust crust to hold it all together. Line the pan with this circle, pressing the dough neatly into the corners, then put it in the fridge to chill for 30 minutes; alternatively, freeze for just 15 minutes if you're in a rush. Rewrap and chill the remaining pastry.

5 While the pastry shell chills, preheat the oven to 400°F. Prepare the eggplant by first cutting it in half crosswise to produce two fat chunks, then thinly slicing these two pieces lengthwise into delicate, floppy slivers. If the slices are rigid when held up by one corner, they're too thick.

6   Now assemble the pie. Layer one-third of the eggplant strips over the bottom of the pastry shell, drizzle lightly with some of the remaining olive oil, and season with salt and pepper. Top with half of the carrot mixture. Repeat the eggplant layer (with olive oil, salt, and pepper), followed by all of the chard, the third and final eggplant layer, and then the remaining carrot mixture. If you have any eggplant strips left, you can top the filling with these. Roll out the rest of the pastry to a circle roughly 8 inches in diameter, lay this over the pie, and crimp the edges to seal. Brush with the beaten egg if you want a deeper color to the top, and make an incision in the top so that steam can escape as the filling cooks. Bake for 15 minutes, then turn the oven down to 350°F and bake for 45 minutes longer. You can eat this pie while it's still hot, but I think it's best cold, and even better the following day. Just leave it to cool in its pan before carefully unmolding. It holds its shape better once cold, too — perfect for cutting into fat wedges for picnics.

BROCCOLI & GORGONZOLA QUICHE

Some whole wheat flour in the pastry lends a welcome nuttiness to this quiche, pairing well with the blue cheese within. You can make this marginally healthier, if you like, by replacing the half-and-half with more milk, but I'm not sure that shaving those few extra calories off is worth the trouble. Just enjoy it with a peppery green salad and rest assured that it's a good deal less fattening than the more common, bacon-laden quiche lorraine.

Makes 1 quiche, serving 6
Pastry
125 grams (1 c) all-purpose flour
75 grams (½ c + 2 tbsp) whole wheat flour
100 grams (7 tbsp) unsalted butter, firm but not fridge-cold, cubed
Large pinch of salt
2 tablespoons water

Filling
150 to 200 grams (5.25 to 7 oz) broccoli florets

7 tablespoons whole milk
½ cup + 2 tablespoons half-and-half
3 large eggs
150 grams (5.25 oz) Gorgonzola
50 grams (7 tbsp) coarsely chopped walnuts
Salt and black pepper

9- to 10½-inch tart pan

📷 page 242

1   First make the pastry. In a large bowl, combine the flours, then rub in the butter until fully combined. Stir in the salt, followed by the water, using a cutting motion to distribute the water until all of the flour comes together in small clumps (see page 235 for more details). Add a few more drops of water if necessary. Press the pastry into a ball, flatten it slightly, then wrap in plastic wrap and chill for at least 30 minutes.

2   Once chilled, roll out the pastry into a circle large enough to line the bottom and sides of the pan. Because of the proportion of bran-rich, whole wheat flour in this dough, it's more crumbly than a standard white flour pastry. Roll it out on a sheet of lightly floured parchment paper, and don't fret if it cracks or breaks as you slide it into the pan; just use scraps to patch up any holes and prevent the filling

from leaking. Chill the pastry in the fridge for 30 minutes, or the freezer for 15 minutes, and preheat the oven to 400°F.

3   Blind bake (see page 234 for more information): line the chilled pastry shell with parchment paper, then fill with pie weights, dried beans, or uncooked rice and bake for 15 minutes. Remove the parchment paper and weights and return the pastry to the oven, uncovered, to cook for another 5 minutes or so, until sandy and firm.

4   Meanwhile, prepare the filling. Boil or steam the broccoli florets for a few minutes — just long enough to rid them of their crispness while leaving them firm. Drain and let cool slightly.

5   Whisk together the milk, half-and-half, and eggs, then crumble in the Gorgonzola. Stir in the walnuts and season with salt and pepper. Cut any large pieces of broccoli into more manageable chunks, then arrange the broccoli over the bottom of the cooked pastry shell. Pour in the milk mixture (you may not need all of it depending on the size of your pan).

6   Decrease the oven temperature to 350°F and bake for about 30 minutes, until set and barely firm to the touch. Let to cool in the pan on a wire rack for at least 15 minutes before serving.

BUTTERNUT SQUASH & MOZZARELLA TARTLETS WITH HERB PASTRY

It's not difficult to make pastry interesting. A scattering of herbs, a spoonful of mustard powder, some ground chiles, or perhaps even a fistful of Parmesan is all it takes to elevate a pastry shell from a cursory vessel to a feature in its own right. The pastry for these tartlets has fresh herbs in the dough, but for a stronger flavor you could use dried herbs instead, decreasing the amount by half.

Makes 8 individual tartlets, or 1 large tart

Pastry
125 grams (½ c + 1 tbsp) unsalted butter, firm but not fridge-cold, cubed
250 grams (2 c) all-purpose flour
¼ teaspoon salt
2 tablespoons finely chopped fresh oregano or sage
3 tablespoons cold water

Filling
1 medium butternut squash, peeled and cut into medium-sized chunks
2 cloves garlic, unpeeled
3 tablespoons coarsely chopped fresh oregano or sage
¼ teaspoon ground chiles
2 tablespoons olive oil
250 grams (8.75 oz) mozzarella
50 grams (½ c) sliced almonds, plus extra for scattering

8 (4- to 5-inch) tart pans, or one 8- to 9-inch round cake, pie, or tart pan

📷 page 245

1   Preheat the oven to 400°F.

2   First make the pastry. In a large bowl, rub the butter into the flour until completely integrated, with no chunks of butter remaining. Stir in the salt and 2 tablespoons of oregano, then add the water, cutting it in with a small knife until all of the flour has been moistened, and begins to come together in clumps (see page 235 for more information on making short-crust pastry). If lots of dry flour remains, add a little extra water, a few drops at a time. Take care not to use more water than is absolutely necessary; too much will leave the dough sticky, and the crust tough once baked. Press the clumps together to form one large disk of pastry, wrap it in plastic wrap, and chill in the fridge for at least 30 minutes (although it can be rested for up to a couple of days as long as it's tightly wrapped).

3   Meanwhile, make the filling. Combine the butternut squash, garlic, oregano, and ground chiles in a roasting pan. Drizzle with the olive oil and toss until evenly coated. Bake for about 30 minutes, until the squash is tender. (If your oven takes a while to preheat, leave it on after roasting the squash. If it heats up quickly, however, save energy by turning it off until you've finished preparing the filling and the pastry shells.)

4   Squeeze the cooked garlic cloves between your thumb and index finger to pop the pulp out from their skins, then mash the garlic with the squash and oregano in a large bowl. Once the mixture is reasonably smooth, roughly tear three-quarters of the mozzarella into pieces and add to the squash, along with the almonds. Stir to roughly combine, then set aside to cool while you prepare the pastry shells.

5   If using small tart pans, roll out the pastry until it's a little more than ⅛ inch thick, then use a pastry cutter to cut 8 circles — at least 1¼ inches wider than the diameters of the pans. If you can't get 8 circles from the pastry, reroll the scraps and cut the remaining circles from this. Don't reroll a second time, however; the pastry may become tough if handled too much, and it will shrink when baked. If using a single, large pan, just roll out the pastry until it's large enough to line the bottom and sides of the pan, but no thicker than just shy of ¼ inch. (If you have any excess pastry, you could try cutting it into fingers, scattering grated Cheddar or crumbled mozzarella over it, and baking for 15 minutes for an easy nibble.)

6   Chill the pastry in the fridge for 30 minutes, or in the freezer for about 15 minutes. Preheat the oven to 400°F. Fill the chilled pastry with the squash mixture, top with the remaining mozzarella (again, torn into pieces) and a scattering of sliced almonds, and bake for 25 to 30 minutes for small tarts or 35 to 40 minutes for a single, large tart, until the cheese is bubbling and golden.

HOT WATER–CRUST PASTRY

Robust and traditionally lard based, hot water–crust pastry is the sort used for pork pies. It's a no-nonsense dough that will neatly overturn everything you thought you knew about pastry making. Oblivious to standard pastry etiquette, it calls for boiling water and melted fat, prefers to be kept warm, and is all the happier for being handled. It couldn't be less like the fragile, standoffishly cold pastry dough we've met so far. It doesn't bake to quite the same crispness as short-crust pastry, but it is far sturdier and easier to work with, which is why it's so well suited to heavy-duty picnic pies.

Because it can be held and handled, hot water pastry is a good dough to start with if you're not yet confident about making pastry. Have the filling more or less ready before you start on the pastry, though. You'll need to roll and shape the dough while it's still supple; if it cools too much, it will become dry and stiff. Although usually made with lard, hot water–crust pastry can be made with butter, too. The pork pie below uses a little butter for flavor's sake (the lard itself, although nicely savory, isn't particularly flavorful), while the Cauliflower Gruyère Pasties (page 248) use an all-butter, vegetarian version.

SPICED PORK PIE

A good pork pie is hard to find. There's something quite Sweeney Todd about the ones in the supermarkets: tough pastry, salty jelly, and a sad block of (ostensibly) pork, gray and bland. Unless you're lucky enough to live in Melton Mowbray, in Leicestershire, you're probably better off making your own. You'll know exactly what's gone into it, and it's really not difficult to make. You can forget about the gelatinous gunk, too. It's there to fill the cavity between the meat (which shrinks during cooking) and the pastry, and to keep the meat moist, but as long as you're not planning to send the slices much further than the dinner table or the lunch box, there's no need for it.

This is a reasonably shallow pie compared to the typical tall wedges of pork pie, but I think that the smaller slices are a welcome relief when the filling is so meaty, spiced, and rich.

Makes 1 large pie, serving 8 to 10

Pastry
75 grams (⅓ c) unsalted butter, firm but not fridge-cold, cubed
300 grams (2⅓ c) all-purpose flour
¼ teaspoon salt
½ teaspoon smoked paprika
½ cup + 1 tablespoon water
75 grams (6 tablespoons) lard

Filling
400 grams (14 oz) pork shoulder, finely diced
150 grams (5.25 oz) unsmoked back bacon or lean bacon, diced
2 teaspoons smoked paprika
½ teaspoon cayenne pepper
Salt (optional)

1 egg, lightly beaten with a pinch of salt, for glazing

8-inch round springform or loose-bottomed cake pan

1   Preheat the oven to 400°F, then make the pastry. In a large bowl, rub the butter into the flour using your fingertips, until the mixture resembles breadcrumbs. Stir in the salt and paprika. In a small pan, heat the water and lard over low heat until the water is steaming and the lard has melted. (I'm not a fan of the smell of melted lard, so I keep the pan at arm's length at this point.) Pour the hot liquid over the flour mixture and stir to combine. Use your hands to bring the pastry together into a ball, then knead just a couple of times under the heel of your palm to help strengthen it. Let cool, uncovered, at room temperature.

2   Meanwhile, make the filling. In another large bowl, thoroughly mix the pork shoulder, bacon, paprika, and cayenne. The bacon should impart sufficient saltiness, but if you're in any doubt about the seasoning, fry a small ball of the filling for a few minutes and then taste it. Adjust the seasoning in the remaining mixture as needed.

3   Check the pastry — it needs to feel just cool to the touch. The temperature of the pastry is important in order to neatly line the tin: warm pastry will be limp, greasy, and soft; cold pastry will harden and crack. Keep an eye on it, and as soon as it's cool and firm enough to be rolled and molded without collapsing or sticking, line the pan. Working on a piece of lightly floured parchment paper, roll out two-thirds of the dough into a circle large enough to line the bottom and sides of the pan. Slide the dough into the pan and use your fingers to press it neatly into the corners and up the sides. Don't be shy about handling the pastry; this is a rare instance where you can hold, reroll, and press the pastry with impunity.

4   Firmly pack the filling into the lined pan. Roll out the remaining one-third of pastry on a lightly floured surface to make a circle 8 inches in diameter, then transfer to the top of the pie. Press the edges of the sides and the top together to seal. Make a hole in the top with a small knife to allow steam to escape during baking. Brush the top with the beaten egg and bake for 15 minutes. Then decrease the temperature to 350°F and bake for 45 to 60 minutes longer. When done, the pie should be a rich golden brown, with the filling bubbling merrily through the hole on top.

5   Let cool completely in the pan on a wire rack. If you try to serve this while it's still warm, it'll fall apart and leak its paprika-stained juices across the plate; you need to wait until it's cooled and set. Once cool, refrigerate until ready to serve.

CAULIFLOWER GRUYÈRE PASTIES

Cauliflower gets bad press, but it's a far more exciting ingredient than it gets credit for. It's particularly good when baked, developing a nutty, toasted flavor and golden-brown color — a far cry from the anemic, sulfurous slop that it becomes when unsympathetically boiled. It's a good match for musky, full-bodied Gruyère.

These pasties are vegetarian, eschewing the standard lard-based hot water–crust pastry in favor of an all-butter version.

Makes 8
Filling
1 cauliflower, broken into florets
3 cloves garlic, unpeeled
1 red onion, peeled and quartered
2 tablespoons olive oil
1 large egg
150 grams (5.25 oz) Gruyère, grated
  (about 1½ c)
Salt and black pepper

Pastry
150 grams (⅔ c) unsalted butter, firm
  but not fridge-cold, cubed
250 grams (2 c) all-purpose flour
Large pinch of salt
3 tablespoons + 2 teaspoons boiling water

1 large egg, lightly beaten with a pinch
  of salt, for sealing and glazing

📷 page 249

1　Preheat the oven to 400°F and line a large baking sheet with parchment paper.

2　First, make the filling. In a roasting pan, toss the cauliflower, garlic, red onion, and oil together. Roast for about 25 minutes, until patches of brown are creeping across the cauliflower and the garlic is soft and aromatic. Let cool briefly.

3　Coarsely chop the cauliflower florets into quarters. Pull apart the onion segments to create thin crescents. Remove the garlic cloves, squeeze the soft insides from the skins into a separate bowl and mash them. Stir in the egg, then add the cheese, cauliflower, and onion. Toss well to combine. Season with salt and pepper to taste.

4　To make the pastry, combine the butter, flour, and salt in a large bowl, and rub the butter into the flour until no visible pieces of butter remain. Pour in the boiling water and stir to combine, then use your hands to gather the mixture together. It should feel soft, pliable, and slightly greasy. Knead very lightly for a few seconds, then let cool, uncovered in its bowl, at room temperature. It's ready when no longer warm to the touch and stiff enough to be rolled and shaped without sticking or collapsing.

5　Divide the dough into 8 pieces. On a floured work surface, roll out one of the pieces into a circle about 6 inches in diameter. Place 1 to 2 heaping tablespoons of the filling onto one half of the circle, leaving a border of about ⅜ inch. Brush the edge of the circle with a little of the beaten egg to help seal the seam, then fold the other half over the top to create a semicircular parcel. Glaze the top with more egg wash, then set aside on the lined baking sheet while you prepare the remaining pasties.

6　When you have made all 8 pasties, bake for 25 minutes, until golden, fragrant, and firm. These are best served while they're still warm, but they're good cold, too — the stuff that midnight feasts are made of.

QUICK PUFF PASTRY

Real puff pastry — triple-folded six times, layered with an entire sheet of flattened butter — is an incredible thing, but not possible unless you have the luxury of spare time. Here's a quicker alternative using chunks of butter and fewer folds to give a marginally less decadent but far less time-consuming pastry. If you want to challenge yourself, the full puff pastry recipe can be found on page 291, but this easy version is more than adequate for typical pies, especially those rougher, pointedly rustic ones, such as the Chicken, Pale Ale & Chicory Pie (page 252). It's still not as quick to make as short crust and can't compete with the instant appeal of the ready-made stuff, but although it takes around 1½ hours to prepare, only a tiny fraction of that is hands-on. Most of the preparation time is spent chilling out — for both you and the pastry.

QUICK PUFF PASTRY DOUGH

The most important thing here is to keep the butter cold and in large chunks. It's these chunks that, as they're rolled out and folded along with the dough, will form layers of butter in the pastry. When the pastry then heats in the oven, the butter will melt and the steam will force the pastry layers apart. The pastry thus rises and develops hundreds of flaky layers.

You won't need all of this pastry for the following recipes, but it does keep well — either in the fridge for a day or two, or in the freezer for a couple of weeks — so it's useful to set some aside, well wrapped in plastic wrap, ready for another day.

Makes enough to cover 2 to 3 large pies
250 grams (2 c) all-purpose flour
Generous pinch of salt

180 grams (¾ c + 1 tbsp) unsalted butter, chilled, in ⅜-inch cubes
8½ tablespoons ice-cold water

1   Combine the flour and salt in a large bowl. Add the cubes of butter and toss together. If you're used to making short-crust pastry, check yourself now — this is usually the point at which I absentmindedly rub the butter into the flour, but it's important not to do this. Leave the chunks of butter as they are, coated in flour.

2   Add the water and quickly but lightly mix in using your hands. The dough will look a mess, but it's meant to look that way: a shaggy mass of flour dotted with cubes of butter. As soon as all of the water has been incorporated, gather the dough into a ball. It should hold its shape.

3   For this step, try to work quite quickly so that the pastry doesn't warm. Lightly flour a work surface and roll out the dough to form a rectangle measuring about 6 by 18 inches, approximately three times as long as it is wide, with a short side facing you. Fold the top third down, then the bottom third up, as if folding a letter. Rotate the dough 90 degrees so that the folds now run down the dough's length, rather than across its width. Roll out to a large rectangle, again about three times as long as it is wide. Fold the top third down, then the bottom third up. You've just completed two "turns" of the dough. Wrap it in plastic wrap and chill for at least 30 minutes.

4   Unwrap the chilled dough and complete another two "turns" — rotating 90 degrees, rolling out, and folding. It's important to remember to rotate each time so that each successive roll and fold is perpendicular to the preceding one, thus building up crisscrossing layers. The dough has now had four turns. Wrap it again and chill in the fridge for another 30 minutes.

5   The pastry is now ready to be used in one of the recipes that follow. Just make sure that you keep it cool until the moment that it enters the oven. This includes keeping it away from hot fillings (if they need to be cooked before baking, give them a while to cool before laying the pastry on top) and not spending too long rolling and shaping it. Puff pastry should always enter an oven that's quite hot — at least 400°F — to give it the blast of heat it needs to rise. You can reduce the temperature midway through baking, but it needs to start out hot.

Variation
Using all whole wheat flour in puff pastry can be hit-and-miss, but if you blend 100 grams (¾ c + 1 tbsp) of whole wheat flour with 150 grams (1 c + 3 tbsp) all-purpose flour, you'll be left with a pastry that's still flaky, but has a rounded, savory flavor. Whether the salutary benefits of whole wheat flour still stand when layered with butter is debatable, but it gives the illusion of being healthier, at least.

CHICKEN, PALE ALE & CHICORY PIE

There's no such thing as an "ultimate" chicken pie, and you should be wary of anyone who claims to have the recipe for one. There are chicken pies for lazy days, the meat plucked from the bones of yesterday's roast, hearty ones packed with mushrooms, and more delicate versions with tender asparagus spears. There are as many chicken pies as there are dinners to be had, and with that in mind I present this one not as formula, dictum, or brag, but as a humble suggestion — and my personal favorite.

Makes 1 large pie, serving 6
½ recipe of Quick Puff Pastry Dough
   (page 251)

Filling
2 tablespoons butter
2 large onions, thinly sliced
150 grams (5.25 oz) unsmoked back
   bacon or lean bacon, diced
1 cup + 1 tablespoon pale ale
1 cup + 1 tablespoon chicken or
   vegetable stock, plus extra as needed

800 to 900 grams (1.75 to 2 lb) skinless
   chicken legs and/or thighs
3 tablespoons all-purpose flour
½ cup + 2 tablespoons heavy cream
Salt and black pepper
Leaves from 2 heads of chicory

1 large egg, lightly beaten with a pinch
   of salt, for glazing (optional)

**Large pie pan, 10 to 11 inches in
   diameter at its rim**

📷 page 253

1   Having prepared the puff pastry as described on page 251, put it in the fridge to chill while you prepare the filling. Over low heat, melt the butter in a large pan, then fry the onions until they begin to soften. Add the bacon, increase the heat to

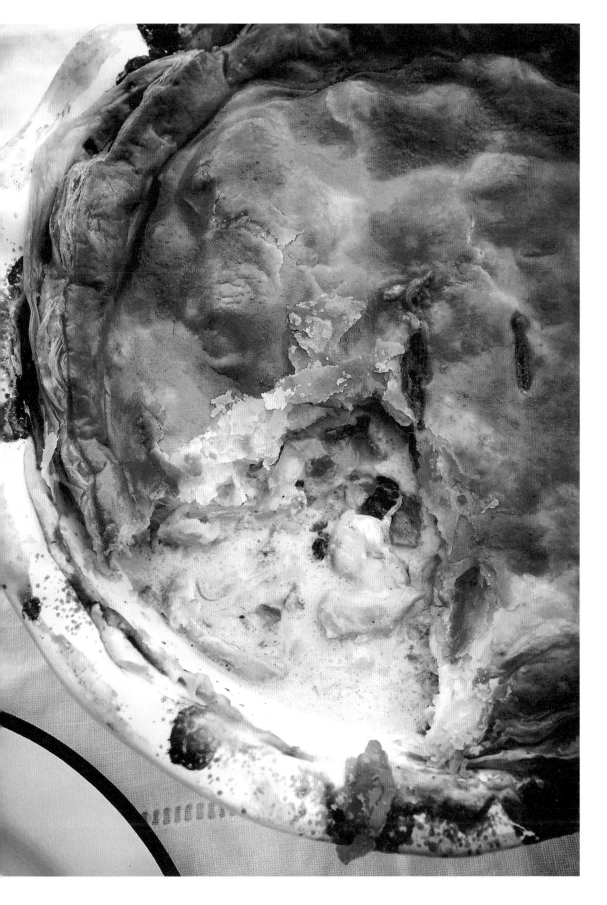

medium and cook for 2 to 3 minutes longer. Add the ale, stock, and chicken (still on the bone). The chicken needs to be just covered by the liquid, so top up with extra stock if necessary. Bring to a simmer, then turn the heat down low enough that the surface of the liquid is just quivering, with only the occasional bubble breaking through. Poach the chicken for 30 minutes this way.

2   After 30 minutes, use a slotted spoon to transfer the chicken to a large cutting board. When cool enough to handle, remove the meat from the bones and set aside.

3   Add the flour to the stock mixture and whisk until smooth. Increase the heat slightly and simmer, stirring, for a couple of minutes to thicken the sauce. Remove from the heat, stir in the cream, and season with salt and pepper to taste.

4   Transfer the chicken meat to the pie pan, add the whole chicory leaves, and toss to combine (the chicory will wilt as the pie cooks). Pour in the sauce — you may not need all of it depending on the size of your pan, but do be generous. Let cool slightly while you preheat the oven to 400°F.

5   Once the oven is hot and the filling has cooled a little (if the pastry goes straight onto the hot filling, the butter will melt and it will lack the crucial "puff"), roll out the pastry into a circle large enough to cover the pie; it should be a little over ⅛ inch thick. Lay it gently over the filling, tucking it down slightly along the sides. Use a sharp knife to poke a hole or score a couple of incisions into the pastry to allow steam to escape during baking. Glaze the top with the egg wash if you want the pie to shine. Bake for 25 to 30 minutes, until the pastry is proudly puffed and flaky and the filling is piping hot. Serve as is only right: with mashed potatoes and tender green beans.

FISH PIE

Dinnertime would grow tiresome if every meal was an exercise in innovation. Here's a pie that salutes all things comforting, homely, and simple. And in the spirit of back-to-basics food, don't feel restricted by the recipe: if you have only frozen fish fillets, use those; if the fish market near you has some good salmon or shrimp available, use that. The only nonnegotiable point here is that you should look out for sustainably sourced fish and steer clear of overfished species, such as cod.

Makes 1 large pie, serving 6
½ recipe of Quick Puff Pastry Dough
   (page 251)

Filling
1½ cups + 3 tablespoons whole milk
½ large onion, peeled but uncut
200 to 250 grams (7 to 8.75 oz) smoked
   fish, such as haddock

300 grams (10.5 oz) white fish, such as
   pollock
2 tablespoons butter
2 tablespoons all-purpose flour
Salt and white pepper
2 to 3 tablespoons fresh tarragon
   leaves, chopped
200 grams (7 oz) prawns, cooked and
   peeled

6 by 9-inch baking pan

1 Having prepared the puff pastry as described on page 251, put it in the fridge to chill while you prepare the filling. In a large pan, warm the milk with the onion until it comes to a simmer, then remove from the heat and let steep for a few minutes while you prepare the fish. Chop both the smoked fish and white fish into large chunks, removing any skin or errant bones as you go. Remove the onion from the milk and discard, then put the fish in the pan. Return the pan to low heat and poach (just shy of a simmer) for 5 minutes, during which time the flavor of the fish should infuse the milk.

2 Drain the fish, collecting the milk in another bowl to be used in the sauce. In another pan, melt the butter over low heat, then whisk in the flour. Let the butter and flour mixture (or roux) sizzle for a minute or two, stirring constantly, to cook out the taste of the flour. Now, very gradually, add the reserved hot milk while whisking continuously. As long as you add the liquid slowly enough and beat well, you should be left with a smooth sauce. Cook for a few minutes, stirring constantly, until it has thickened to a custard-like consistency. Season with salt and white pepper to taste, although with the amount of fish in here, it really shouldn't need much salt. I'd steer clear of black pepper in a dish as creamily mild as this.

3 Put the poached fish into the baking dish, add the tarragon and prawns, and toss throughly with your hands. Pour in the sauce and jiggle the dish lightly to help settle the mixture. Let cool slightly while you preheat the oven to 400°F.

4 Roll out the pastry on a cool, lightly floured surface until it's big enough to cover the pie and a little over ⅛ inch thick. Drape it on top of the filling, trim to fit, and poke a couple of holes in the top to allow steam to escape. Bake for 25 minutes, until the pastry is well risen and the filling bubbling.

Variation
As devoted as I am to all things pastry-crusted, I have to admit that fish pie is incredible the traditional way, too: topped with mounds of buttery mashed potatoes and, perhaps sacrilegiously, some grated Cheddar cheese.

BANANA THYME TART

This was initially an improvised dessert scraped together from the leftovers in the fridge and half a dozen old bananas, but it has since become one of the recipes of which I am most proud. If you're in any doubt about the pairing of fruit and herb, just take a good sniff of ripe banana and a sprig of thyme side by side. The heady, Mediterranean aromatics of thyme sit as naturally with creamy banana as if they were made for one another. Like any great romance worth its salt, it's a perfectly odd, oddly perfect couple. But whatever you do, don't use dried thyme, which will overpower even the ripest bananas.

Makes 1 tart, serving 4 generously
½ recipe of Quick Puff Pastry Dough
   (page 251)
5 to 6 large, ripe but not overripe
   bananas

4 to 5 tablespoons Demerara sugar
Leaves from 2 sprigs of thyme
   (about 1 tablespoon)

📷 page 256

1   Having prepared the puff pastry as described on page 251, put it in the fridge to chill. Preheat the oven to 425°F and line a large baking sheet with parchment paper.

2   Cut the bananas into chunky slices about ¾ inch thick. In a large bowl, toss the bananas with the sugar and thyme until encrusted with sugar crystals and little thyme leaves.

3   Roll the pastry into a rectangle measuring about 8 by 10 inches and lay it on the lined baking sheet. Arrange the coated banana slices all over the pastry, leaving about a ¾-inch border around the edges. Bake for 20 to 25 minutes, until caramelized patches begin to creep across the tops of the bananas and the pastry is flaky and crisp. Serve warm, with vanilla ice cream (preferably homemade; page 312) melting over the lot and, better still, drizzled with Chocolate Sauce (page 322).

SWEET SHORT-CRUST PASTRY

The sweet pies and tarts that follow all use a slightly enriched short-crust pastry. Eggs often take the place of water, giving the dough a golden glow. A spoonful of sugar helps to sweeten the pastry and gives it a deeper color once baked. This pastry behaves in much the same way as the plainer short-crust pastry earlier in the chapter, so refer to pages 235 through 237 if you're unsure how best to handle the dough. The only difference you might find is that this variation is slightly more crumbly when rolling.

PEAR, SESAME & CHOCOLATE TART

For those bored with traditional almond frangipane, here's a version made with ground sesame seeds instead. Despite their diminutive size, sesame seeds really pack a flavor punch, and their nuttiness sits well with the sweet pear and dark chocolate.

Makes 1 large tart, serving 6 to 8
90 grams (6 tbsp + 1 tsp) unsalted butter, firm but not fridge-cold, cubed
175 grams (1⅓ c + 1 tbsp) all-purpose flour
Pinch of salt
1 tablespoon superfine sugar
1 tablespoon + 1 teaspoon water

Filling
100 grams (⅔ c) sesame seeds
100 grams (7 tbsp) unsalted butter, softened
100 grams (½ c) light brown sugar
1½ teaspoons vanilla extract

¼ teaspoon almond extract
Zest of 1 lemon
Large pinch of salt
1 large egg
60 grams (½ c) all-purpose flour
1 teaspoon baking powder

Topping
2 ripe firm pears (such as Bosc or Comice)
50 grams (1.75 oz) dark chocolate

6 by 9-inch rectangular cake pan, or 8-inch round cake or pie pan

📷 page 258

1   Preheat the oven to 400°F. If your pan isn't loose-bottomed, line it with parchment paper to help with unmolding later.

2   In a large bowl, rub the 90 grams (6 tbsp + 1 tsp) butter into the flour until the mixture resembles breadcrumbs, then stir in the salt and superfine sugar. Add the water and use a butter knife to cut it into the flour until it comes together in small clumps. If there's still dry flour left, gradually add a few more drops of water. The pastry should hold together in a ball when pressed between your hands. Wrap it tightly in plastic wrap and chill in the fridge for at least 30 minutes.

3   Meanwhile, make the filling. On a baking sheet or small roasting pan, toast the sesame seeds for 12 to 15 minutes, until they're a couple of shades darker — a rich, golden color. Let cool, but don't turn off the oven. Once cooled, grind the seeds to a coarse powder in a coffee grinder or food processor. If you don't have either but do have plenty of patience, use a mortar and pestle instead.

4   In a large bowl, beat the butter and brown sugar together until completely smooth, then stir in the vanilla and almond extracts, lemon zest, and salt. Stir in the ground sesame seeds and the egg. In a separate bowl, combine the flour and baking powder, then add to the sesame seed mixture and stir until smooth.

5   On a lightly floured surface, roll out the pastry to a rectangle (or circle, depending on your pan) no thicker than a scant ¼ inch, then carefully transfer to the pan. Press gently into the corners and up the sides, then trim off any excess. Chill in the fridge for 30 minutes or in the freezer for 15 minutes.

6   While the pastry chills, prepare the topping. Peel and core the pears and slice them into even segments, each wedge about ⅜ inch thick at its widest point. Spoon the sesame filling into the pastry shell and arrange the pears on top however you please, perhaps in lines, concentric circles, or zigzags. Bake for 10 minutes, then turn the temperature down to 350°F and bake for 20 to 30 minutes longer. The cooked tart should feel just firm to the touch in the middle. Let cool in the pan on a wire rack.

7   Melt the chocolate either in the microwave or in a small, heatproof bowl suspended over a pan of simmering water. Drizzle the chocolate over the cooled tart and let set before serving. This is even better with an orange zest–flecked ice cream.

CHERRY PIE

This is *Twin Peaks* on a plate. Crisp golden pastry and sour-sweet crimson cherries. Enjoy with a "damn fine" cup of black coffee.

Despite using primarily sweet cherries, what really makes this pie exciting is the comparatively small quantity of sour cherries, preferably Morello cherries, mixed into the filling. You're more likely to find Morello cherries in a jar or dried than fresh; just use whichever type you can get your hands on.

I'll admit that this isn't a cheap fruit pie — it's far from the frugal sort cobbled together from a few windfall apples and a sheet of premade pastry. To make it cheaper you can use frozen cherries, decrease the amount of sour cherries, or even swap in a couple of apples to bulk out the filling.

Makes 1 large pie, serving 8 generously

Pastry
400 grams (3 c + 3 tbsp) all-purpose flour
200 grams (¾ c + 2 tbsp) unsalted butter, firm but not fridge-cold, cubed
½ teaspoon salt
3 tablespoons superfine sugar
¼ cup cold water

Filling
500 to 600 grams (3½ to 4¼ c) cherries, frozen or fresh, pitted
Juice of 1½ lemons
3 tablespoons cornstarch

¼ teaspoon almond extract
75 grams superfine sugar (⅓ c) or granulated sugar (6 tbsp)
200 grams (7 oz) sour cherries (preferably Morello), either dried or from a jar

1 large egg beaten with 1 tablespoon of milk, for glazing

Large pie pan, 10 to 11 inches in diameter at its rim

📷 page 261

1   First, make the pastry. Measure the flour into a large bowl, then use your fingertips
    to rub the cubes of butter into it until completely combined. The mixture should
    resemble fine breadcrumbs. Stir in the salt and sugar, then drizzle in the water.
    Use a butter knife to cut through the mixture repeatedly (as opposed to stirring)
    to break up any wet lumps of flour and evenly distribute the moisture. It should
    come together into small clumps before long. If it doesn't, add a splash more
    water. Quickly but firmly press the mixture together with your hands, form it into a
    flattish disk, and wrap it tightly in plastic wrap. Refrigerate for at least 30 minutes.

2   To make the filling, put the sweet cherries in a medium-sized pan over low heat (if using frozen cherries, there's no need to thaw them first). Cook gently until the cherries begin to release their juices, then continue to cook for a couple more minutes, stirring all the while.

3   Add the lemon juice and cornstarch to the now-juicy cherries. Cook for a few minutes, until the juices begin to thicken. As soon as the juices have the consistency of heavy cream, remove from the heat. Stir in the almond extract, sugar, and sour cherries, then set aside to cool.

4   Divide the chilled pastry into two pieces, one 400 grams (14 oz) and the other about 300 grams (10.5 oz). Return the smaller piece to the fridge, again wrapped in plastic wrap. Roll out the larger piece into a circle big enough to line the bottom and sides of the pan (doing this on a lightly floured sheet of parchment paper will make it easier to transfer to the pan), then line the pan with the pastry and chill it for 30 minutes. Meanwhile, preheat the oven to 400°F.

5   Once the pastry shell is chilled and the filling has cooled, spoon the filling into the shell. Roll out the smaller piece of pastry into a circle big enough to cover the pie. Lay the crust on top of the filling. Brush the edges with a little milk, then press the edges together to seal. You could crimp the edges with a fork, but it's not essential.

6   Brush the top of the pastry with the egg and milk glaze, make a couple of incisions to allow steam to escape, and bake for 20 minutes. Decrease the temperature to 350°F and cook for 25 minutes longer.

Variations

Fruit pie will take whatever you throw at it. Below is a recipe for a traditional apple pie, to which you could add a handful of blackberries, raspberries, dried currants, or even grated marzipan. The only thing to bear in mind when playing around with fruit pie recipes is how wet the filling will be. Cherries risk cooking down to mush if no cornstarch is used to thicken the mixture, whereas apples are far drier but still benefit from a few tablespoons of flour to soak up any juices.

1 recipe of the pastry from the
    Cherry Pie (page 260)
6 Golden Delicious or Braeburn apples
100 grams (7 tbsp) superfine sugar

½ teaspoon ground cinnamon
3 tablespoons all-purpose flour
Juice of ½ lemon

Prepare, chill, and shape the pastry as in steps 1 and 4, above. Peel, core, and slice the apples. Toss them with the sugar, cinnamon, and flour, then stir in the lemon juice. Fill, seal, glaze, and bake as in steps 5 and 6, above.

LEMON & BASIL TART

Although lemon basil, with its distinctive citrus scent, would make sense in this lemon tart, I prefer the more common sweet basil. Because it's so deeply perfumed, just a few leaves are all that's needed to accent the sharpness of the lemon with notes of clove and spice. It's not always easy to balance two such robust flavors, but mellowed by the cream and sugar, they work beautifully here. Serve with perfectly ripe strawberries.

Serves 8

Pastry

175 grams (1⅓ c + 1 tbsp) all-purpose flour

90 grams (6 tbsp + 1 tsp) unsalted butter, firm but not fridge-cold, cubed

Pinch of salt

1 tablespoon superfine sugar

1 large egg yolk

1 tablespoon milk

Filling

¾ cup + 1½ tablespoons heavy cream

Small handful of fresh basil leaves

4 large eggs

125 grams (½ c + 1 tbsp) superfine sugar

Zest and juice of 5 small lemons (you'll need 8½ tbsp of lemon juice)

8- to 9-inch round tart or cake pan

1　First, make the pastry. In a large bowl, rub the flour and butter together with your fingertips until the mixture resembles fine breadcrumbs, then stir in the salt and sugar. In a small bowl, beat the egg yolk with the milk, then add this gradually to the flour mixture. Cut the liquid into the dry ingredients using a small knife, bringing the mixture together in small clumps. Once there's no dry flour left, press the dough together into a flat disk, then wrap it in plastic wrap and refrigerate for 30 minutes.

2　Meanwhile, start making the filling. Put the cream and whole basil leaves in a small pan over medium heat. As soon as the cream comes to a gentle boil, remove from the heat and set aside to cool and infuse.

3　Once the pastry has chilled, roll it out on a floured surface to make a circle large enough to line the bottom and sides of your pan; it should be between ⅛ inch and just shy of ¼ inch thick. Lower the pastry gently into the pan and, taking care not to stretch it, press it into the corners and against the sides. Trim off any excess and chill the pastry shell for 30 minutes in the fridge, or 15 minutes in the freezer. Meanwhile, preheat the oven to 400°F.

4　Line the chilled pastry shell with parchment paper, fill it with a layer of pie weights or dried beans, and blind bake (see page 234) for 15 minutes. Remove the parchment paper and weights and bake for 5 minutes longer, to crisp it up. Remove from the oven and decrease the temperature to 300°F.

5　To finish making the filling and bake the pie, lightly whisk the eggs in a large bowl, then beat in the sugar. Strain the basil-infused cream into the bowl and discard the basil leaves. Add the lemon zest and juice and whisk gently to combine. Pour this into the baked pastry shell and bake for about 25 to 30 minutes, until the edges are set but, when the tart is lightly shaken, the center still wobbles slightly. If you wait until it's set in the center, you'll have cooked the tart too long, and the filling will shrink and crack as it cools. Let cool on a wire rack before serving. Although it's best to store this in the fridge, the flavors will be brightest at room temperature, so factor in some time for it to warm slightly if preparing the tart in advance.

ROSEMARY

Rosemary is an herb replete with romance and symbolism thanks to its heady scent, Mediterranean roots, and even the etymology of its name (it's said that the Virgin Mary herself turned the flowers blue). But even great love can turn bitter, and rosemary is no exception. Used with a heavy hand, it becomes astringent. When chopped or bruised, its pungent oil is released and it tends to overpower. The spiky leaves of a rosemary sprig look very similar to pine needles, and if not cooked with care they'll end up tasting like pine, too — forest floor, Christmas tree, toilet cleaner.

It's best to let rosemary's flavor permeate gradually. The Rosemary Pecan Pie recipe that follows works by this principle, steeping the rosemary in hot syrup to gently draw out its flavor. And because it is so aromatic, rosemary works well even in the dry heat of the oven: I've yet to find a better use for it than just studding little sprigs into the doughy dimples of a focaccia.

ROSEMARY PECAN PIE

The result of a childhood spent in thrall to US television was that those strange, distinctly American confections — key lime pie, pecan pie, peach cobbler, pumpkin pie — took on a mythical status in my mind. These fantastical pies conjured up fantasies of suburban bliss, shopping malls, yellow school buses, and, crucially, huge portions. Even watching the film *American Pie* couldn't dispel these daydreams. In this version of pecan pie, rosemary adds a woody herbal note that complements the butteriness of the toasted pecans.

Makes 1 large pie, serving 8 to 10

Pastry
125 grams (½ c + 1tbsp) unsalted butter, firm but not fridge-cold, cubed
250 grams (2 c) all-purpose flour
2 tablespoons superfine sugar
Generous pinch of salt
1 large egg, lightly beaten

Filling
200 grams (1 c) soft dark brown sugar
7 tablespoons light corn syrup
100 grams (7 tbsp) unsalted butter
½ teaspoon vanilla extract
¼ teaspoon salt
3 sprigs of rosemary
3 large eggs
200 grams (1¾ c) pecan halves

Large pie or tart pan, 10 to 11 inches in diameter at its rim

📷 page 266

1   First, make the pastry. In a large bowl, rub the butter into the flour using your fingertips until no large, visible pieces of butter remain. Use swift motions and lift the flour and butter up from the bowl as you crumb them together so that the heat of your hands doesn't soften the butter. Stir in the sugar and salt. Pour in the beaten egg, a little at a time (you might not need all of it). Using a butter knife to cut through the mixture, combine the wet and dry ingredients. You'll notice the mixture beginning to come together in clumps. Once it's mixed, quickly and lightly use your hands to press the dough into a ball. Flatten slightly, wrap in plastic wrap, and let chill for 30 minutes or so.

2   Preheat the oven to 350°F. To make the filling, combine the brown sugar, corn syrup, butter, vanilla extract, and salt in a pan over low heat. Add 2 of the rosemary sprigs and bring to a very gentle boil. Simmer for 2 minutes, then remove from the heat and let cool. After 10 minutes, pull out the rosemary sprigs, beat in the eggs, and let cool completely.

3   Spread the pecans on a baking sheet in a single layer and bake for about 10 minutes (check them after 6 or 7 minutes). Set aside to cool and leave the oven on.

4   Once the pastry is chilled, roll it out to make a circle roughly 11 to 12 inches in diameter — large enough to line the bottom and sides of your pan, with a thickness no greater than a scant ¼ inch. It helps to roll on a piece of floured parchment paper to prevent the pastry from sticking to the work surface, and to make it easier to transfer the rolled pastry into the pan. Line the pan with the pastry, patching up any holes or cracks with scraps. (Any leftover pastry can be

rerolled, cut into shapes, and baked to make simple butter cookies.) Gently press the pastry into the sides of the pan and push it just above the rim so it stands about ⅛ inch above the rim. Chill for 30 minutes, or freeze for 15 minutes.

5   Coarsely chop the pecans, leaving a few whole to decorate the top of the pie. Stir the chopped pecans into the filling mixture, then pour into the pastry shell. Pull the needles off the remaining sprig of rosemary and sprinkle them on top, along with the whole pecans.

6   Bake for 30 to 45 minutes. The time will depend on the dimensions of your pan (wide and shallow will cook more quickly than small and deep), but you should be able to judge when it's ready by how set it feels: if, when jiggled, the pie filling ripples and sways, it needs longer; if there's barely a wobble, it's done.

STEM GINGER TART

It was on holiday in Dorset, on the ketchup-stained back page of a tattered pub menu, that I first came across stem ginger tart, and although I didn't have the appetite to try the dessert at the time, those words echoed tauntingly in my mind for the rest of the week. I had barely been home from the holiday a few hours before I took to the kitchen to finally put my craving to rest. If I was hoping for some sort of closure, I failed miserably. I've been hankering for more of this sweet, ginger-spiced tart ever since.

Makes 1 large tart, serving 8
Pastry
90 grams (6 tbsp + 1 tsp) unsalted butter, firm but not fridge-cold, cubed
175 grams (1⅓ c + 1 tbsp) all-purpose flour
Pinch of salt
1 tablespoon superfine sugar
1 large egg, lightly beaten

Filling
¾ cup light corn syrup

Zest of 2 lemons
125 grams (about 2 c) fresh breadcrumbs
2 inches fresh ginger, coarsely grated
75 grams (about ⅓ cup) finely chopped stem ginger
1 egg
2½ tablespoons dark brown sugar
¼ teaspoon salt

8- to 9-inch round springform cake pan or pie pan

📷 page 268

1   First, make the pastry. In a large bowl, rub the butter into the flour using your fingertips until the mixture resembles fine breadcrumbs. Stir in the salt and sugar. Add the beaten egg a little at a time to moisten the flour until it all comes together in small clumps (you won't need all the egg — half to three-quarters of it should suffice). Use a cutting motion through the mixture with a knife to distribute the moisture. When it's well combined, quickly but firmly press the dough into a ball, wrap it in plastic wrap, and refrigerate for at least 30 minutes.

2   Once the pastry has chilled, roll it out on a piece of lightly floured parchment paper so that it ⅛ inch to just shy of ¼ inch thick and large enough to line the

bottom and sides of your pan. Line the pan with pastry, taking care not to stretch it or handle it too long, then patch up any cracks in the dough. Refrigerate for at least 30 minutes, or freeze for 15 minutes if you're in a hurry. Meanwhile, preheat the oven to 400°F.

3   Line the chilled pastry shell with parchment paper, add a layer of pie weights or dried beans, and blind bake (see page 234) for 15 minutes. Remove the parchment paper and pie weights and bake for 5 minutes longer, until the crust feels reasonably dry and sandy.

4   While the tart shell is blind baking, prepare the filling. Combine the corn syrup, lemon zest, breadcrumbs, fresh and stem ginger, egg, sugar, and salt in a large bowl and gently stir together.

5   Once the tart shell is ready, decrease the oven temperature to 350°F and pour the filling into the crust. Bake for 40 to 50 minutes, until the filling is set and barely firm to the touch. Let cool in the pan on a wire rack for 15 minutes.

SPICED CHOCOLATE TART

This was my first ever chocolate tart, and my favorite. I used to chew on anise hard candies every day on the way home from school — small purple sweets in a tissue-thin, white paper bag. At some point I discovered bubble gum — sweet, colorful, fun — and stopped buying the faintly medicinal, unfashionable anise, but the flavor is still one I love. The fennel seeds here impart that same warm, aromatic flavor.

   With dark chocolate, there's often the temptation to brighten and to lift. Forget that. This tart uses fennel to play to the licorice notes in the chocolate, coloring its darkness with spiced warmth. The honey, too, is crucial: somehow just one tablespoon brings the whole thing into focus.

Makes 1 tart, serving 8 with small-but-rich slices

Pastry
90 grams (6 tbsp + 1 tsp) unsalted butter, firm but not fridge-cold, cubed
175 grams (1⅓ c + 1 tbsp) all-purpose flour
Pinch of salt
1 tablespoon superfine sugar
1 large egg yolk
1 tablespoon milk

Filling
6 tablespoons milk
½ cup + 2 tablespoons heavy cream

1 tablespoon fennel seeds
3 star anise
300 grams (10.5 oz) dark chocolate (70% cocoa solids), coarsely chopped
1 large egg
3½ tablespoons superfine or granulated sugar
¼ teaspoon ground chiles
1 teaspoon ground cinnamon
1 tablespoon honey

8-inch round springform or loose-bottomed cake pan

📷 page 271

1   First, make the pastry. In a large bowl, toss the butter cubes with the flour and — using only your fingertips — rub the two together until the mixture resembles

breadcrumbs and no visible chunks of butter are left. Try to work quickly and lightly, keeping the mixture cool so that the butter doesn't melt (this would leave the pastry greasy and tough). Stir in the salt and sugar. Lightly whisk the egg yolk and milk together, then add this to the dry ingredients. Use a small knife to cut through the mixture until all of the flour has been moistened. If a lot of dry flour remains, add a few more drops of milk. Once it's combined, use your hands to quickly but firmly press the pastry together into a ball. Flatten it into a disk, wrap it in plastic wrap, and refrigerate for at least 30 minutes, or as long as overnight.

2   Once the pastry has chilled, roll it out on a piece of lightly floured parchment paper. Don't go too heavy on the flour — use just enough to prevent the pastry from sticking to the surface. Roll out to a circle about 9 inches in diameter and ⅛ to a scant ¼ inch thick. Line the pan with the pastry, taking care not to stretch it but gently pressing it into the corners for sharp edges. Chill for 30 minutes, or freeze for 10 minutes. Meanwhile, preheat the oven to 400°F.

3   Scrunch up a large piece of parchment paper into a ball and then smooth it back out again (this makes it much easier to work with). Line the pastry shell with the parchment paper and fill with pie weights or dried beans. Push the beans up toward the sides a little to help prevent the steep pastry walls from slipping. Bake for 15 minutes, then remove the parchment paper and bake pie weights for 5 minutes longer.

4   While the pastry is blind baking, start preparing the filling. Combine the milk, cream, fennel seeds, and star anise and gently heat, either in a bowl in the microwave or in a small pan over low heat. Remove from the heat just before the mixture starts to boil — it should smell heavily aromatic and redolent of aniseed.

5   Put the chocolate in a bowl and strain the still-scalding cream mixture over it to remove the fennel seeds and star anise. Let it sit for just a minute, then gently stir. The chocolate should melt smoothly into the hot cream. If chunks of unmelted chocolate remain, you can heat the mixture very gently (either in the microwave or over a pan of simmering water) until it is smooth. In a separate bowl, whisk the egg together with the sugar, ground chiles, cinnamon, and honey, then fold this into the chocolate mixture.

6   Once the pastry shell is baked, decrease the temperature to 325°F. Spoon the filling into the pastry, filling it to about ⅛ inch below the rim. Bake for 20 minutes, until just set with only a slight wobble at its center. Let cool completely before serving, during which time it will firm up. Keep the tart chilled if not eating it the same day, but give it time to come back to room temperature again before eating; otherwise the filling will set too hard.

PASTRIES

THE BREAKFAST CLUB

DANISH PASTRY & CROISSANT DOUGH

CHERRY DIAMONDS • JAM PINWHEELS

CUSTARD ENVELOPES • PAIN AU CHOCOLAT

FRANZBRÖTCHEN • CROISSANTS

A BETTER LUNCH BOX

SALMON & CREAM CHEESE PARCELS

ZUCCHINI, STILTON & PECAN ROUNDS

PUFF PASTRY • FIG & WALNUT ECCLES CAKES

MARMALADE ALMOND GALETTE • MILLE-FEUILLE

BEFORE MIDNIGHT

ÉCLAIRS • DILL & MUSTARD CHOUX BITES• BAKLAVA

Here are some of the most challenging recipes in this book, but if you can muster the courage to give them a try, you'll find them the most rewarding, too. They require patience and some planning ahead, but the processes themselves are not compage licated and the finished pastries will taste all the better for the time that has gone into them. Once you've tasted homemade croissants, Danish pastries, and choux buns, you'll want to eat them all day, every day — and you can! I've divided this chapter into breakfast, lunch, and dinner pastries for those who, like me, cannot have too much of a good thing.

THE BREAKFAST CLUB

Breakfast should never be boring. There are the sensible options of porridge and muesli, the masochistic smoothies, and the meager cereal bars. At the other end of the spectrum lie hangover breakfasts thrown headlong into the frying pan, feasts of leftovers, and bacon sandwiches. And somewhere in between, for breakfasts where the aim is just pleasure — not nutrition, refueling, or belated sobering up — there are pastries. They roll leisurely onto the scene midmorning, with coffee and orange juice, to set a good day quietly in motion.

Danish pastries and croissants use laminated dough — a bread dough layered, or laminated, with fat. It's a hybrid of bread and pastry, straddling the two disciplines and yet more delicious than either of them. It has the complex flavors of bread (with even more depth, thanks to the long, cold rising periods) and the richness and flaking texture of puff pastry.

Pastries aren't quick: be prepared to set aside 6 to 7 hours from start to finish, or 4 hours if you have time to prepare the dough base the night before. The wait is well worth it, however, and only a fraction of this time is hands-on. Most of the preparation time is spent waiting for the butter to chill, the yeast to ferment, or the dough to relax. I can't pretend that these are easy recipes, but they shouldn't be unmanageable as long as you take a moment to read through the method before you get started and get to grips with just how this particular dough works.

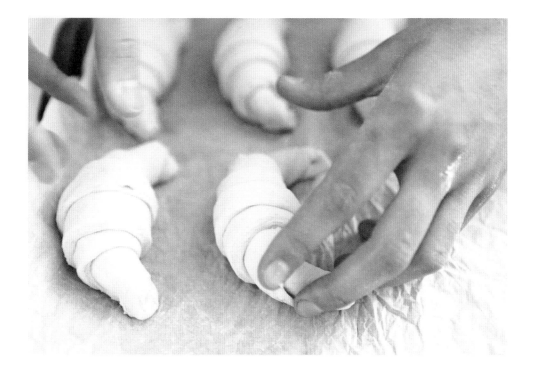

WHY IS MY DANISH PASTRY...

...SOFT AND STICKY WHEN ROLLING?

— The dough may be too warm. Return it to the fridge for an extra 15 minutes to help set the butter.

— It might be that the dough has ripped, leaving the butter at the surface. If this happens, try to fold the dough in a way that moves the tear to the inside.

— Dust the surface with flour as you roll to minimize sticking, but take care not to use too much.

...DIFFICULT TO ROLL OUT OR SPRINGING BACK AS I ROLL IT?

Because it's quite dry and contains bread flour, Danish pastry dough tends to be difficult to roll out. And unfortunately, it becomes gradually more difficult to roll to size with each turn. There's no escaping this tug-of-war, but there are a few things you can do to avoid defeat.

— If the dough has too little resting time, it will be almost impossible to roll. That resting time is important not only for helping the butter to stay firm, but also for letting the gluten relax. Worked too hard and with too little rest, dough becomes uncooperative, inflexible, and tired. Return it to the fridge for an extra 15 minutes to let it chill out, then try again.

— You might have dusted with too much flour. Although a small amount of flour helps to prevent sticking, too much can toughen the dough. Be sparing with it, and brush any excess off as you fold the dough.

...LEAKING BUTTER AS IT BAKES?

— When Danish pastry dough is underproofed, it won't have risen enough and the structure will be too tight when it first hits the oven. The result is that the butter layered inside is left with no place to go but out onto the baking sheet, pooling at the feet of the pastries and leaving them greasy. Next time, proof the shaped pastries for slightly longer, until they're very puffy. When poked gently with your little finger, they shouldn't spring back into shape immediately — the indentation should slowly refill most of the way.

— It could be that the dough was too warm when proofing, causing the butter to melt prematurely. Normal room temperature will suffice for proofing — never put the pastries in a warm place, such as a proofing box, to rise.

See also the tips on pages 85 through 87 for more common problems with yeast doughs.

The instructions below might look daunting, but they actually cover just a few basic steps. The dough is mixed and rested before being chilled for a few hours. Once chilled, it's wrapped around the butter (which has been pounded into a sheet) and left to rest in the fridge for 30 to 45 minutes. It is then given three turns — that's rolling, folding, and rotating the dough three times — with a chilling period of around half an hour between turns. The dough is then ready to be rolled and shaped however you please. The recipes for croissants, *franzbrötchen*, and both sweet and savory Danish pastries all use this dough as their base. Except for the croissants and *franzbrötchen* (which are easiest to cut and shape in bigger amounts), I've given quantities for only a small batch of each. This way, you can make several different types of pastry from one large batch of basic dough; having spent so long preparing the dough, it's good to be able to experiment with it. There are a couple of savory Danish pastry recipes coming up in the next section, too. These pastries are always best eaten while fresh, but if you want to serve them any longer than a few hours after baking, they can be revived in a 350°F oven for 5 to 10 minutes.

A mixture of all-purpose and bread flour in this dough gives a good balance between crispness, rise, and ease of rolling and shaping. For more information on bread flour, see page 73.

Makes just over 1 kilogram
(about 2.25 lb) dough

350 grams (2¾ c) white bread flour
150 grams (1 c + 3 tbsp) all-purpose flour
3½ tablespoons unsalted butter,
    chilled and cubed
2¼ teaspoons (1 packet) instant yeast
1½ teaspoons salt
2 tablespoons superfine sugar
½ cup + 2 tablespoons cool water
½ cup + 2 tablespoons whole milk
200 grams (¾ c + 2 tbsp) block of
    unsalted butter, chilled

1   Combine the flours in a large bowl, then rub in the cubed butter using your fingertips. Add the yeast and stir to combine, then stir in the salt and sugar. Pour in the water and milk and use your hands to roughly combine everything, mopping up any dry flour to bring the ingredients together and form a dry, shaggy dough. Don't knead this: it needs to be only barely mixed. If worked too vigorously at this early stage, gluten will develop and make the dough incredibly difficult to roll out later on. Cover the bowl with plastic wrap and let the dough rest for 30 minutes. Gently deflate the dough if it has risen, then transfer to the fridge to chill for at least 3 hours, or as long as overnight. Make sure that the bowl is tightly covered with plastic wrap; otherwise the dough will dry out and form a skin.

2   Once the dough has thoroughly chilled, prepare the block of butter. Heavily dust it with flour, then place it between two sheets of parchment paper and use a rolling pin to pound it into a square measuring about 10 by 10 inches. Return the slab of butter to the fridge for a few minutes while you prepare the dough. Remove the dough from the fridge, turn it out onto a work surface, and roll it into a large rectangle measuring about 12 by 20 inches. Lay the sheet of butter over one half of the dough, then fold the other half over to completely cover the butter. Gently smooth this parcel to press out any air bubbles (which will burst and ruin the layers in the pastry if they get trapped), then seal the edges together by pressing

down with either your fingers or the length of a rolling pin. You should be left with a completely sealed, dough-wrapped parcel of butter. Wrap this in plastic and return it to the fridge for 30 minutes to allow the dough and butter to reach roughly the same temperature.

3   Gently roll the chilled dough out on a lightly floured surface to a large rectangle at least twice as wide as it is long. The precise dimensions aren't important, but it ought to be rolled to a thickness no greater than ⅜ inch. This first roll is a tricky one: work slowly to avoid squeezing the butter out of the sides or forcing it through the dough. Start by gently pressing down all over the dough with your rolling pin to flatten it slightly and evenly distribute the butter. Then roll carefully but firmly, making sure the dough doesn't stick to the work surface. Lightly dust any excess flour off the surface of the dough, then fold the left third of the rectangle over and then the right third on top. Rotate the dough 90 degrees so that the fold lines run across the width of the dough rather than toward you. Wrap the dough in plastic wrap, then let rest in the fridge for 30 to 45 minutes. You've just completed one turn of the dough.

4   Give the dough two more turns, rolling, folding, rotating, and chilling each time. It will become progressively more difficult to roll out as you go on, thanks to the gluten in the flour. You might have to put your weight behind the rolling pin by the time you come to the final turn, but do stick with it. If you find yourself in a stalemate with the dough, let it win: it doesn't need to reach exactly the same size each time, so just fold it as it is and then return it to the fridge. Better this than handle the dough for so long that the butter melts.

5   After the final turn and chill, the dough is ready to be rolled and shaped. It should be smooth, taut, and neatly folded into a rectangle — very different from the rough mass of dry dough you started with. Whatever shapes you choose, remember that because these pastries are yeast-leavened, they need time to rise before baking — 1 to 2 hours depending on the pastry. This second rise may be done overnight in the fridge, but it's far quicker to do it at room temperature. Proofing at room temperature might seem counterintuitive, considering the lengths you've gone to in order to keep the dough cool all along, but as long as the pastries are left at normal room temperature (no higher than 72°F, preferably) they'll be fine. The butter will soften slightly during the proofing period, but because there's yeast here to give the pastries their rise (unlike puff pastry, which relies only on steam from the butter), this isn't a problem.

CHERRY DIAMONDS

Cherry danishes are sour, fruity, buttery, and sweet all at once, and in perfect balance. They're a classic for a reason.

Makes 4

¼ recipe of Danish Pastry Dough (page 277)

Filling

150 grams (about 1 c) cherries, pitted
Juice of ½ lemon

2 tablespoons superfine sugar
1 to 2 teaspoons cornstarch

1 large egg, beaten with 1 tablespoon milk, for glazing

📷 page 281

1   Prepare the filling before rolling and shaping the dough, leaving time for it to cool before making the pastries. Combine the cherries, lemon juice, and sugar in a small pan and heat until the cherries begin to soften and release their juices. Whisk in 1 teaspoon of the cornstarch and let the mixture simmer for a minute to thicken. Add another teaspoon of cornstarch if necessary — the juices ought to be thick enough to coat the back of a spoon. Let cool completely.

2   Roll out the prepared dough into an 8-inch square. Cut it into 4 pieces, each 4 by 4 inches. Using a very sharp knife, make four long incisions in each piece of dough: imagine that you're cutting a smaller square out of the piece of dough, ¾ inch shorter and narrower than the original, thus leaving a ⅜-inch border around the sides (see the upper right photo opposite). But instead of completely cutting out this smaller square, you need to leave it attached to the larger one at two opposite corners. In other words, make two L-shaped cuts, each following the edges of the original square, with neither L shape touching the other.   •

3   Fold one of the unattached corners of the larger square diagonally across and over to align with the opposite corner of the small, interior square. Gently press into place. Now fold the opposite corner of the larger square over to align with the opposite corner of the small square. The pastry should now have a rough diamond shape with a smaller diamond indentation in the middle.

4   Place a spoonful of the cooled cherry mixture in the indentation in the middle of each diamond. Put the pastries on a large parchment-lined baking sheet and loosely cover with plastic wrap. Let proof at room temperature. How long they take will depend on the room temperature and how much they've been handled, but 1 hour is about right. They're ready when they are puffy and spongy — rather than springy — to the touch. Preheat the oven to 425°F.

5   Brush the risen pastries with the egg wash, then bake for 10 minutes. Decrease the temperature to 350°F and bake 10 to 15 minutes longer. The finished pastries should be golden brown and crisp.

JAM PINWHEELS

I prefer a dark jam such as blackberry or damson plum jam for these, but anything will do. Even cheap strawberry jam works well against the richness of the pastry.

Makes 4

¼ recipe of Danish Pastry Dough
  (page 277)
¼ cup jam

1 large egg, beaten with 1 tablespoon
  milk, for glazing

📷 page 282

1   Roll out the prepared dough into an 8-inch square, then cut it into 4 smaller, 4-inch squares. Use a sharp knife to make four incisions in each one, cutting 1½ to 2 inches diagonally from each corner in toward the center. You should have a square with four "not-quite" triangles. Fold the corner of one of the triangles over into the center of the square. Repeat with the same corner of each of the remaining triangles until you're left with a pinwheel shape. Press the corners firmly down at the center, then place a tablespoonful of jam over the seam. Place the pastries on a large, parchment-lined baking sheet, then loosely cover with plastic wrap. Let proof at room temperature for about 1 hour, until almost doubled in size. While you wait, preheat the oven to 425°F.

2   Brush the pastry of the pinwheels with the egg wash, then bake for 10 minutes. Turn the oven down to 350°F and bake 10 to 15 minutes longer, until crisp. Transfer to a wire rack to cool before eating, and be careful of the dangerously hot jam.

CUSTARD ENVELOPES

This recipe is more proof, should you need it, of the versatility of humble pastry cream. This time it's wrapped in a square of flaky pastry. Tuck in a couple of raspberries or even a spoonful of rhubarb compote if you like.

Makes 4

¼ recipe of Danish Pastry Dough
  (page 277)
½ recipe of Pastry Cream
  (page 312), chilled

1 large egg, beaten with 1 tablespoon
  milk, for glazing

1   Roll out the prepared dough into an 8-inch square, then cut into 4 smaller, 4-inch squares. Place a dollop of pastry cream in the center of each square. Fold one corner of the square diagonally over toward the center, over the pastry cream, then fold the opposite corner down over this. This should leave you with a flattened, open-ended tube with pastry cream inside. Pinch the two layers of dough together on top to keep the tube from unfurling — lift the layers slightly and press only gently; otherwise the custard will squish out.

2   Place the pastries on a parchment-lined baking sheet and loosely cover with plastic wrap. Let proof at room temperature for about 1 hour, until the dough has almost doubled in thickness. Meanwhile, preheat the oven to 425°F.

3   Brush the risen pastries with the egg wash, then bake for 10 minutes. Decrease the temperature to 350°F and bake for 10 to 15 minutes longer. Transfer to a wire rack to cool.

PAIN AU CHOCOLAT

Call these by their anglicized name — "chocolate bread" — and that aura of French refinement falls quickly away. They are, after all, just chunks of chocolate wrapped in a butter-laden dough. They may be a dietitian's nightmare, but I can't think of a better start to the day.

Makes 4
¼ recipe of Danish Pastry Dough
   (page 277)

80 grams (2.75 oz) dark chocolate, coarsely chopped
1 large egg, beaten with 1 tablespoon milk, for glazing

1   Roll out the prepared dough into an 8-inch square, then cut it into 4 smaller, 4-inch squares. Lay one-quarter of the chocolate along one half of each square, then fold over the other half and pinch shut to seal. Place the pastries on a parchment-lined baking sheet and cover loosely with plastic wrap. Let proof at room temperature for 1 hour. Preheat the oven to 425°F.

2   Brush the risen pastries with the egg wash, then bake for 10 minutes. Decrease the temperature to 350°F and bake for 10 to 15 minutes longer. Transfer to a wire rack and let cool slightly before serving with a mug of milky coffee.

FRANZBRÖTCHEN

These German pastries have cinnamon and sugar swirled into them. What I like most about *franzbrötchen* is the shape: they're rolled up and then squashed down under the handle of a wooden spoon so that spirals of dough ripple out either side.

Makes 12
3½ tablespoons unsalted butter
1 recipe of Danish Pastry Dough
   (page 277)
150 grams (⅔ c) superfine sugar

2 teaspoons ground cinnamon
1 large egg, beaten with 1 tablespoon milk, for glazing

📷 page 285

1   Melt the butter in a small pan, then let it cool slightly while you roll out the prepared dough. The butter shouldn't be too hot when it comes into contact with the dough — no more than slightly warm.

2   Roll out the dough into a rectangle measuring about 12 by 24 inches. It can be a struggle to get it to this size, especially as it has already been handled so much, but a bit of firm rolling and rerolling should do it. If it proves really difficult, let it rest for 5 minutes and then try again. Don't worry about reaching exactly those dimensions, though.

3   Brush the rolled dough with the melted butter. Stir together the sugar and cinnamon and sprinkle this all over the buttery dough. Roll up the dough tightly from long edge to long edge to make a roll roughly 24 inches long. Trim off the uneven ends of the roll, then cut it into 12 slices. Leave the slices sitting upright as they are, ready for shaping. To give the pastries their distinctive shape, lightly flour a wooden spoon handle and press it down along the middle of each slice, parallel with the cut edges, almost as though cutting the slice into two, smaller slices. Press down firmly, pushing about three-quarters of the way through the dough so the swirls splay out on either side. Take care not to push too far, or you'll accidentally halve it.

4   Arrange the pastries on a parchment-lined baking sheet, leaving room for them to expand as they proof and bake. Cover loosely with plastic wrap and let proof at room temperature for about 1 hour, preheating the oven to 400°F in the meantime.

5   Bake for 15 minutes, then remove from the oven, glaze with the egg wash, and bake for 5 minutes longer. (These pastries are glazed partway through the cooking time because the raw edges of the pastry layers face outward — if you were to glaze before baking, the egg would set, fusing the layers together.)

CROISSANTS

The original breakfast pastry. Don't rush these as they proof: it's during the rising period that they'll begin to develop the buttery honeycomb structure that makes croissants so good. If you shorten that time, the baked croissants will be heavy and chewy, and the butter will leak from them as they bake.

Makes 12   ◻ pages 287 & 288

1 recipe of Danish Pastry Dough
    (page 277)
1 large egg, beaten with 1 tablespoon
    milk, for glazing

1   Roll out the prepared dough into a rectangle measuring about 8 inches high by 27 inches long. It will be difficult to roll the very elastic dough this thinly, so you'll need a little perseverance. Throughout this rolling process, take care not to use too much flour on the work surface, as this can toughen the pastry. As you go, gently lift the dough by one edge and flap it against the work surface to loosen it and give it a chance to relax. If you don't give it this opportunity to spring back a little now, it will shrink and deform later when you're cutting it into shape. Continue to gently roll and reroll it, giving it a 5 minute rest if it's really resistant, until it stays at 8 by 27 inches.

2   Cut the dough into 12 triangles 4 to 5 inches across at their bases and 8 inches tall. It's worth using a ruler or tape measure at this point to get even shapes. The triangles should tessellate — imagine 6 of them lined up with their bases along the bottom edge of the dough, and 6 more upside-down in the gaps between them. When you've cut these triangles out, you'll also have a couple of half-triangle scraps from the ends of the dough, which you can fashion together into a thirteenth croissant for a full baker's dozen, if you want.

3   To shape each croissant, stretch the triangle by its bottom two corners, slightly elongating its 4- to 5-inch base so that it flares out. Quite fittingly, it'll look a bit like the Eiffel Tower. Now roll the triangle tightly up from base to tip, stretching the tip slightly as you do so, then curve the ends around slightly to give it a crescent shape. It should now resemble the final croissant. Transfer the croissants to a large, parchment-lined baking sheet, cover loosely with plastic wrap, and let proof at room temperature. Preheat the oven to 425°F in the meantime.

    How long these take to rise will depend on the temperature of your kitchen, but I find that they usually need 1½ to 2 hours. Check yours after an hour or so and then at intervals thereafter: they're ready when they've doubled in size and feel marshmallow soft. Gently poke one, and if it's springy rather than spongy, give it slightly longer.

4   Brush the risen croissants with the egg wash, trying to keep the egg only on the smooth tops of the swirls and not on the cut edges (otherwise it'll bind the flaky layers together). Bake for 20 minutes, then transfer to a wire rack to cool slightly. Eat them while they're still a little warm: spreading them with salted butter, giving it a moment to melt into the soft pastry, then tucking in.

A BETTER LUNCH BOX

The pastries in this section are a change from the usual sad sandwiches and wilted salads. They're not as quick to make as just slapping a piece of ham between two slices of buttered bread, but they're about a thousand times more interesting. For quicker versions of these pastries, swap the Danish or puff pastry for Quick Puff Pastry (page 251) or even an all-butter store-bought puff pastry (although it really won't taste the same).

SALMON & CREAM CHEESE PARCELS

Danish pastries don't have to be sweet. These encase smoked salmon and soft cream cheese in a neat pastry parcel. A sprinkling of chopped chives or a slick of mild mustard works nicely in them, too.

Makes 4

¼ recipe of Danish Pastry Dough (page 277)
75 grams (2.5 oz) cream cheese
30 grams (1 oz) smoked salmon, cut in slivers
1 large egg, lightly beaten with 1 tablespoon milk, for glazing

1   Roll out the prepared dough into an 8-inch square, then cut it into 4 smaller, 4-inch squares. Put a dollop of cream cheese in the center of each then drape one-quarter of the salmon over the cheese. Fold the corners of the dough inward to meet at the center and press them very firmly together. Transfer to a parchment-lined baking sheet, cover loosely with plastic wrap, and let proof for about 1 hour at room temperature. Preheat the oven to 400°F in the meantime.

2   Brush the pastry with the egg wash, then bake for 10 minutes. Decrease the temperature to 350°F and bake for 10 minutes longer. Transfer to a wire rack to cool.

ZUCCHINI, STILTON & PECAN ROUNDS

Salty-sharp blue cheese, zucchini, and buttery pecans make these open tarts a lunch to savor. Use a mandoline (with extreme caution) or a vegetable peeler to get very thin slivers of zucchini, so that it grows meltingly soft as it cooks.

Makes 4

¼ recipe of Danish Pastry Dough (page 277)
½ zucchini, sliced into ribbons
50 grams (1.75 oz) Stilton
50 grams (7 tbsp) coarsely chopped pecans
Black pepper
Olive oil, for drizzling
1 large egg, lightly beaten with 1 tablespoon milk, for glazing

1   Roll out the prepared dough into an 8-inch square, then cut it into 4 smaller, 4-inch squares. Heap a large spoonful of the zucchini ribbons in the center of each square, then sprinkle with crumbled Stilton and pecans. Grind black pepper over the top and drizzle with olive oil. Fold in the tips of the corners, then roll the edges of the square in slightly to create a rounded shape with a raised border. Transfer to a parchment-lined baking sheet, cover loosely with plastic wrap, and let proof for about 1 hour, until very puffy and risen. Preheat the oven to 400°F.

2   Glaze the pastry edges with the egg wash, then bake for 20 minutes. Transfer to a wire rack to cool.

PUFF PASTRY

Puff pastry undergoes perhaps the most impressive transformation of any of the doughs in this book. When first mixed, it is scraggy, dry, and pale. Throughout the long process of rolling and folding, it remains anemic and dull. But it's what's inside that counts: look closely at the cut edge of a thick block of raw puff pastry and you'll see faint yellow striations through the dough. These are streaks of butter — and the key to this pastry's success. When baked, the butter melts and the water in it evaporates, producing steam that provides the "puff." The dough then sets around these pockets of air, separating into (quite literally) hundreds of tissue-thin layers. It's so airily light that you'd be forgiven for not realizing that it contains almost as much butter as it does flour. The crisp, golden pastry that emerges from the oven couldn't be further from the ugly duckling it was in the mixing bowl.

Puff pastry isn't a quick or easy dough to make: it needs plenty of time in the fridge to rest and chill, a lot of rolling, and at times some forcible pounding. If at any point during this process the dough begins to feel sticky or the butter leaks out, return it to the fridge right away to firm up. The trick is to keep the dough cool at all times. Granted, this isn't easy when you have to roll and handle the dough this much, but it is important. If your kitchen is particularly warm, you might even want to chill the dough for 20 to 30 minutes after every turn, rather than just after every other turn. If you're in a hurry, try Quick Puff Pastry (page 251) instead. But, although it takes a while, the method here really isn't too taxing — it's very similar to the method for Danish Pastry Dough (page 277): mixing, several turns of the dough (six turns for proper puff pastry), plenty of time in the fridge, and then a quick bake at a high temperature.

Temperature is the secret to perfect puff pastry — everything needs to be kept cool until the moment the pastry is baked. The butter needs to be firm enough that it stays in distinct layers, but not so cold that it breaks, tearing the pastry as you roll. The temperature of the oven is crucial, too: it must be hot enough (at least 400°F) to rapidly turn the water in the butter layers into steam. If puff pastry is put into a cool oven, the butter will melt but there won't be enough steam power to pry apart the layers, leaving the pastry greasy and flat.

This is a reasonably dry dough, but that's necessary if the pastry layers are to be tough enough to encase the butter without tearing. Unfortunately, that dryness can make puff pastry a little difficult to roll out. You should find it simple enough for the first couple of turns, but later rolls might require a firmer hand. However, the added lemon juice provides a touch of acidity, relaxing the dough and making rolling easier. If your dough is particularly tricky to tease into shape, give it an extra 15 minutes resting time in the fridge before the next turn; this gives the gluten in the flour a chance to relax, making for a more pliable dough.

500 grams (4 c) all-purpose flour
½ teaspoon salt
3½ tablespoons unsalted butter, firm but
not fridge-cold, cubed

¾ cup + 3 tablespoons cold water
1 tablespoon lemon juice
350-gram (1½ c + 1 tbsp) block of
unsalted butter, chilled

1 Mix together the flour and salt in a large bowl, then rub in the cubes of butter using your fingertips until there are no visible pieces left. Add the water and lemon juice and use your hands to bring the mixture together into a rough dough. It ought to be combined, but it doesn't matter if it still looks slightly shaggy at this point — the important thing is not to overwork it, as too much mixing will tighten the dough, making it harder to roll out. Wrap the dough in plastic wrap and refrigerate for at least 30 minutes.

2 Use a rolling pin to pound the block of butter between a couple of well-floured pieces of parchment paper, making a square measuring about 8 by 8 inches. Wrap in parchment paper or plastic wrap and return to the fridge to firm up again for 10 minutes or so while the dough finishes chilling.

3 Roll out the chilled dough to a rectangle measuring about 12 by 20 inches. Place the square of butter over one half of the dough, then fold the other half over to make a roughly square parcel of dough and butter. Take care to smooth out the dough to avoid sealing any air pockets inside. Use your rolling pin to press down the edges, sealing the butter inside. This is important; otherwise the butter may seep out during rolling or baking. Wrap the parcel in plastic wrap and return to the fridge for a further 30 to 60 minutes, allowing the dough and butter to settle at roughly the same temperature.

4 Now for the first "turn." Unwrap the chilled dough and, on a lightly floured work surface roll it out to a rectangle twice as wide as it is high — about 12 by 24 inches. Be gentle with the dough for this first roll, as the butter is still fairly thick and needs to be carefully teased out into a thinner layer. If you simply roll straight from one end of the dough to the other, you risk squeezing the butter along the dough and straight out the other side. To avoid this, press down lightly with your rolling pin at intervals along the dough to flatten it slightly, then roll from the middle upward and from the middle downward.

   Fold the left third over toward the center and then the right third over that to give a squat rectangle measuring about 8 by 12 inches. Now rotate this rectangle 90 degrees so that the folds run from side to side rather than from top to bottom. You've just finished the first turn. Repeat for a second turn: roll to around 12 inches high by 24 inches wide, fold into thirds, then rotate. Now wrap the dough in plastic wrap and chill in the fridge for 30 to 45 minutes.

5 Do two more turns, then chill the dough for a further 30 to 45 minutes. Give the dough a final two turns to bring the total up to six turns, then wrap and let rest in the fridge for at least 1 hour. During these final turns you might find the dough more difficult to roll out: the more it is stretched, the tighter it becomes. Just be patient and don't get too hung up on rolling the dough to exactly 12 by 24 inches each time. As long as you roll it to a reasonable size and fold neatly, it will work out.

6   The dough is now ready to use — a cool, silky-smooth slab faintly layered with butter. This recipe makes a lot of puff pastry, as there isn't much point making a small, single-use batch when it's so time-consuming. Save half of it for another project, either in the fridge for a couple of days or in the freezer for several weeks.

FIG & WALNUT ECCLES CAKES

Named after a town in Manchester, Eccles cakes are small, round cakes filled with currants. Technically these aren't real Eccles cakes, as there's not a currant in sight. Filled with sticky fig, walnut, and rose water, they feel more Middle Eastern than from Manchester. I like the delicate floral flavor of these, but do feel free to experiment with your own flavor combinations: perhaps dried apricots with grated marzipan, or diced apples and raisins, or even sweet mincemeat.

Makes 8 to 12

175 grams (1¼ c) dried figs, finely chopped
1 teaspoon baking soda
2½ tablespoons light brown sugar
1 teaspoon vanilla extract
Pinch of salt
A few drops of rose water

30 grams (¼ c) coarsely chopped walnuts
½ recipe of Puff Pastry (page 291), or 1 recipe of Quick Puff Pastry (page 251)
1 egg, beaten with a pinch of salt, for glazing

📷 page 295

293

1   Preheat the oven to 400°F. Line a large baking sheet with parchment paper.

2   Toss the figs and baking soda together in a large bowl, then add just enough boiling water to cover them. Let soak for 10 to 15 minutes, during which time the leathery dried figs will soften.

3   Once tender, drain the figs, then put them in a medium bowl and stir in the sugar, vanilla extract, and salt. Add the rose water a few drops at a time, to taste — it's strong stuff and can easily overpower. Stir in the walnuts. The mixture needs to be completely cool before the next step, so set it aside for a short while if necessary.

4   Roll out the prepared pastry thinly to a rectangle measuring about 14 by 20 inches. Use a 3¼- to 4-inch round pastry cutter (or something approximately the same size) to stamp out 16 to 24 circles. If you need to reroll the scraps, layer them carefully on top of one another, then roll again. Don't just gather the scraps into a ball as you might for short-crust pastry — it will ruin those layers of butter that you've so carefully created.

5   Puff pastry needs to be kept cold until the moment it enters the oven, so it's best to move half of the circles to the fridge at this point — on a baking sheet, covered loosely with plastic wrap — until you're ready for them. Arrange the remaining circles on the lined baking sheet and prick them with a fork. Dollop a heaped teaspoonful of the fig mixture onto the center of each circle. The trick is to fill them generously without adding so much that you can't seal the parcel. Leave a generous ½-inch border around the edges of each circle.

6 Retrieve the second half of the pastry circles from the fridge and drape one on top of each mound of filling. Firmly pinch the edges of the pastry bases and tops together to seal in the filling. Brush the tops of the pastries with the beaten egg, then use a small knife to pierce two or three holes in each lid to allow steam to escape.

7 Bake for 20 to 25 minutes. The filling will be very hot immediately after baking so transfer to a wire rack and let cool before tucking in.

MARMALADE ALMOND GALETTE

Traditionally, this would be a French *galette des rois* — an Epiphany treat made of two disks of crisp puff pastry encasing a fat dome of almond filling. My version has an extra layer of marmalade inside to balance the sweetness of the filling, while a couple of tablespoons of whiskey provide depth without leaving it tasting boozy.

Serves 8

150 grams (⅔ c) unsalted butter, softened
100 grams (½ c) soft light brown sugar
3½ tablespoons superfine sugar
Zest of ½ orange
2 tablespoons whiskey

2 large eggs
150 grams (1½ c + 1 tbsp) ground almonds
50 grams (6½ tbsp) all-purpose flour
Pinch of salt
½ recipe of Puff Pastry (page 291)
5 to 6 tablespoons marmalade
1 large egg, lightly beaten with 2 teaspoons water, for glazing

1 Preheat the oven to 400°F. Line a large baking sheet with parchment paper.

2 Beat together the butter and sugars in a large bowl until smooth and creamy. Add the orange zest, whiskey (to taste), and eggs and mix. Don't worry if the mixture looks slightly curdled. Stir in the ground almonds, flour, and salt, stirring until just combined. Set aside while you prepare the pastry.

3 Halve the prepared pastry and roll out one piece out on a lightly floured surface into a circle about 10 inches in diameter, trimming with a sharp knife to neaten the shape. Lay this circle on the lined baking sheet and spread with the marmalade, leaving a border of about 1 inch. Gently spoon the almond mixture on top, heaping it more toward the center to create a dome shape. Brush the border lightly with some of the egg wash. Roll out the second half of the pastry into a slightly larger circle (about 11 inches) and, using your rolling pin to help you lift it, lay it over the base and filling. Press down gently around the border to seal so that the filling doesn't leak as it bakes, but keep the edges of the layers exposed.

4 Use a pastry brush to glaze the top with the remaining egg wash. Take care not to let the egg run down the edges of the pastry, or it'll fuse the layers together as it cooks. You can decorate the top at this point if you want to: use a sharp knife to very gently score a pattern partway into the top pastry. Press only lightly with the blade; otherwise you risk cutting right through the top.

5   Bake for 15 minutes. Decrease the temperature to 350°F and bake 25 to 35 minute longer, until the pastry is crisp and golden and the filling set.

Variations
For a sweeter galette, swap the marmalade for good-quality raspberry jam. You could even stud the almond mixture with pitted cherries for a fruity filling.

MILLE-FEUILLE

Mille-feuille translates as "thousand layers," and although it sounds like a grand claim to make of a dessert, it's not as hyperbolical as it sounds: each mille-feuille slice has three sheets of caramelized pastry — each containing around seven hundred flaky layers — two tiers of custard, and a dusting of confectioners' sugar to top it all off.

The pastry sheets used in this dessert need to be weighed down as they bake. If puff pastry is allowed to rise freely, it can grow to six times its original thickness — such thick pastry would leave the mille-feuille bloated and unwieldy. Baked under the weight of a baking sheet, however, the pastry will still develop its characteristic layers, but in more elegant proportions.

These really aren't difficult to make, but they do involve a bit of juggling of equipment: you'll need to bake three sheets of pastry, and each requires two baking sheets, so unless you've got a lot of equipment and oven space, you'll probably have to bake in batches. Just make sure you keep the pastry cool while rolling and cutting it; otherwise the butter will melt and you'll lose those thousand layers.

Makes 6 large slices   📷 page 298

½ recipe of Puff Pastry (page 291)
100 grams (¾ c + 1 tbsp) confectioners' sugar
2 recipes of Pastry Cream (page 312), well chilled

1   Preheat the oven to 400°F and have a few large baking sheets at hand.

2   Divide the prepared pastry into 3 equal pieces. Wrap 2 of the pieces in plastic wrap and refrigerate. On a lightly floured surface, roll out the remaining piece into a rectangle measuring about 6 by 12 inches. Sprinkle confectioners' sugar generously over the top of the pastry and lightly rub it over the pastry to coat. Turn the pastry over, dust with more confectioners' sugar, and smooth again. This coating will caramelize as the pastry cooks, lending a slight sweetness and a deep golden color. Transfer the pastry to a parchment-lined baking sheet, then drape another piece of parchment paper over the top of the pastry. Place a second baking sheet on top to weigh the pastry down. If you only have very lightweight trays, perch a couple of small ovenproof ramekins or something similar on top. Bake for 20 minutes, then remove the weights and the upper sheet of parchment paper and bake for 5 minutes longer. Lift the pastry from the baking sheet, peel off the bottom piece of parchment, and let cool on a wire rack. Repeat with the remaining two pieces of pastry, to yield three sheets of baked, caramelized puff pastry.

3   The next step can be done in two ways. The first produces neat sides, with the custard flush to the edges of the pastry. The second is easier but less polished.

Method 1

Once the pastry sheets are cool, trim them slightly to about 5 by 10 inches. They may have shrunk slightly in the oven already, so if there's not much to trim, don't worry. Spread half of the pastry cream over one of the sheets, using a frosting spatula or something similar to usher it right to the very edges. Place the second pastry sheet on top and spread the remaining pastry cream neatly over it. Cut the final pastry sheet into a row of 6 rectangles, each around 5 by 1½ inches. Lay these rectangles on top of the pastry cream, aligning them neatly with the layers underneath. You should now have, from bottom to top, layers of pastry, custard, pastry, custard, and the 6 small rectangles of pastry on top.

   Use a very sharp knife to slice down cleanly through the pastry and custard layers and yield 6 slices, using the precut top pieces as a guide. (If you wait to cut the top layer of pastry once it's already perched on top of the custard, you might find that the custard gets squeezed out and the layers slide apart.) If the custard is too soft, try freezing the whole thing for 10 to 15 minutes, then trying again.

Method 2

Trim the cooled pastry sheets to even rectangles measuring about 5 by 10 inches. Cut each of these into 6 smaller rectangles, measuring about 5 by 1½ inches. You'll have 18 identical pieces of pastry. Use a piping bag with a wide nozzle (or a tablespoon and spatula) to divide the pastry cream between 12 of the pastry pieces. Perch 6 of these custard-laden slices on top of the other 6, then top with the remaining rectangles of pastry. You should have 6 stacked pastries, slightly rough around the edges.

4   Dust the tops of the mille-feuille slices with confectioners' sugar, perhaps using a strip of parchment paper as a template to create a pattern. Serve right away, as the pastry will soften if left sandwiching the filling for too long.

BEFORE MIDNIGHT

I developed the next three recipes with midnight snacks and late-night feasts in mind. They taste all the better for being a little clandestine — eaten furtively under the duvet or by lamplight. I'm not suggesting that you round off every day with an éclair, but there's no harm in indulging from time to time.

CHOUX PASTRY

This is a pastry that works under its own steam: without any help from either yeast or baking powder, it puffs to double or even triple its original size in the oven. The resulting pastries are light, crisp, and almost hollow, and can then be filled with creams, custards, jams, ice cream, or even savory fillings.

Choux pastry is the exception to just about every rule in pastry: it is mixed while hot, twice-cooked, and barely a thick paste when it enters the oven. The first period of cooking is done on the stove top. There are many important processes happening at this stage — gluten is developed (helping the pastries stretch in the oven) but also partly broken down by the heat (preventing the pastry from springing back again once puffed). Meanwhile, the starch in the flour absorbs a great deal of water and forms a paste that will help to form a bubble to trap the steam as the choux bakes and expands.

The paste is then mixed with the eggs, piped into shapes, and baked. Choux pastry relies solely on steam power for its rise, so it's important to start it off in a very hot oven: as the water in the dough evaporates, the steam produced forces the choux upward and outward. But until the outer surface of the pastry begins to set, the choux shapes remain incredibly fragile. Even a slight drop in temperature could cause the pastries to collapse, which is why it's crucial not to open the oven door, even for a second, during the first 20 minutes of the cooking time.

As the pastries continue to bake, the crusts set and the whole structure stabilizes. But you shouldn't assume that the choux is ready the instant the surface is golden brown; the pastries will soften again once out of the oven, so if they're anything less than completely firm — almost brittle — when first baked, they'll collapse as they cool. If you plan to fill the pastries with cream or custard, this is particularly important, as they will soften once contact with the fillings.

ÉCLAIRS

You can tell a lot about a person from their reaction to a plate of éclairs. Some happy hedonists will reach straight for the fattest one and eat it gleefully with their fingers; others will politely take a small one and eat it, with curbed enthusiasm, with a knife and fork. The last group will insist that they are too full, or on a diet, or that they "don't have a sweet tooth," only to tiptoe back to the kitchen table once everyone else has gone to bed, sit squarely down in front of the plate of éclairs, and, guiltily, tuck in.

Pastry Cream (page 312) can be used as an alternative filling.

Makes 10 to 12

3½ tablespoons unsalted butter
⅓ cup milk
⅓ cup water
Pinch of salt
65 grams (½ c + 1 tsp) all-purpose flour
2 large eggs, lightly beaten

Filling
¾ c + 1½ tbsp heavy cream

2 tablespoons confectioners' sugar
150 grams (5.25 oz) raspberry jam
  (about ½ c)

Ganache
½ cup + 2 tablespoons heavy cream
100 grams (3.5 oz) good-quality dark
  chocolate, finely chopped
1 tablespoon light corn syrup

📷 page 302

1   Preheat the oven to 425°F. Lightly grease a large baking sheet (this will help to hold the parchment paper steady when you pipe on the choux), then line the baking sheet with parchment paper.

2   In a small pan, combine the butter, milk, water, and salt. Heat gently until the butter has melted and the liquid is scalding. Pour the flour in all at once and immediately start beating the mixture with a wooden spoon, keeping the pan on the heat. It will quickly thicken and begin to sizzle. Cook the paste for 2 minutes or so, stirring continuously.

3   Remove the pan from the heat and let cool for 5 minutes. Once slightly cooled, beat in the eggs a little at a time; if you add them all at once, the mixture will form lumps. Once you've added about half of the egg, or when the paste is slightly less stiff, switch to a wire whisk and gradually beat in the remaining egg. The mixture should be smooth, thick, and glossy.

4   Prepare a piping bag with a ⅜-inch metal nozzle, or just cut the tip of the bag to leave a ⅜-inch-wide hole. Spoon the choux paste into the bag, taking care not to seal in any large air pockets. Don't overload the piping bag — you can pipe in two batches if necessary. Twist the top of the piping bag to seal it shut, then, with the nozzle pressed close to the parchment on the lined baking sheet, pipe 10 to 12 thick, 4-inch-long lines of choux paste. Leave at least 1¼ inches between the lines, as they will expand when baked.

5   Bake for 15 minutes, then decrease the temperature to 350°F and bake for 15 to 20 minutes longer, until the pastry is browned and crisp. It's crucial that you don't open the oven door, even for a second, during the first 20 minutes of the cooking time (see page 300). The cooked pastries should be firm and crisp — almost overcooked — as they'll soften once filled with cream and jam.

6   As soon as the pastries are out of the oven, use a serrated knife to split them in half. Leave their top and bottom halves cut side up on a wire rack to cool. Meanwhile, make the filling. Whisk the cream and confectioners' sugar together in a large bowl until just thick. Don't overwhisk, or the cream will separate as it's piped. Press the jam through a fine-mesh sieve into a small bowl to remove the seeds.

7   To prepare the ganache, heat the cream in a small pan until scalding. Put the chocolate in a large bowl and slowly pour the hot cream over it. Let the mixture sit for a minute, then gently stir to combine. Add the corn syrup. The ganache should be smooth, glossy, and thin enough to drip from a spoon.

8   Now assemble the éclairs. Fill a fresh piping bag with the cream mixture and pipe this onto the bottom halves of the cooled choux buns. Spoon or pipe the jam on top of the cream. Dip the tops of the buns in the ganache or carefully spoon the ganache onto the buns — whichever way works best for you. Place the ganache-topped lids on the filled buns and serve.

DILL & MUSTARD CHOUX BITES

These choux morsels are my snack of choice when the appeal of the usual film-night fodder — popcorn, chips, takeout pizza — wears thin. Serve with mustard-laced crème fraîche to dip them in.

Makes 25 tiny bites

1 tablespoon + 2 teaspoons unsalted butter
2½ tablespoons milk
2½ tablespoons water
1 teaspoon Dijon mustard
Pinch of salt
30 grams (¼ c) all-purpose flour

1 large egg, lightly beaten
Leaves from 2 to 3 sprigs of dill, finely chopped

Dip
½ cup + 2 tablespoons crème fraîche
1 to 2 teaspoons Dijon mustard
Pinch of salt

1   Preheat the oven to 425°F. Lightly grease a large baking sheet (this will help to hold the parchment paper steady when you pipe on the choux) then line the baking sheet with parchment paper.

2   In a small pan, combine the butter, milk, water, mustard, and salt. Heat gently until the butter has melted and the liquid is scalding. Pour the flour in all at once and beat continuously, still on the heat, for 2 minutes, while the paste sizzles and thickens.

3   Turn off the heat and let cool for a few minutes, then beat in the egg a little at a time, stirring vigorously after each addition. Once all the egg has been added and the mixture is smooth and glossy, stir in the dill. Either pipe the mixture onto the prepared baking sheet using a piping bag or sturdy freezer bag with a ⅜-inch nozzle or hole, or spoon it onto the baking sheet, making 25 very small blobs, each no more then 1 inch wide. If the choux shapes have any peaks, pat these gently down with a wetted finger; otherwise they'll burn.

4   Bake for 10 minutes, then decrease the heat to 350°F and bake for 5 to 10 minutes longer, depending on how crispy you like them. They should be golden brown and firm to the touch. Once they're baked, make a small incision in each (to let the steam escape, so that they don't soften) and transfer to a wire rack to cool while you stir together the crème fraîche, mustard, and salt for the dip.

I stop short every time I pass the grand displays of baklava in the windows of the Turkish shops near my flat in north London. It's a glutton's dream: row upon row of tiny, honeyed pastries dusted with jewel-green pistachios. These pastries are intensely sweet and buttery — overindulge at your peril.

You can make filo pastry at home, but I wouldn't recommend it. It takes a lot of time, space, and strenuous kneading to develop the dough and stretch it to such impossibly thin layers. The stuff you can find in the freezer case is a far easier option, and — unlike puff or Danish pastry — there's not much difference between homemade and store-bought filo in terms of taste.

Makes 20 to 25 pieces
75 grams (1/3 c) unsalted butter
150 grams (5.25 oz) filo pastry

Filling
200 grams (1½ c + 2 tbsp) pistachios
2 tablespoons superfine sugar
Pinch of salt
1½ teaspoons vanilla extract
½ to 1 teaspoon rose water
Zest of 1 lemon

Syrup
Juice of ½ lemon
3 tablespoons water
75 grams (1/3 c) superfine sugar
3½ tablespoons honey

8-inch round loose-bottomed or springform cake pan

📷 page 306

Pastries

305

1 Preheat the oven to 400°F. In a small pan, melt the butter over low heat, then set it aside.

2 To prepare the filling, process the pistachios in a food processor or coffee grinder until finely ground. Set aside 2 tablespoons of the pistachios, then mix the remaining pistachios with the sugar, salt, vanilla extract, rose water, and lemon zest. It won't look like much at this point — just a nutty rubble — but once it's baked and doused in syrup it'll be very different.

3 Using the bottom of your pan as a guide, cut the filo sheets to make 8-inch circles. Brush the pan with some of the melted butter, then begin to layer the filo pastry in the bottom of the pan, brushing each layer with butter before adding the next. Keep the remaining sheets of filo under a damp tea towel until you're ready to use them to prevent them from drying out. Once you've stacked half of the sheets, spoon on the filling and press down lightly to form an even layer. Stack the remaining sheets of filo on top, brushing with butter as you go. Brush the top with butter, too. (I usually end up with 4 to 6 sheets of filo on either side of the filling, but this will depend on the thickness and dimensions of the filo you use.)

4 Use a sharp knife to cut small diamond shapes, each piece no larger than 1¼ inches per side (they're very rich). It's important that you cut the pieces now rather than after baking, as cutting the crisp, baked pastry will just shatter it.

5   Bake for 20 to 25 minutes, until golden. In the meantime, prepare the syrup. Combine the lemon juice, water, sugar, and honey in a small pan and simmer over medium-low heat for a few minutes, until syrupy. As soon as the baklava is baked, put the pan on a baking sheet to catch any syrup that might leak and pour the syrup all over the top. It should soak down into the hot pastry and filling. Leave the baklava to absorb the syrup for a few minutes, then, while it's still warm, unmold from the tin and separate the pieces. Sprinkle a little of the reserved ground pistachios on top of each slice. Finally — and this might just be the only acceptable use for mini muffin liners — place each piece of baklava in a paper liner for serving.

Variation

For walnut baklava, swap the pistachios for walnuts, the lemon zest and juice for orange zest and juice, and the rose water for orange blossom water.

EXTRAS

MILK

CUSTARD • PASTRY CREAM

VANILLA ICE CREAM

SUGAR

CARAMEL • TOFFEE SAUCE

MARZIPAN • BASIC WATER ICING

CHOCOLATE

SPREADABLE GANACHE

POURING GANACHE • CHOCOLATE SAUCE

FRUIT

JAM • LEMON CURD

Here are the unsung heroes of baking: curds, sauces, custards, ice creams, ganaches, and jams will bring your cakes, breads, and pastries to life. A cheapage jam or tub of ice cream will suffice when time is short, but if you want to give your baking the final flourish it really deserves, it pays to make your own.

MILK

CUSTARD

Instant custard is a godsend when time is short and the cupboard is bare — and I am fond of it — but everyone should have a recipe for real custard, too. Until I ate my first egg custard, I had assumed that all custards were canary-yellow and thick enough to stand a spoon up in. The real thing is very different: rich, silky, and smooth. It's in a league of its own.

Purists will insist that a true custard sauce should be thickened with egg yolks alone, but it will be far less likely to curdle if you swallow your pride and add a couple of teaspoons of cornstarch. This stabilizes the mixture and creates a slightly thicker consistency. You will still need to be gentle with the egg yolks, though, to avoid scrambling them. Add the scalding milk slowly to the egg yolks, and never the other way around. This step is called tempering. And once the ingredients are combined and thickening on the stove top, keep your eye on the pan and don't stop stirring.

If you have a vanilla bean, you can use it instead of the vanilla extract, heating it along with the milk and letting it infuse for a while before you get started. For a richer custard, replace half of the milk with half-and-half.

Serves 2, as an accompaniment
¾ cup + 1½ tablespoons whole milk
2 large egg yolks

3 tablespoons superfine sugar
2 teaspoons cornstarch
1 teaspoon vanilla extract

1   Warm the milk in a small pan over low heat. Whisk the egg yolks and sugar together in a medium bowl for at least 2 minutes, until thick, smooth, and paler in color, and then whisk in the cornstarch.

2   Once the milk is scalding, pour it into the egg yolks in a thin stream, whisking continuously. Once combined, pour everything back into the pan and return to low heat. Keep stirring the custard for 5 to 10 minutes. Follow a figure-eight pattern with your spoon or spatula across the bottom of the pan to prevent the custard from sticking. It won't be long before the mixture begins to thicken; it will stop sloshing as you stir and instead move in shallower ripples, and soon it will feel heavier and take on the consistency of heavy cream. Eventually it will be thick enough to coat the back of the spoon. Don't let the mixture boil, though — keep the pan over low heat and you should find that it thickens well before reaching the boiling point.

3   As soon as the custard has thickened, remove from the heat, stir in the vanilla extract, and serve right away.

PASTRY CREAM

This is a very thick custard, made using extra cornstarch for a smoother, firmer set. Thanks to the cornstarch in this recipe, it's mercifully very difficult to accidentally curdle the mixture; as long as you stir continuously, you should have no problems. Use this in mille-feuilles or custard doughnuts or as an alternative filling for the éclairs on page 300. Keep the custard covered once cooked, or it will form a thick skin.

As in the custard recipe on the previous page, you can use a vanilla bean instead of the vanilla extract, if you want.

Makes about 1¼ cups
1¼ cups whole milk
3 large egg yolks

3 tablespoons + 1 teaspoon superfine sugar
3 tablespoons cornstarch
1½ teaspoons vanilla extract

1   Heat the milk in a pan over low heat until scalding. Meanwhile, whisk the egg yolks and sugar together in a large bowl for 2 minutes, until thick and creamy, and then whisk in the cornstarch. Once the milk is just shy of boiling, pour it into the yolks very slowly, whisking constantly. When all the milk has been added, pour the custard back into the pan and cook over low heat, stirring continuously. Make sure that you cover every part of the bottom of the pan with your spoon; otherwise the custard will stick.

2   As you heat the custard, you'll notice it rapidly thickening. This is the work of the cornstarch; when heated, its molecules disperse into the surrounding liquid and thicken it. After a few minutes, the mixture should be noticeably thicker. Once the first bubble breaks the surface, continue to cook, stirring constantly, for 1 minute, until unctuously thick and heavy.

3   As soon as it's cooked, transfer the pastry cream to a clean, dry bowl, beat in the vanilla extract, and cover with plastic wrap, laying it across the surface of the custard itself (otherwise a thick skin will form). Let cool to room temperature, then refrigerate if not using right away. As it cools, the pastry cream will continue to thicken, so don't be alarmed if it has solidified to a jellylike block after a spell in the fridge — just beat it well before using, and press it through a sieve if you want it perfectly smooth.

Variations
Add 2 tablespoons of softened unsalted butter just after the cream has finished cooking for a slightly richer custard. You can flavor pastry cream with spirits, too — a capful of rum or whiskey works well.

VANILLA ICE CREAM

Once you've seen how easy it is to make your own ice cream — and tasted how much richer and smoother it is than store-bought varieties, you'll find it hard to return to those cheap half-gallon tubs. You don't need an ice cream maker, either.

There are different ways of making ice cream, but the one that produces the best texture uses a simple custard base. Unlike the custard recipe on page 311, it's best not to use cornstarch here, so the cooking process can be slightly more difficult. Fortunately, you only need the custard to be just thick enough to coat the back of a spoon, so as long as you keep the heat low and stir continuously, the mixture shouldn't become so hot that it separates and curdles.

Making good ice cream is all about minimizing the formation of large ice crystals, which result in a crunchy consistency and slightly watery taste. The yolks in the custard help with this. Sugar and fat minimize crystallization, too, but the only way to make a truly smooth ice cream is to churn or mix it as it freezes. By regularly beating it, you break apart any large ice crystals and encourage smaller crystals to form instead. In an ice cream maker, this is no problem; it does the hard work for you, chilling and churning until the ice cream is very cold and smooth. Without an ice cream maker it's more effort, but not nearly as hard as it's purported to be. You'll just need to beat the ice cream vigorously every 30 to 60 minutes until it's very thick.

I like to make this with a vanilla bean (the speckling of tiny black vanilla seeds looks fantastic against the cream), but it's far from essential. Stir a couple of teaspoons of vanilla extract into the cooked custard if that's all you have.

Makes about 500ml, serving 4
1 vanilla bean
1½ cups + 3 tablespoons whole milk
4 large egg yolks

75 grams (⅓ c) superfine sugar
½ cup + 2 tablespoons heavy cream

📷 page 315

Extras

313

1   Split the vanilla bean lengthwise and scrape the seeds into a medium pan with the point of a knife. Add the vanilla bean and milk and cook over low heat, stirring occasionally, until the milk is scalding. Remove from the heat and let infuse for at least 30 minutes.

2   Once infused, remove the vanilla bean and return the pan to low heat until the milk is steaming. While it warms, whisk the egg yolks with the sugar in a large bowl until very creamy and thick — this will take 5 minutes or so. The air incorporated at this stage will give a softer set to the ice cream once frozen. Pour the scalding milk slowly into the egg yolk mixture while whisking continuously, then pour the mixture back into the pan and return to low heat.

3   Cook the custard very gently, stirring constantly, until it's just thick enough to translucently coat the back of the spoon. It's crucial not to overheat it, or the eggs will overcook and the custard will separate. (It can help to have a sink of cold water ready while you do this. If the custard looks like it's on the verge of curdling, just dip the bottom of the pan in the water to cool the mixture and stop the cooking.) Once the custard has slightly thickened, turn off the heat and stir in the heavy cream. Transfer to a large bowl and let cool, then transfer to the fridge to chill thoroughly.

4   Once the custard is completely chilled, pour it into an ice cream maker if you have one and follow the manufacturer's instructions. Otherwise, tranfer it to a large, lidded tub (the shallower the better, as this will help the ice cream to

freeze faster) and put it in the coldest area of your freezer. Remove the tub after 30 minutes and use a fork to beat the ice cream, paying special attention to the edges (which will freeze more quickly than the center). Return to the freezer for a further 30 minutes. Continue to beat the ice cream at regular intervals for 2 to 4 hours. Once it's very thick and slushy, you can leave it until frozen. There's no need to panic about stirring the ice cream precisely every half hour — as long as you break up the crystals every hour or so, it will be fine.

5   When it comes to serving the ice cream, let it soften in the fridge for 15 minutes or so beforehand. Store-bought ice creams are easy to scoop straight from the freezer thanks to the high proportion of air whipped into them. This ice cream isn't as airy, so it has a denser, creamier consistency — a small price to pay for a result that is 100 percent ice cream, not 50 percent ice cream, 50 percent air.

Variations

CLOTTED CREAM ICE CREAM Vanilla ice cream is — apparently — plain ice cream, and we often include vanilla without even thinking. But this does a disservice not only to the vanilla (whose inimitable flavor is anything but plain) but also to the milk and cream that are at the ice cream's heart. Dairy is delicious, and it's not until it's showcased without its usual vanilla crutch that its flavor can really come to the fore. To make a version that celebrates the flavor of the best cream, leave the vanilla out of the above recipe, and replace the heavy cream with clotted cream, sometimes called Devon or Devonshire cream.

RHUBARB RIPPLE ICE CREAM Rhubarb and custard are made for one another. In this ice cream, the rhubarb is swirled through the vanilla ice cream in thick ripples.
      Make a rhubarb compote by cutting 200 grams (7 oz) of rhubarb into ¾-inch chunks. Put it in a pan, add 3 tablespoons of superfine sugar, and cook over medium-low heat, stirring often, for 10 minutes or so, until the rhubarb is soft but still blushing pink. Mash any large rhubarb chunks lightly with a fork, then let cool completely. Swirl the mixture into the vanilla ice cream recipe above when the ice cream is very thick but not yet fully frozen. Return to the freezer until set.

GINGER ICE CREAM Sour cream leaves this ice cream fresher and brighter than the usual heavy cream varieties. Don't scrimp on the ginger. Follow the vanilla ice cream recipe above, leaving out the vanilla and adding 1¼ cups of sour cream to the cooked custard instead of the heavy cream. Stir in 150 grams (1 c) of finely chopped crystallized ginger, then grate in 2 inches of fresh ginger and the zest of 1 lemon. Cool and freeze as above.

SUGAR

CARAMEL

I have to admit that, even now, setting a pan of white sugar over high heat feels like a game of Russian roulette. Some days the sugar melts smoothly to a clear, deep golden caramel; other days — and with no discernible change in technique — I find myself standing over a cracked, crystallized failure: burnt in parts, set solid in others. Left none the wiser about exactly where it all went wrong, it's easy to fall into superstition ("It only works if I swirl the pan clockwise") or disillusionment ("Caramel just doesn't like me").

But although caramel is tricky, it isn't impossible. There are some factors that make caramel more likely to fail, and others that will put you on the path to success. The two most common problems are crystallization (where the dissolved sugar forms back into crystals, creating a granular, crunchy texture) and burning. If you can avoid these pitfalls, you'll make a perfect caramel. Patience, care, and a clear head are crucial — some of my worst caramel experiences happened when I was in a rush or a bad mood.

A NOTE ON SAFETY

I've broken down the process into manageable steps in this recipe, but before you get started, here are some important cautions:

— Usher small children out of the kitchen, and make sure that you can devote your full attention to the caramel.

— Have a sink of cold water ready to plunge the base of the pan into if the caramel looks like it may be on the brink of burning.

— It sounds obvious, but don't touch or taste the caramel until it's completely cool, although I appreciate that it's tempting when the smell of toffee begins to fill the kitchen. If you do, the hot caramel will stick to your skin and give you a very painful burn.

There are two ways to make caramel. The first, and the one described here, is the wet method, which adds water to the pan along with the sugar. The second approach uses only sugar. The dry method burns far more easily, whereas the wet method is prone to crystallization. And if the choice is between a crystallized mess and an acrid, burnt mess, I can't help feeling that failure with the wet method is the lesser of two evils.

This caramel hardens quickly as it cools, so make sure you know what you're going to do with it before you get started. Something similar is used in the Rye Apple Upside-Down Cake (page 47), or you could add cream and butter for a softer set, as in the Toffee Sauce (page 319). Alternatively, dip toasted almonds or hazelnuts in the hot caramel to make caramelized nut clusters.

Makes about ½ cup   📷 page 317
100 grams (½ c) granulated sugar
2 tablespoons water

1   Choose an appropriate pan: nonstick pans aren't suitable for caramel as they tend to encourage the sugar to crystallize. Make sure that the pan is wide enough to accommodate the sugar in a reasonably shallow layer (no thicker than ¾ inch) but not so wide that the sugar barely covers the bottom. The pan should be very clean, too — even just a little dirt could cause crystallization.

2   Combine the sugar and water in the pan, stirring to ensure that no dry sugar crystals are left. Place the pan over medium heat and stir very gently with a metal spoon just until the sugar has all dissolved. At that moment, stop stirring and keep the spoon well clear of the mixture for the rest of the cooking time, as any agitation will encourage the sugar to regroup into crystals.

3   The syrup should now be clear and bubbling. The next 5 minutes or so are all about avoiding crystallization. Keep the heat constant, don't even think about stirring, and if any small crystals form around the sides of the pan, use a small pastry brush dipped in hot water to brush them away. The crystals should dissolve upon contact with the brush, but any large clumps should be brushed upward, away from the syrup.

4   After about 5 minutes, the syrup should be just beginning to take on a light golden color. If it's coloring unevenly, very gently tilt the pan to swirl the mixture, but don't succumb to the temptation to stir it. Continue to let it bubble until it's a uniformly golden color.

5   What happens over the next minute will seal the fate of your caramel. Take it off the heat too soon and it'll be blandly sweet, but leave it too long and it will blacken and burn. Keep a very close eye on it as it darkens to golden brown, then to an amber color. This is the perfect time to remove the pan from the heat — the sugar will continue to cook for a short while longer, so it's better to stop cooking when the caramel is slightly too pale than too dark. If you take the caramel too far and it begins to smoke, immediately remove it from the heat and plunge the base of the pan in a basin of cold water (be careful of any spluttering or a rush of steam) to stop the cooking. If you're planning to mix this with cream or butter, or if you like the slight bitterness of a dark caramel, you can cook the mixture very slightly longer for a deeper flavor, but I find it's best to err on the side of caution.

TOFFEE SAUCE

This toffee sauce has a deep, caramelized flavor. It will thicken slightly as it cools, but you can easily bring it back to a pourable consistency by heating it gently over low heat. Drizzle it over cakes, spoon it into doughnuts, or use it for choux buns.

A little salt can make a big difference to toffees and caramels: use salted butter and an extra pinch of salt for a bold flavor in this sauce, or stick with unsalted butter for a simpler sweetness.

Makes about ⅔ cup
100 grams (7 tbsp) superfine sugar
2 tablespoons water

5 tablespoons heavy cream
1 tablespoon butter, softened
Pinch of salt (optional)

1   Make a caramel with the sugar and water, following the instructions for the caramel recipe opposite. Have the cream and butter measured and ready to add as soon as the caramel is cooked.

2   Once the caramel reaches a rich amber color, turn off the heat and immediately whisk in the cream. The mixture will bubble up as you add the cream, so keep the pan at arm's length and take care to avoid any sputters of the hot sauce. Once combined, stir in the butter and salt. Let cool slightly before serving, or let cool completely and refrigerate for up to a few days.

MARZIPAN

Homemade marzipan is incredibly easy to make. It's not quite as smooth or pliable as the lurid store-bought stuff, so if you want to roll it thinly to cover a cake, you might be better off buying it ready-made. But for most purposes — studding cupcakes (see page 27), filling a stollen (see page 159), or just to nibble on — this marzipan is perfect. There's also a recipe for a pistachio version on page 159.

This recipe contains raw egg white, so if you're concerned about eating unpasteurized eggs, it's worth buying a carton of the pasteurized egg whites from the supermarket instead of using a fresh egg.

Makes about 450 grams (1 lb)
200 grams (2 c + 2 tbsp) ground almonds
200 grams (1⅔ c) confectioners' sugar

Pinch of salt
1 large egg white (3 tbsp)
1 teaspoon almond extract

1   Mix the ground almonds, sugar, and salt together in a large bowl. Beat the egg white and almond extract together in a small bowl then add this, a little at a time, to the almond mixture, using a fork to mash the liquid into the dry ingredients as you go. It will seem far too dry at first, but as you continue the mixture will come together. Use only as much of the egg white mixture as is absolutely necessary to bind the almonds; otherwise the marzipan will become sticky and difficult to work with. Once the marzipan is made, use right away, or wrap tightly in plastic wrap and store in the fridge for up to 1 week.

BASIC WATER ICING

I'm not keen on slathering a cake with buttercream — more often than not, it adds sweetness without subtlety and leaves the whole thing excessively rich — but I'm not averse to a thin layer of frosty glaze or a messy zigzag of icing. It livens up a cake, pastry, or cookie without smothering the flavor. There's really no hard-and-fast formula for water icing; it's just confectioners' sugar, water, and any additional flavors, mixed to a consistency appropriate for the occasion. A thicker icing — almost paste-like — can be neatly piped over buns in bright white streaks. Make a version with more liquid, and it can be drizzled messily off a spoon or used as a shiny glaze.

Regardless of how thick or thin you want the icing to be, it's important to add the water very gradually. Add too much at once, and the sugar will clump and you'll have to strain the icing. The first few drops of water should be enough to create a thick paste, and every drop thereafter is about fine-tuning the consistency. Be warned that water icing always seems thicker in the bowl than it will be when used; dilute it too much, and the icing will be too watery to even drizzle. The temperature of the thing you're icing will make a difference, too. Pour a thick icing onto a hot cake, and it will loosen and run off the sides, while the same icing will sit neatly on top of a cooled cake.

In terms of flavoring, water icing is very adaptable. Use lemon juice and zest in place of the water for a citrus version, add a teaspoon of vanilla extract to tone the sweetness, or stir a little cocoa powder into the confectioners' sugar.

CHOCOLATE

SPREADABLE GANACHE

Ganache is just dark chocolate and cream, melded together to create a rich, glossy icing or glaze. It's very simple to make and really requires little instruction; as long as you chop the chocolate finely and avoid heating the ingredients too much once combined, it's difficult to get ganache wrong.

This thick, spreadable ganache is suitable for filling or frosting cakes such as the Chocolate Fudge Cake (page 54).

Although it is possible to make ganache with white or milk chocolate, I wouldn't recommend it — the result is too sickly sweet and doesn't have the same thickness or glossy sheen as the dark version. And because dark chocolate and cream are the foundations of ganache, they should be of good quality: no economy-brand chocolate or ultra-high temperature pasteurized cream.

I like ganache to be very dark and bittersweet, but you can add a couple of tablespoons of sugar, dissolving it in the cream, if you prefer it a little sweeter.

Makes enough to fill and cover one
  8-inch round layer cake
200 grams (7 oz) good-quality dark
  chocolate, finely chopped

¾ cup + 1½ tablespoons heavy cream

1   Put the chocolate in a large bowl. Gently heat the cream in a small pan over low heat until almost boiling, then pour it over the chocolate. Let stand for 1 minute, then gently stir until thick and smooth. If any stubborn chunks of unmelted chocolate remain, heat the ganache very slightly in its bowl, suspended over a pan of simmering water. Take care not to overheat it, though, or it'll lose its shine.

2   Let the ganache cool slightly to a spreadable consistency before using. Alternatively, refrigerate until firm, roll into smooth balls, and toss in cocoa powder to make chocolate truffles.

POURING GANACHE

Use this pourable ganache for a shiny glaze, like the one used on the Coffee & Black Currant Opera Cake (page 65). The addition of a bit of corn syrup gives this ganache a high-gloss finish.

Makes enough to glaze the top and
   sides of one 8-inch round cake
150 grams (5.25 oz) good-quality dark
   chocolate, finely chopped

1 cup + 1 tablespoon heavy cream
1 tablespoon light corn syrup

1   Follow the method on the previous page, stirring in the corn syrup after the chocolate and cream have been stirred together. If it's very thin, let cool for a few moments. Otherwise, use it right away, pouring it onto the top of a cake and letting it flow across the cake and down the sides. Use a frosting spatula or something similar to level it where necessary. For a very smooth finish, it helps to give the cake a thin coating of buttercream first. This crumb coat will gloss over the uneven surface of the cake to ensure a perfectly level layer of ganache on top.

Variations

Add any of the following to the cream as you heat it in the pan to infuse the cream with aromatics: a tablespoon of fennel seeds, a cinnamon stick, a vanilla bean, a dried red chile, or a couple of whole star anise. Strain them out before pouring the scalding cream over the chocolate. Whatever flavors you use, they need to be bold if they're to stand their ground against the robust dark chocolate.

CHOCOLATE SAUCE

Chocolate sauce is the difference between a good ice cream sundae and one that's sublime. It's not bad with bananas either (see page 257).

   This recipe uses exactly the same principle as the ganache recipes that precede it: chocolate is melted in scalding cream. The difference is that in this recipe, the high proportion of corn syrup keeps the sauce from setting and takes away ganache's grown-up, bitter edge.

Serves 4 generously, with ice cream
½ cup + 2 tablespoons heavy cream
100 grams (3.5 oz) good-quality dark
   chocolate, finely chopped

3 tablespoons light corn syrup
Pinch of salt

1   Put the chocolate in a medium bowl. Heat the cream in a small pan over low heat until almost boiling, then pour it over the chocolate. Stir until smooth and glossy, then stir in the corn syrup and salt.

2   If you're not serving this immediately, keep it in the fridge for up to 4 days, reheating it gently on the stove top when you're ready to use it.

FRUIT

JAM

I wish I could subscribe to the view of jam making as a cathartic exercise — homely and therapeutic — but in truth it's not very relaxing at all, standing over a pan of fiercely bubbling sugar and fruit. It's hot work, and you have to be very careful to avoid burns. But, fortunately, the results are worth it.

You can use more or less any fruit in jam: foraged blackberries or fistfuls of black currants work particularly well, and tender stems of rhubarb will see you through the winter months. But you need to be mindful of the pectin content of the fruit you choose. Pectin, which helps jam set, can be found in most fruits, but some contain far more than others. High-pectin fruits include blackberries, oranges, lemons, apples, plums, red currants, and gooseberries, whereas strawberries, raspberries, cherries, rhubarb, blueberries, and apricots have less.

To compensate for lower pectin levels, there are a few things you can do:

— Add a small amount of a high-pectin fruit to a low-pectin fruit jam. A chopped apple, for example, can help a batch of strawberry jam set.

— Stir in the juice of half a lemon along with the fruit. The acidity will help set the jam.

— Use a special jam sugar, which contains added pectin and acid. But you really shouldn't need it if you add a little high-pectin fruit and a spritz of lemon juice.

The amount of sugar needed in this recipe depends on the fruit you use: high-pectin fruits will require less, but low-pectin fruits should be cooked with an equal weight of sugar. If using plums, simmer them with a scant ½ cup of water for 30 minutes before adding the sugar and lemon juice.

Makes 2 to 3 cups
400 grams (14 oz) fruit, pitted
  (if necessary) and coarsely chopped
300 to 400 grams (1½ to 2 c) granulated
  sugar

Juice of ½ lemon

2 or 3 (8-ounce) jam jars

page 323

1   Sterilize a few 8-ounce jam jars: scrub them well, then rinse with boiling water. Let dry upside down on a wire rack while you make the jam. (If you have a dishwasher, you can use them straight from there.)

2   Combine the fruit, sugar, and lemon juice in a large nonreactive pan over low heat. Cook, stirring occasionally, until the fruit begins to soften and release its juices, then let bubble for 10 to 15 minutes, stirring often.

3   The temperature at which jam sets — its setting point — is 220°F, so if you have a candy thermometer, hook it onto the side of the pan to monitor the temperature. You don't need one, though. I actually find the old-fashioned test more reliable: place a small plate or saucer in the fridge while the jam simmers, and after about 10 minutes, spoon a small amount of jam onto the cold plate. Return it to the fridge for a minute or two, then slowly push your finger through the layer of jam. If it wrinkles as you push it, it's ready.

4   Let the jam cool for 15 minutes; it'll settle during this time, and the fruit will be more evenly distributed. Pour into the sterilized jars and seal immediately. Let cool to room temperature. As long as the jars were properly cleaned and the jam reached the setting point, it will keep for up to 1 year in a cool, dry place. Once opened, keep the jar in the fridge and use within 6 weeks.

Variations
Jam is versatile, so don't be afraid to combine different fruits and flavors. Add a vanilla bean to a pot of simmering rhubarb jam, or even a splash of rose water to a strawberry one.

LEMON CURD

This curd has less butter and marginally less sugar than you might be used to. The result is a cleaner tasting, brighter, zestier curd, and although it won't keep for quite as long as other versions, you should have no trouble using it up. If it's a little sharp for your taste, just add more sugar. I've included quantities for an all-yolk version, too, which can be useful if you've made a meringue, mousse, or sponge that has left you with a glut of spare yolks — the Lemon Meringue Roulade (page 210), for example. If you like, you can swap the lemons for limes or even passion fruit, as in the Passion Fruit Curd Jelly Roll (page 64).

Makes about 1 cup

Zest and juice of 2 large or 3 smaller
  lemons

1 large egg plus 1 yolk, *or* 4 large egg yolks

90 grams (6 tbsp + 1 tsp) superfine sugar

2 tablespoons + 2 teaspoons unsalted
  butter, cubed

**1 (8-ounce) jam jar, sterilized
  (see page 324)**

📷 page 325

1   Bring a couple of inches of water to a very gentle simmer in a small saucepan.
    Combine all the ingredients in a large heatproof bowl. Suspend the bowl over the
    saucepan, making sure that the base of the bowl isn't touching the water; this curd
    needs to cook slowly, using only the heat of the steam.

2   Keep a very close eye on the curd, stirring almost continuously. The mixture won't
    look promising at first, but before long the butter will melt, the sugar will dissolve,
    and it'll start to thicken. It'll take 10 to 15 minutes for the curd to cook, and it
    needs to be kept moving throughout this time. Patience is crucial. The curd is ready
    when it is viscous enough to coat the back of the spoon. It should leave a layer of
    yellow curd that will hold the track left by a finger swiped through it — not a thin,
    translucent film. It will thicken as it cools, however, so don't worry too much.

3   Remove the curd from the heat, pour it into the sterilized jar, and seal immediately.
    Let cool to room temperature, then store in the fridge for up to 4 weeks. If you're
    planning to use the curd within a few days, perhaps in a cake or dessert, then of
    course you needn't go to the trouble of jarring and sealing it — just keep it in the
    fridge in any covered container.

ACKNOWLEDGMENTS

To my parents, without whose patience, unfaltering support, and cookbook collection this would never have been possible. Åsa, Caitlin, and Tessa: thank you for being such understanding flatmates and caring friends. I'm sorry for making such a mess in the kitchen.

Thank you to Parisa and Poppy for believing in this book and for making it the best that it could be. I couldn't have hoped for kinder or more knowledgeable editors. To Nato and Anna, thanks for the wonderful photos, and the fun had along the way. Kate and Tim at Hyperkit, I'm so grateful to you for bringing these many disparate elements together and turning them into such a beautiful book. To Clare, Marion, and Myra, for their sharp eyes and suggestions. To Stuart, who had all those conversations I didn't have the nerve for. And, of course, Rukmini: I wouldn't have been able to do it without you. Thank you.

I cannot thank the rest of the Baker's Dozen enough for their reassurance, their guidance, and their wealth of baking tips: Ali, Beca, Christine, Deborah, Frances, Glenn, Howard, Kimberley, Lucy, Mark, Rob, and Toby. You are great friends to me — *Bake Off* would've been nothing without you. And thanks to everyone at Love Productions and on the *Bake Off* crew for giving me the opportunity to do this and for your help throughout. To Amanda Console in particular, who was there at the most difficult moments and stopped me from throwing in the towel.

Finally, to everyone who had to endure those early days of my terrible baking — this book is for you: Curtis, Rosa, and Noah; Sheila and Violet, whose pride has spurred me on; everyone at Oasis in Lisbon, especially Jackson, my most dedicated taste tester; Jess; the Philosophy common room regulars; Zoe at Bake-a-Boo, who made such exquisite cakes and let me read pastry books on the job; Ben — and his mum — for all the éclairs; and to everyone else whose company I so sorely missed while frantically writing this book. And last of all, to Adam, for always being there for me.

INDEX

329